MW00334526

Erotic Faith

Erotic Faith

Desire, Transformation, and Beloved Community
in the Incarnational Theology of Wendy Farley

EDITED BY

Mari Kim

FOREWORD BY Ellen T. Armour
AFTERWORD BY Marcia W. Mount Shoop

PICKWICK *Publications* · Eugene, Oregon

EROTIC FAITH
Desire, Transformation, and Beloved Community in the Incarnational Theology
of Wendy Farley

Pickwick Publications
An Imprint of Wipf and Stock Publishers
199 W. 8th Ave., Suite 3
Eugene, OR 97401

www.wipfandstock.com

PAPERBACK ISBN: 978-1-5326-9510-0
HARDCOVER ISBN: 978-1-5326-9511-7
EBOOK ISBN: 978-1-5326-9512-4

Cataloging-in-Publication data:

Names: Kim, Mari, editor. | Armour, Ellen T., 1959–, foreword. | Mount Shoop,
Marcia W., afterword.

Title: Erotic faith : desire, transformation, and beloved community in the incarnational theology of Wendy Farley / edited by Mari Kim ; foreword by Ellen T.
Armour ; afterword by Marcia W. Mount Shoop.

Description: Eugene, OR : Pickwick Publications, 2022 | Includes bibliographical
references.

Identifiers: ISBN 978-1-5326-9510-0 (paperback) | ISBN 978-1-5326-9511-7 (hard-
cover) | ISBN 978-1-5326-9512-4 (ebook)

Subjects: LCSH: Farley, Wendy, 1958–. | Feminist ethics. | Feminist theology. |
Christian ethics. | Sexual ethics.

Classification: BJ1395 .E74 2022 (print) | BJ1395 .E74 (ebook)

To my beloved parents,
Chang-Yull Gold Kim and Jeong-Ji Jane Kim

"Contemplation is a journey of self-knowledge in which we come to know ourselves and all other beings as God-bearers, luminous through connection to all creation."

—Wendy Farley
Gathering Those Driven Away

Table of Contents

Theology as Intimate Address:
Wendy Farley's *Gathering Those Driven Away*

ELLEN T. ARMOUR

IT IS BOTH AN honor and a pleasure to lay some groundwork for the rich conversation that this volume both embodies and seeks to prompt with the work of the eminent theologian Wendy Farley, whom I have known for over thirty years now. My thanks to Dr. Mari Kim for bringing this volume to fruition and for inviting me to contribute to it.[1] The essays that follow all engage with Farley's 2011 book, *Gathering Those Driven Away: A Theology of Incarnation.* Her fourth published monograph (a fifth, *The Thirst of God: Contemplating God's Love with Three Women Mystics* [2015], was barely conceived when these essays were written, and a sixth is currently in progress), *Gathering* carries forward and expands upon ethical and theological concerns that have motivated Farley's work from its beginning. The lodestone of her *oeuvre* is Christianity's need for a theological response to radical suffering. She grounds that quest in an impassioned critique of normative or dominant theological positions that not only fail as responses to suffering but exacerbate it. Critique opens the way to retrieval and creative reworking of resources (theological and otherwise) in support of a theology of love-in-relation

---

1. Like some other contributions to this volume, this essay originated as my contribution to a panel on *Gathering Those Driven Away* that Mari organized for the Theology and Philosophy of Religion Section at the Pacific Northwest American Academy of Religion in Spokane, WA, held on May 14, 2010.

as compassion and desire. While this goal is consistent throughout her *oeuvre*, Farley's approach to it took a decisive and distinctive turn starting with *The Wounding and Healing of Desire* (2005) that continues in *Gathering Those Driven Away*. Both books are informed by standard academic sources and practices, but they also incorporate sources and practices that are rarely engaged in academic theology, at least—listening to music, practicing yoga, engaging in meditation and contemplative prayer (Buddhist and Christian). And even traditional academic sources are incorporated in a different way. When she wrote *Wounding*, posttraumatic stress disorder had robbed Farley of the ability to read. Thus, the textual sources that made it into that book were those that she had (literally) incorporated through her years of study and teaching. Though her ability to read has largely returned, *Gathering* continues to stretch the boundaries of academic theology, yielding a text that, like *Wounding*, seems to me markedly different in its address to and impact on the reader than most theological writing of our time. It's that difference that I want to reflect upon here.

Wounding and *Gathering* constitute a distinctive genre of theology, but I'm not sure we have a term in our taxonomy adequate to it. In some ways, these works hearken back to the writings of the medieval mystics that have been so influential on Farley. In some ways, her recent work might fit under the rubric of what her father, the late Edward Farley, called *theologia*: theological wisdom or theology *as* wisdom.[2] Indeed, (Wendy) Farley refers to theology in *Gathering* as *sapientia*, as "motivated by a 'longing for wisdom.'"[3] While *theologia* and *sapientia* may help elucidate what *Gathering* seeks to offer its readers, they do not quite do what genres are supposed to do: provide the key to *how* to read the text before us. How do we/should we/can we read this text, then?

We know from the first page of the introduction that we are not in a standard theology text. This volume time travels. We start on a fictional Christmas Eve in nineteenth-century Germany, with the (so-called) father of modern theology, Friedrich Schleiermacher. And from there we jump back to the prophet Micah (ever-so-slightly updated) and then (whoosh!) back to almost-the-present: 2010, the date of the publication of Shawn Copeland's magnificent *Enfleshing Freedom*, with a little Gregory of Nyssa thrown in. A brief pause to catch our breath, and at

2. Edward Farley, *Theologia*.
3. Wendy Farley, *Gathering Those Driven Away*, 1.

last, a direct address from the author—one that takes that freshly caught breath away. "For me," Farley writes, "the genesis of theology is pain." Pain replaces faith as that which seeks understanding and "erupts in writing," she writes.[4] Theology can be a balm for pain when it is doing its rightful business. Working that space between words and what exceeds them "throws [our] minds and hearts toward the eternally erotic abyss which is our heart's desire."[5]

Gathering is, I will suggest, a theology of intimate address: to the reader, yes, but also to that too-often maligned or forgotten company of saints that have been and are being driven away (here, especially, queers in all our particularity) and, in and through and around us/them, also to the divine—as that within whom we live and move and have our being and as the source of that which, Farley insists, we most truly are: bearers of the divine image.

Farley originally subtitled Gathering "An Erotic Theology of Incarnation." The adjective was dropped for publication—understandably, given its contemporary connotations. Yet eros remains the mode and manner of divinity's relation with humanity, of the Word made flesh, if you will, not only in Jesus the Christ but in all of us, on Farley's read, manifest in and as our ownmost desire. That mode and manner wants no truck with those who would use the claim to incarnation to license the logic and practice of domination, humiliation, and exclusivism (Athanasius serves as paradigm here). As a counter to such usage, Farley seeks to awaken in her readers their relationship to the divine and to provide essential nutrients it needs to survive and (hopefully) flourish in a world of institutional and individual (de)formations that seem hell-bent on its suffocation. For even if Love's enemies can't get the ultimate last word (the power of love is the depth of the deepest abyss, Farley insists), they persist.

What are those nutrients? In part, they are ideas gleaned from texts (ancient, medieval, contemporary) given a new frame (more about that in a minute), but they are also practices: meditation with scripture, faith presented as task and path, rather than intellectual assent. These practices are, in the best sense of the word, practices of re-formation, of undoing as much as doing. Re-formation starts both from the outside in (reforming the traditions that have shaped us) and from the inside out (reforming our shaping by traditions). Both projects require disentangling theology

4. Wendy Farley, Gathering Those Driven Away, 1.
5. Wendy Farley, Gathering Those Driven Away, 1.

from its deformation by fear and trauma into tribalist idolatries and re-connecting it to its ever-generous and generative source in divine kenotic love.

These elements are framed by and in a subtle rewording/renaming of the guiding motif of the project: the Incarnate One at the heart of Christian tradition. Every now and then, this One appears in the standard guises (as Jesus—of Nazareth, Christ, our Savior, etc.), but much more consistently we find enigmatic references to "the Beloved" or "our Beloved." Farley is even bold enough to insert such references into the epigraphs she's chosen from scripture and elsewhere. "The/our Beloved" is more than a felicitous turn of phrase; rather, it performs what lies at the heart of Farley's project in *Gathering*. It is, I think, a key to how to read this book. "The Beloved"—of whom, by whom, is this so-named one loved? (I'll return to this topic shortly.)

What makes *Gathering* resemble the texts of medieval contemplatives, though, isn't just the similar vocabulary for the divine (one centered around love)—nor is it the fact that Farley explicitly draws on their writings. Rather, one has the sense in reading *Gathering* that one is reading the words not only of a well-trained theological mind conversant in her own field and those that adjoin it, but a spiritual adept, not one who has withdrawn from the world to some cloister, the better to practice her arcane arts (as the stereotype of "the mystic" would have it), but one who has in her own very ordinary life and (maybe not-so-ordinary) practice struggled with deformation and reformation, who knows the pain of trauma *and* the healing grace of love.

This distinctive authorial voice is manifest in the sometimes disconcerting immediacy of Farley's engagement with texts and traditions, an immediacy we might associate more with devotional practice than academic writing. It is also manifest in Farley's use of the second person plural throughout. It is "we"—author and reader together—whose ego-minds fall into self-deception, who will learn the difference between faith in the gods of our own making and trust in the power of divine love only in fits and starts, if at all. This is a deeply pedagogical text—in the best sense of the word—and that, perhaps, is what links it most substantively to those we call "mystics." The masterful and enlightening readings of theologians (including Mechthild and Porete) that Farley provides herein are compelling accounts of the content of their thought, but that is not Farley's primary aim. These readings school us in practices of undoing and unsaying the logic of domination, a logic whose effects extend beyond text and tradition into the very marrow of those shaped by them. Undoing a logic so deeply imbibed and embedded requires more than mere intellectual critique, though that is essential. It requires the slow and patient cultivation of new disciplines—of reading, of saying and see-ing, of breathing, of prayerful contemplation, of compassion, disciplines that will help us undo old habits of thinking and being and cultivate new ones—habits more suited to living out of and into awareness of the abyssal love of God. (*Gathering*'s structure arguably embodies this. The first third, more or less, undoes the logic of domination that surrounds orthodox theology and Christology; only then does the task of rebuild-ing—from the ground up—begin.)

I do not mean to suggest that these are easy lessons to learn. Farley is clear, in the chapter on apophatic theology, for example, that this is not the case. Stepping out of the known—no matter toxic we know it to be—into the unknown is frightening and takes courage and patience. And just reading a book—even *this* book—will not make it happen. But if any book can serve to lure us toward such labor, it may just be this one.

The explicit motivation for *Gathering* is the church's insistent ex-clusion of queerness as incompatible with Christianity. The particular strength of this text, I think, is in its connecting of religiously-based queer-phobia—and its overcoming—to a larger theological critique and reconstruction. Both sides of Farley's project draw on insights gleaned from companion forms of "othering" that have engendered their own powerful articulations of overcoming. Her work is steeped in that of contemporary fellow travellers like Laurel Schneider, Catherine Keller, Horace Griffin, Marcella Althaus-Reid, Kelly Brown Douglas, Robert Goss, and Paul Knitter, just to name a few.

If these are the resources Farley gathers for her readers, what does that gathering yield—specifically, by way of an erotic theology of incar-nation? As noted earlier, this part of her project doesn't show itself until we're several chapters in. It needs the space prepared by the foregoing exercises in ground-clearing, by practices of unsaying. In that space, on that ground, we encounter anew language and concepts from the oldest Christian traditions—orthodox and heterodox, familiar and non—all woven together in a creative synthesis with insights they share, Farley ar-gues, with other religious traditions (particularly Buddhism). Here's that synthesis, in sum. All that is, is God incarnate—God understood now as abyssal *eros* that bodies forth creation in all its wild abundance and lures it toward Godself in love. We access this abyssal *eros* initially through the testimony of witnesses that run the gamut of social location; luminaries named and unnamed—from the African women whose experience Mercy Oduyoye lifts up, to the Dalai Lama, whose own luminosity to the divine rescued for Farley the very category of incarnation. They are witnesses not only to divine *eros* but to loss and wounding wherever in the world it occurs (which is to say, everywhere). The incarnation proffers love and healing to suffering and woundedness because, in it, love and suffering, life and death, are intertwined. Among the salves it offers us is a severing of the connection that seems to come so naturally to us between suffering and guilt. The life and ministry of Jesus of Nazareth as described in the gospels, Farley argues, incarnate this. The story of crucifixion and resurrection that is its culmination witnesses to the power of love. Divine *eros* seeks us out in the very depths of debasement and humiliation, pain, suffering, and death—not in offering up the sacrifice that absolves us of our debt, as traditional atonement theory would have it, but in the form of intimate address that reaches out to meet us where we are, no matter how far that would seem to be from the realm of the holy.

With those insights in mind, let me make good on my promise to return to the figure of "the Beloved," "our Beloved." I claimed earlier that tracking "the Beloved" might be the key to how to read *Gathering*. By whom is "the Beloved" beloved? Well, by the divine, of course, whose love is made incarnate in "the Beloved." As *Gathering* proceeds, "the Beloved" gathers significances and meanings. It becomes, in the end, a multivalent term. Yes, the Beloved is Jesus—of Nazareth, the Christ. But "Beloved," as well, are all of us—including those whom we don't/can't/won't know, whom we disavow, reject, or abject. "Beloved" as well is/are all that is, ever was, or ever will be—including what we don't/can't/won't know, what we exclude or extinguish, excavate or exploit, often without thinking twice. To read *Gathering* is, on one level, to open ourselves—slowly, creakily, and maybe crankily—to this theo-logic. To *really* read *Gathering*, though, is to in-corporate it, to incarnate this insight, to respond to its intimate address by binding ourselves to Love, committing ourselves anew to its furthering and flourishing, to be-loving *as doing* so that it might increase in being. May it be so.

Bibliography

Copeland, Shawn. *Enfleshing Freedom: Body, Race, and Being*. Minneapolis, Fortress: 2009.

Farley, Edward. *Theologia: The Fragmentation and Unity of Theological Education.* Minneapolis: Augsburg Fortress, 1994.

Farley, Wendy. *Gathering Those Driven Away: A Theology of Incarnation.* Louisville, KY: Westminster John Knox, 2010.

———. *The Wounding and Healing of Desire.* Louisville, KY: Westminster John Knox, 2005.

———. *The Thirst of God: Contemplating God's Love with Three Women Mystics.* Louisville, KY: Westminster John Knox, 2015.

Preface

IN THE SUMMER OF 2009, across the Atlantic, the farseeing Stockholm School of Theology in Sweden hosted a conference on the work of Wendy Farley. Meanwhile, here in North America, there was a realization that not even a panel concentrating on Farley's work had been organized. I contacted Jon Berquist in the spring of 2010 with the intention of rectifying the situation. He agreed that a volume should be put together, and in preparation, two panels—the first reflecting on the uses of her past works, *Tragic Vision* and *Eros for the Other*, and the second discussing her upcoming work, *Gathering Those Driven Away*—were presented at the Pacific Northwest American Academy of Religion at Gonzaga University. Among the presenters were Verna Ehret, Annie Bullock, Kendra Hotz, Carl Levenson, Ellen Armour, and Douglas McGaughey. In November of 2011, John Thatamanil presided while Serene Jones, Monica Coleman, Catherine Punsalan-Manlimos, and Edward Farley further considered the merits of *Gathering Those Driven Away*, released a few months prior.

This volume marks the fulfillment of an intention to bring to greater awareness the contributions and gifts of contemporary North American constructive theologian and theological ethicist Wendy Farley. As the authors of this volume will reveal, Farley's work requires us to see, with clear and unwavering gaze, the truth of our suffering and our belovedness. She invites us to resist that which diminishes the divine image in us. In her work we discover the truth of our own complicity in the violations that undermine our ethical commitments to the other, what Farley calls sin, and also the persistent power of divine *eros*—that grows within and flows through our very lives—to transform and redeem the same.

Through her perspective, we discover the presence of a capacity for what I call *erotic faithfulness*, that orientation of desire that compels us beyond disappointment, shame, or complacency to seek still-greater realization of divine love in our lives. Farley's voice is a clarion call for the

American context from which she writes. Her work calls us to embody that compassion capable of resisting the injustice that dehumanizes, to awaken and challenge the sin that pervades from within and without; and, most of all, when we are tempted to despair, she reminds us that hope, at times against all evidence, refuses to give up on the promise of justice and wholeness, for each and all of us. Radical hospitality, creative liberation, and deep listening emerge as more than ethical values for Farley; they are the enduring spiritual practices with the capacity to help us discover and confirm our identity as the "god-bearers" Dorotheus of Gaza reminded us we are.

Farley's work prophetically calls from and to the community that self-identifies as disciples of Jesus Christ: to re-member him in the living of our lives, to em-body that Christic love in the choices we make about how to walk with the most vulnerable of the earth, and to know that such discipleship will take us beyond the bounds of all that generations of communities within the Christian tradition have traditionally held sacred, to discover anew what and where sacredness dwells. The intention of this volume is to allow rumination, reflection, and perception of the powerful presence of desire within us, the truth of inescapable fragility, vulnerability, and suffering, and the long, complex, unscriptable struggle that marks the transformation that calls to us.

Explorations of Farley's thought have continued in classrooms and conference presentations and more recently also in pulpits and contemplative retreats. Farley's work stimulates new interest and consideration because of the way in which it ruptures the binary between the prophetic and the mystical and reweaves elements that should never have been torn asunder. In this time of pandemic, robust struggles for racial justice, and political turbulence that threatens to tear nations apart, we need to hear and heed Farley's call to healing desire more than ever.

As in many rich conversations between colleagues, the years that have passed since we first considered our learning together have served to heighten rather than diminish our awareness of the profound generativity of Farley's thought. With the help of Charlie Collier, this volume passes the torch to you. It is an invitation for readers to join in the growing discovery of how Farley's exploration of desire, transformation, mysticism, and healing permit us to see and speak the reshaping of reality into one that embraces hospitality over hostility. My hope is that one day soon we will host our own conference based on Farley's work in North America.

Until then, may volumes like this and many others continue engaging Farley's thought and finding paths toward creating beloved community.

Mari Kim, PhD
Editor

Contributors

Ellen T. Armour holds the E. Rhodes and Leona B. Carpenter Chair in Feminist Theology and is Associate Dean for Academic Affairs at Vanderbilt Divinity School. She is the author of *Deconstruction, Feminist Theology, and the Problem of Difference: Subverting the Race/Gender Divide* (1999) and co-editor of *Bodily Citations: Judith Butler and Religion* (2006). Her latest book, *Signs and Wonders: Theology after Modernity* (2016), uses photographs to diagnose and respond to shifts in our relationship to bio-disciplinary power as channeled by a fourfold of "man" and "his" others (sexed/raced, animal, and divine). Its sequel, *Seeing and Believing: Theology, Visual Culture and New Media* (under review at Columbia University Press), builds upon *Signs and Wonders* by drawing on theological resources to address photography's import for and impact on our life together thanks to its role in our new (digital and social) media landscape.

Monica A. Coleman is Professor of Africana Studies at the University of Delaware. Her research investigates the intersection of process and womanist theologies, religious pluralism, and mental health and faith. Coleman is author or editor of six books including *Making a Way out of No Way: A Womanist Theology* (2008) and *Bipolar Faith: A Black Woman's Journey with Depression and Faith* (2016).

Ian Curran is Lecturer of Religion at Georgia Gwinnett College in Lawrenceville, Georgia. He is also an Associate of Green Bough House of Prayer in Scott, Georgia. He teaches classes in World Religions, Environmental Ethics, and the Christian tradition. His academic interests include Christian theology, Christian spirituality, the theology of Teilhard de Chardin, religion and science, and religion and ecology. He has published articles in *Irish Theological Quarterly, ET-Studies, Liturgy*, and

The Christian Century. He is currently writing a book entitled *The Vision of Transfiguration.*

Kristen Daley Mosier is a PhD candidate at Garrett-Evangelical Theological Seminary. Based in the Seattle area, her research takes a watershed-oriented approach to theology and sacramentality informed by ecofeminist writers. She serves as co-chair for the Women in Religion unit in the Pacific Northwest Region of the American Academy of Religion. Daley Mosier has published in *Liturgy* and is a contributing writer to the blog womenintheology.org.

Edward Farley (1929–2014) was Drucilla Moore Buffington Professor of Theology, emeritus, at Vanderbilt Divinity School in Nashville, Tennessee. Educated at Centre College in Kentucky and Louisville Presbyterian Seminary, and receiving his PhD from Union Theological Seminary/Columbia University, he taught at Pittsburgh Theological Seminary for a short time before coming to Vanderbilt Divinity School in 1969. His distinguished writing is expansive and interdisciplinary, extending through multiple volumes and scores of articles. *Ecclesial Man: A Social Phenomenology of Faith and Reality* (1975) and *Ecclesial Reflection: An Anatomy of Theological Method* (1982) are among his earliest works, developing philosophical theological themes based on phenomenology that later informed his systematic theology, notably in *Good and Evil: Interpreting a Human Condition* (1990) and *Divine Empathy: A Theology of God* (1996). Over the years, Farley also wrote influential volumes on theological education, such as *Fragility of Knowledge: Theological Education in the Church and the University* (1988) and *Theologia: The Fragmentation and Unity of Theological Education* (1994). Other writings show the breadth of his scholarly resources, including *Deep Symbols: Their Postmodern Effacement and Reclamation* (1996), *Faith and Beauty: A Theological Aesthetic* (2001), and *Practicing Gospel: Unconventional Thoughts on the Church's Ministry* (2003). He published an intellectual autobiography, *Thinking About Things and Other Frivolities: A Life* (2014), shortly before his death. Farley received Vanderbilt's prestigious Earl Sutherland Prize for Achievement in Research in 1991, and the 1997 American Academy of Religion Award for Excellence in Constructive-Reflective Studies for *Divine Empathy.* He was father to Wendy Farley.

Emily A. Holmes is Associate Professor in the Department of Religion and Philosophy at Christian Brothers University in Memphis, TN. She is the author of *Flesh Made Word: Medieval Women Mystics, Writing, and the Incarnation* (2013) and the co-editor of *Women, Writing, Theology: Transforming a Tradition of Exclusion* (2011) and *Breathing with Luce Irigaray* (2013). Her teaching and research interests include women's writing practices in Christian history, feminist theology, religious pluralism, and the spirituality and ethics of eating.

Kendra G. Hotz is the Robert R. Waller Professor of Population Health, Associate Professor of Religious Studies, and Director of the Health Equity Program at Rhodes College. She is the co-author of four books: *Dust and Breath: Faith, Health, and Why the Church Should Care About Both* (2012); *What Do Our Neighbors Believe? Questions and Answers from Judaism, Christianity, and Islam* (2019); *Shaping the Christian Life: Worship and the Religious Affections* (2006); and *Transforming Care: A Christian Vision of Nursing Practice* (2005). Kendra's research focuses on the relationship between religious belonging, social inequalities, and health.

Mari Kim teaches social ethics and philosophy for the Division of Communications and Social Sciences at Everett Community College. She writes on experiences of ambiguity, ambivalence, and desire in cultural identity. Her essay "Very Reverend Sang Chul Lee: A Legacy of Justice and Hospitality" appears in *Religious Leadership: A Reference Handbook* (2013), and her dissertation, *Eros in Eden: A Praxis of Beauty in Genesis 3,* is under contract. Kim's current research engages issues of justice around diversity, equity, and inclusion informing cultural competency, as she explores social justice and racial equity movement-building. Kim serves as Vice President of the Pacific Northwest Region of the American Academy of Religion.

C. A. Levenson, who did his doctoral work under David Tracy, Mircea Eliade, and Paul Ricoeur at University of Chicago, served as Professor of Philosophy at Idaho State University. He is the author of *Socrates Among the Corybantes: Being, Reality and the Gods* (1999) and is currently working on *The Socrates Project*, a study of Plato's Socrates in the light of prophetic, historical, and literary traditions.

Marcia W. Mount Shoop is Pastor/Head of Staff at Grace Covenant Presbyterian Church in Asheville, NC. Mount Shoop is the author of *Let the Bones Dance: Embodiment and the Body of Christ* (2010) and *Touchdowns for Jesus and Other Signs of Apocalypse: Lifting the Veil on Big-Time Sports* (2014). She co-authored *A Body Broken, A Body Betrayed: Race, Memory, and Eucharist in White-Dominant Churches* (2015) with Mary McClintock-Fulkerson. Mount Shoop has also contributed chapters on embodiment, race, and trauma to several anthologies. She co-hosts a radio show for Blue Ridge Public Radio, "Going Deep: Sports in the 21st Century," with her husband, John. www.marciamountshoop.com

Janelle Peters is a Visiting Assistant Professor at Loyola Marymount University. She is the author of *Paul and the Citizen Body.* Her journal articles have appeared in *Biblica, Neotestamentica, Journal of Early Christian History, Journal for the Study of Pseudepigrapha,* and *Postscripts.*

Leigh Pittenger teaches at Rhodes College and Christian Brothers University in Memphis, TN, having earned her PhD in the Comparative Literature and Religion program at Emory University. Wendy Farley guided her dissertation research on the role of moral imagination in Hannah Arendt's writing. Pittenger's current teaching, research, and writing interests include women's religious autobiographies and environmental ethics.

Catherine Punsalan-Manlimos is Assistant to the President for Mission Integration at University of Detroit Mercy. She held the Stamper Chair in Catholic Intellectual and Cultural Traditions at Seattle University, where she was the Inaugural Director of the Institution for Catholic Thought and Culture. Her current research focuses on the intersection of Catholic social thought, Catholic higher education, and marginalized voices. Her work has been published in *American Journal of Theology and Philosophy, Asian Horizons,* and *East Asian Pastoral Review,* among others.

Thomas E. Reynolds is an Associate Professor of Theology at Emmanuel College of Victoria University in the University of Toronto and the Toronto School of Theology. He is author of *The Broken Whole: Philosophical Steps Toward a Theology of Global Solidarity* (2006) and *Vulnerable Communion: A Theology of Disability and* Hospitality (2008). Currently he is writing a book on the theology of care.

Kristine Suna-Koro is Associate Professor of Theology at Xavier University in Cincinnati, OH. She is a diasporic Latvian-American theologian who works at the intersections of postcolonial studies, sacramental and liturgical studies, and modern historical theology, while engaging migration and diaspora discourses. She is the author of the trailblazing study in postcolonial sacramental theology *In Counterpoint: Diaspora, Postcoloniality, and Sacramental Theology* (2017) and numerous articles and book chapters engaging liturgical-sacramental theology, postcolonialism, migration, and theological aesthetics. She currently serves as the Delegate for Membership of the North American Academy of Liturgy (NAAL) and co-chair of the Religions, Borders, and Immigration seminar at the American Academy of Religion (AAR). Since her ordination in 1995, she has served as a pastor in the Latvian Evangelical Lutheran Church Worldwide in Great Britain, Germany, and the United States and continues to serve as the denominational liaison of the Latvian Evangelical Lutheran Church in America with the Lutheran Immigration and Refugee Service (LIRS).

John J. Thatamanil is Associate Professor of Theology and World Religions at Union Theological Seminary. His research takes up comparative theology, theologies of religious diversity, Hindu-Christian dialogue, and Buddhist-Christian dialogue. Thatamanil is author of *The Immanent Divine: God, Creation, and the Human Predicament* (2006). He has recently completed a second book, entitled *Circling the Elephant: A Comparative Theology of Religious Diversity* (2020).

Michelle Voss Roberts is Professor of Theology and Past Principal at Emmanuel College, a multireligious theological school in the University of Toronto. She is the author of three book-length works in comparative theology: *Dualities: A Theology of Difference* (2010); *Tastes of the Divine: Hindu and Christian Theologies of Emotion* (2014), which received the Award for Excellence from the American Academy of Religion; and *Body Parts: A Theological Anthropology* (2017). She edited a volume that brings interreligious comparison to the introductory study of theology, *Comparative Theology: Insights for Systematic Theological Reflection* (2016). Her most recent project was co-editing the *Routledge Handbook of Hindu-Christian Relations* (2020) with Chad Bauman.

Thinking the Unthinkable: Theology as Pain, Joy, Anger, Compassion, Justice, Tradition, and Many Other Things

Edward Farley

NEVER BEFORE HAVE I taken up such a difficult interpretive task. To interpret the textual face of another human being is always daunting, as it invites the interpreter's own narcissistic ideologies that erase the textual face in the very process of drawing it. To take up and express in language Wendy Farley's textual face is to be confronted not simply with a set of texts—philosophical, polemical, personal, and beautiful—but with a concreteness that has already de-stabilized these texts. It is a project that undermines itself as a straightforward articulation. This essay has one primary aim: to assist readers of these texts to discover in and behind them the (non)project of the textual face. I may have it all wrong. I may do it poorly. But this is the task I take up in three themes: poetic thinking, traditions (the uses of the past), and the concepts and vision of (non) theodicy.

Poetic Thinking

Farley's writings are offered to people in academia, church leadership, and everyday life settings. These readers surely experience a kind of initial puzzlement, if not even shock, when they peruse her pages. Readers outside of the fields of academe find themselves struggling with ancient and modern philosophical works by figures they have never heard of. Academics find themselves drawn into a world and a discourse of pain, passion, and intense joy. Thus, readers may not be sure whom the writings are addressing. I think we can start by saying that the author is addressing herself: her own pain, joy, and puzzlements. To say this is not to accuse the author of religious or theological solipsism. She explicitly addresses her works to those who are afflicted, excluded, and marginalized.[1] But exclusion first applies to herself as she is afflicted, tempted, and celebrates a joyous freedom. The style of her writing shows that there is no self-isolated author. Many of the marginalized are part of her own everyday life, and beyond them are vast numbers of those who have been "driven away." But this distinction is never sharply drawn for the reason that all, and in fact everything in creation, is fragile as it makes its way in life; these writings have no strictly designated readership. Academic readers may be perplexed when they would track down the author's "method," her first principles, her steps of argument. And while these writings do cite texts, argue points, and clarify meanings, they typically do not proceed from A to B to C, each step accompanied by cognitive justifications. What, then, do we have before us when we would interpret, learn from, and assess this textual face?

Readers will recognize many ways of thinking in Farley's works: historical analyses, social criticism, and phenomenological insight.[2] Yet there is something new and different that is the result of how all of these ways come together. Hers is a thinking that is deeply personal, touched by who she is and what she has experienced.[3] It may be also analytical and critical, and it is always a thinking that displays passion: the eros (erotic reason) at work in the world and in herself. Farley's thinking, though personal, is simultaneously ethical.[4] However existential or historical the

1. Farley, *Gathering Those Driven Away*.

2. For a very convincing proposal of how the many thinkings come together in the genre of intimate address, see Ellen T. Armour, "Theology as Intimate Address: A Response to Wendy Farley's *Gathering Those Driven Away*" (unpublished paper), presented on May 14, 2010, for a panel on "Erotic Faith: Reflections on Farleyan *Eros*" for the Theology and Philosophy of Religion Section at the 2010 meeting of the Pacific Northwest Region of the American Academy of Religion.

3. While all of Farley's books reflect her person and experiences and arise from her contemplative life, the one most shaped by her experiences is *Wounding and Healing*. See also "Most Beautiful Face," chapter 7 in *Gathering Those Driven Away*.

4. The following passages are examples of the ethical dimension of Farley's work: *Eros for the Other*, 12–13, 89; *Gathering Those Driven Away*, chapter 9, "Truth and Ethics."

subject, she never forgets the exiles and victims of the world. When she interprets an ancient creed or makes use of a philosophical concept, ethical issues set the aim and tone of the writing. And when the voices of her life experience resound in a passage of writing, the voices of others who struggle and suffer are always there, including those from the world of nature. The poetic thinking manifest in this textual face is a disciplined contemplation shaped by scholarship and study. For her, theological (erotic) thinking is a practice: not simply the practice of scholarship but of life itself. Even when it engages in self-, textual, and institutional criticism, it is at the same time the practice of a joyous freedom.

Let us begin with the concept of the concrete, a term Farley uses only occasionally.[5] This concept is our first and most important clue; namely, the author's cognitive antennae and sensibility are always alert to the particular. Concrete particulars—events, persons, and experiences—precede, found, and shape her knowledge, definitions, and inferences. Here we have what may be the most basic paradox of this textual face. That which is concrete is always a particular that we are, that we experience, that constitutes the world. As such, it is necessarily elusive. All particulars are therefore mysteries, and their mystery increases as we experience them and come to know them. All genres of literature (novels, short stories, poetry, memoirs) display a sensibility to the concrete. No language, even that which attempts precise quantitative description, replicates what it describes. Poets are acutely aware of this and attempt a kind of linguistic enchantment, describing yet letting their words be reshaped by the mystery of the concrete. Their metaphors both express the concrete and fail to capture it, and that is their very success. Farley's writing may not be poetry as such, but it displays a poetic element. (Perhaps all genuine theological thinking does.) In passage after passage, the reader is shaken by a discourse that uses metaphor and negation to display particulars in their mystery. To say that these writings originate in and display concreteness and particularity is to say something very abstract. There is no single, unchanging particularity that is the subject of these writings. This is because the writings have to do with victims, including the author herself; institutions; events and movements; and even God. Amidst all of these subjects is a fundamental particularity, and here we have the Kierkegaardian strain of these works: a persistent refusal to suppress the personal dimension of the author's life experiences.

5. On concreteness and particularity, see Farley, *Eros for the Other*, 111–14, 127ff., 178–41, 196–97; and *Gathering Those Driven Away*, chapter 7.

This theological, poetic, life-transforming thinking engenders several distinctive features of the author's writing. First, however much the inquiry has to do with texts and issues of the world of scholarship, and however much it focuses on the issues and causes of the victimized and the excluded, its reach has no boundaries. Its words pass beyond special readerships to any and all who struggle in their fragility and need solace and transformation. Second, poetic thinking creates its own peculiar, beautiful style of writing. For instance, Farley frequently uses nouns and even abstract terms as if they were subjects of action. Thus, compassion "is *open* to the pain of the world."[6] It is "the genius of tragedy that it *recognizes* complexity and responsibility."[7] More is going on here than shortcuts or condensed writing. The style bespeaks the author's poetic sense that everything in and about the world is a mysterious agent of power and action. Third, the most prominent feature of Farley's style may be the recurrence and persistence of what rationalists would identify as contradictions and which poets sense as the inevitable tensions which constitute the world. She is less apt to explain her subjects (the tragic, evil, Christ) than simply to display them. As concrete particulars, these subjects not only elude and resist precise articulation but show their features as self-canceling and their actions as contradictory behaviors. Thus, as soon as readers are satisfied that the author has simply dismissed creeds, confessions, and authorities, they are faced with an eloquent and profound appropriation of the Nicene Creed and the *homoousion*. As soon as they are convinced by the negative theology that nothing can really be said, they find themselves in the midst of a vast and beautiful garden of metaphors. When they become quite certain that the vision and program are by and for individual human beings in the drama of their lives, they discover that the vision is as much about politics and justice and social and institutional power. When they find themselves drawn into the fascinating world of particular things, they are shocked to run across passages of speculative flight. And when they adapt themselves to the dark world of pain, a world that will never be different from what it now is, they are, to quote the famous evangelical C. S. Lewis, "surprised by joy." Such is the (non)method, the poetic thinking, of this project that awaits future readers.

6. Farley, *Eros for the Other*, 75.
7. Farley, *Tragic Vision and Divine Compassion*, 24.

Traditions

Farley's writings are personally and socially contextual, passionate and compassionate. As poetic writings, they display a sensibility to multiple issues, events, and states of affairs. But they are not simply expressions of the author's experiences or analyses of current situations. Every work is shaped by her study of the authors, periods, and texts of Christian history. Here the reader senses ambiguity and tension in the author's relation to Christianity, discovering that her texts exhibit a deep sympathy and appropriation coupled with fierce criticism and rejection.[8]

I begin with the observation that the author's poetic thinking is very much shaped by and filled with the Christian textual past. This very shaping is marked by ambiguity because it does not arise from some theory of an authoritative past that bestows on the traditions of Christian history a guarantee of truth. On the other hand, the Christian past is never simply dismissed as passé, mythical, meaningless, or morally bankrupt.[9] Why does the Christian past survive at all in Farley's poetic thinking? The general answer is that she has antennae for truth, eyes and ears oriented to wisdom wherever and however it occurs. This is why she can appropriate, expound, and argue for explicit texts, figures, and movements of that history—for instance, the fourth- and fifth-century ecumenical Councils—and why she delightedly uncovers and uses the suppressed and marginalized strands of Christian history found in medieval women contemplatives, heretical movements, Neoplatonic theologians like Origen and Nicholas of Cusa, nineteenth-century liberal Protestant theologians, and present-day feminist and womanist theologies. Furthermore, the eyes and ears of the author range far beyond the orthodoxies and heterodoxies of the Christian past. Like Christian thinkers throughout that past, from Justin Martyr to Paul Tillich, she finds truth and wisdom in the broader culture: in literature, philosophy, and even other religious faiths, especially Tibetan Buddhism.

The other side of Farley's use of the Christian past appears in her fierce, sometimes angry, criticisms that effect departures from much of

8. Christianity, classical Christian theologies, and traditions are treated primarily with scattered references in *Tragic Vision*; *Wounding and Healing*, chapter 2; and *Gathering Those Driven Away*, chapter 1.

9. Farley's participation in, sympathy for, and continuity with "classical" Christian theologies are apparent in a number of passages. See her interpretation of the motif of "ransom" in *Wounding and Healing*, 30–31, 106ff. Note also the strong Nicene element in her Christology in *Gathering Those Driven Away*, chapters 2, 7.

what has been identified as ecclesial and Christian. She is conscious of being part of a centuries-long cloud of witnesses who have voiced many of these criticisms: Christian philosophers, mystics, medieval women, agape theologians, liberal Protestants, and womanists. The works of Nicholas Berdyaev, the Russian émigré to Paris, scream objections to "the logic of domination" and the monarchical metaphor for God. The process thinker Charles Hartshorne has exposed contradictions in the classical metaphysics of divine immutability. Farley's works add a dimension of social radicalism directed at both the institutions and narratives of classical Christianity. Institutions and narratives are linked because power and its operations are never absent from ratiocinations, confessions, and intellectual controversies. Farley's criticisms have a radical character not simply because of themes of social corruption and domination but because the author is convinced that something went wrong early on in Christian history. Like William Blake's late epic works, her texts depict the Christian past as a "fallen" history, proceeding from a kind of expulsion from the Edenic period of its origin. Accordingly, the Christian church and its institutions are not simply fallible but fallen, living under a dark shadow of self-absolutization and uniformity often enforced by violence. Is this fall the tragic fate of any and all communities when they institutionalize their initial vision, or a contingent and even avoidable historical accident? She does not say.

Viewed institutionally, the "Fall" of Christianity took place when it made an officially defined uniformity of doctrine, polity, liturgy, and casuistry the very condition of salvation.[10] Since God (him)self brought about this uniform institution and narrative, the propriety of violent enforcement was self-evident. Following from this, the "Fall" continued when the Christian movement assimilated the centuries-long sexism of Greek, Roman, and Asian cultures, thus incorporating the marginalization and even oppression of women into its social structure. The "Fall" continued as the church defined its leadership structure by way of ancient homophobias. The result was a religious community in which exclusions formed its very heart and social structure.[11]

10. Farley's criticisms of the authoritarian and institutional uniformity of the branches of classical Christendom can be found in *Wounding and Healing*, chapter 2; and *Gathering Those Driven Away*, Introduction. See especially her description of the historico-political events of the fourth century that marked a stage in the defining of the heretical other in Christianity (*Gathering Those Driven Away*, chapter 2).

11. Farley, *Gathering Those Driven Away*, Introduction, especially 16–19.

Farley's criticisms apply not only to institutional power and policy but also to themes in Christian narrative traditions: convictions of faith, doctrines, images, and metaphors. Although Farley speaks in the singular of "the old narrative," her departures from classical orthodoxy have to do especially with two centuries-old Christian metaphors that sometimes obtain the status of metaphysical, cosmic descriptions. Both metaphors arise from ways human society organizes itself and pursues its aims: thus, by way of *law* and the law court and by way of authoritarian, hierarchical, and monarchical modes of *governance* or *domination*. Legal systems provided the Christian movement with forensic metaphors and their attendant concepts of guilt and penalty, and the state or ruling power gave it metaphors of *domination* with their attendant concepts of control, direct causality, enforcement, and violence. These two clusters of metaphors pervade and shape the traditional narrative and its themes of the human condition, suffering (theodicy), sin, salvation, divine action, and eschatology. They so closely describe the actions and character of God, the world, and salvation history that the Christian message narrows to a narrative about a law-promoting monarch determining the dualistic heaven–hell outcome of all creation.

In the forensic metaphor, concepts drawn from law courts, such as guilt and punishment, are used to interpret God, human evil, and salvation.[12] Farley's criticism of the metaphor is not intended to replace the concept of guilt with "guilt feelings" but to question the centrality of the metaphor. When it becomes the sole or primary way of thinking about the human condition, it displaces and obscures the ambiguity of that condition as fragility and affliction. Further, it displaces salvific freedom—solace, transformation, and compassion—with a focus on the legal status of being condemned or pardoned. This centrality of guilt and penalty transforms everything: belief, liturgy, piety, and church organization. In the Christian narrative, the metaphor has a cosmic and even divine reach, with its notions of the divine lawgiver presiding over a heavenly court, issuing judgments, condemnations, and pardons in a final, world-ending event. The second metaphor, what Berdyaev calls the logic of domination, is closely linked to the forensic metaphor.[13] This metaphor

12. For criticisms of the forensic or punishment metaphor, see *Tragic Vision*, chapter 4, 120f.; *Wounding and Healing*, chapter 2; and *Gathering Those Driven Away*, 18, 157ff.

13. Passages critical of the monarchical or domination metaphor include *Tragic Vision*, 13, 9–90, 124; and *Gathering Those Driven Away*, Introduction, 9, 160ff.

of unqualified divine power and rule depicts God and God's activity as a unilateral willing of whatever happens and the necessary causal activity it requires. This too is a literalized or cosmological metaphor because it purports to be a direct description of the foundation, origin, and framework of the history of creation and salvation. Like the law court, this metaphor of domination pervades Christian history, creating a discourse and a social structure and providing the content of piety, prayer, doctrine, and organization. This is the metaphor behind traditional Christian notions of the final outcome of cosmos and history as preset heaven/hell destinies of all human beings and is also presupposed by most rationalistic theodicies. This summary account does not include the real, decisive reasons for Farley's criticisms and departures. To do that calls for an explication of her notions of Divine Eros and the centrality of the metaphor of love. To that we now turn.

A (Non)Theodicy

To dwell on Farley's style of thinking and writing and her appropriative and critical use of Christian traditions, as I have, may obscure and distort her textual face, the project itself. Her poetic thinking and historical appropriations and criticisms are paths to something else, not the textual face. To grasp that "something else" is the interpreter's primary challenge.

At this point, interpreters familiar with Christian theology may face something they do not quite recognize. This is because scholars, church leaders, and others tend to measure a theological project by how it is organized into the great themes or doctrines of Christian history: God, Christ, and salvation. To be sure, these themes are very much a part of Farley's writings. One can even say they constitute the very substance of some works. To say this, however, would promote an unfortunate distortion. The heart and soul of these works is a panorama of concepts and metaphors, all closely interrelated, which are the author's ways of specifying and setting forth the great themes. To interpret the textual face of Farley's works is, in part, to grasp how these concepts alter and express the themes. But we distort the textual face if we conclude that a set of metaphors is what is distinctive about her work. For what alters and fills out the great themes are different genres of things, even dimensions of reality. Thus, the interpreter confronts not just metaphors (e.g., eros, the erotic) but truth, practice, individual passions, gender exclusion, institutional corruption, and contemplation.

Four general areas (doctrines) recur in Farley's four books: God, the human condition (suffering, affliction, evil), Christ, and redemption (freedom). God is the primary theme of *Tragic Vision and Divine Compassion*, and the human condition and liberation are the focus of *Eros for the Other* and *The Wounding and Healing of Desire*. All the themes are brought together in *Gathering Those Driven Away*. A quick and superficial reading of these works may take these themes to be restatements of the great doctrines. Indeed, they reflect the long sweep of classical Christian texts. God is triune, the creator of all things. Jesus is the particular historical embodiment of the divine *logos* or Wisdom, which itself is the creativity and Word of God. Human beings exist in a shadow world of suffering, individual evil and despair, and social and institutional corruption. Solace, liberation, and joy are available to them as they partake in that strand of history that unrolls from the incarnation. Yet we do not have in this summary the actual meaning and reality of God, Christ, and the human condition. For that we must attend to the textual face of Farley much more closely.

There is no way an interpreter can do justice to the conceptuality of this project in a few pages. Thus, I risk perpetuating abstraction and misunderstanding by selecting a few important concepts that shape and express all of the theological themes. Altogether, these concepts and metaphors do not add up to a conceptual system such as we find in Friedrich Schleiermacher or Paul Tillich. They do, however, hang together in coherence. Although they resist systematization because they express different genres and dimensions, they do have a coherent relation to each other. Among the many concepts in Farley's works, six especially stand out: desire, suffering, compassion (love), mystery, practice, and contemplation. A seventh concept, totality, functions as a contrast and even endangerment to all six. *Desire*, coupled with Plato's concept of Eros, has no single definition.[14] Desire is the broadest and most universal metaphor for expressing the ground of all things (the Divine Eros) and describing the most pervasive feature of created existence (striving, need) and the depth structure of human beings. Although *ideas* (another key concept) are also important in Farley's poetic thinking, they are more expressive

14. The theme of desire (Eros) is pursued and elaborated in *Eros for the Other*, *Wounding and Healing*, and *Gathering Those Driven Away*. Farley's most extensive philosophical analysis of the concept, including a discussion of a major source (Levinas), can be found in *Eros for the Other*, chapter 3. Desire is the unifying theme of *Wounding and Healing*. See also *Gathering Those Driven Away*, chapters 5, 8.

of the powers of things than of essences, precisely because desire keeps both the creative and the created ever on the move.[15] The term *suffering* occurs frequently in Farley's works.[16] It names the many ways creatures can experience temptation, fear, and demise. All actual things are fragile, vulnerable to the accidents and built-in mortalities of being part of a world in the making. Human beings in their bio-social complexity move through time by way of unfathomed, deep structures of the soul, structures which can turn into soul-destroying dispositions (passions). Their deepest structure, desire, opens them to temptation, or the tendency to make too much of the goods on which they depend. In other words, as both individuals and communities, human beings can and do become self-absorbing, predatory, and cruel.[17]

There are many dark passages in these works, but *love* (compassion) is never forgotten. In one sense, love is identical with Eros—which in its truest aspect is never simply need or striving but a disposition to become, be part of, and further the well-being of whatever is at hand.[18] This is why Eros has a compassionate face turned toward whatever is fragile, which means everything that exists. *Mystery* (the apophatic) applies not only to God but to anything that exists.[19] This concept has both Semitic (Hebrew prophets) and Hellenic (e.g., Plato) roots and obtains poetic and philosophical expression in the Neoplatonist Pseudo-Dionysius and the negative theology he introduced. The apophatic exposes the limits of all the other concepts and metaphors. Powerful as they may be, they never obtain the status of utter presence, unambiguous meaning, or linguistic replication. The apophatic shadows all language, all terms, even all entities themselves. It is the unthinkable mystery of all particulars and the unthinkable mystery of what brought them into being. If we stopped our analysis with these four concepts, we would give the impression that they fall together in a metaphysics of world and God, a universalization of whatever is. The apophatic does set limits to such an account, but so does

15. See *Eros for the Other*, chapter 4.

16. The themes of fragility, suffering, and affliction appear in all of Farley's works. See especially *Tragic Vision*, Introduction, chapter 2 on "individual suffering," chapter 5; and *Wounding and Healing*, chapters 4–5.

17. On themes of human evil (sin, cruelty), see *Tragic Vision*, 44–50, chapter 2. On the "betrayal of eros," see *Eros for the Other*, 90–109.

18. On themes of love and compassion, see *Tragic Vision*, chapter 3; and *Gathering Those Driven Away*, chapters 6, 9.

19. See especially *Gathering Those Driven Away*, chapters 3–4.

another concept that introduces a different dimension altogether: *practice*.[20] This concept draws all the other concepts into the push and pull of events, persons, conflicts, and the flow of actual history and biography. Practice transforms all of these concepts from speculative-descriptive agents of knowing to a kind of marching orders. Desire is something to be practiced. So are love, suffering, and even negative theology. So is the incarnation (divine indwelling) itself. And we surely will miss what Farley's project is about if we omit the function of concepts in the practice of living. *Contemplation* is part of the central core of concepts in Farley's theology. This is because the divine indwelling (incarnation) and the freedom that comes with it are never simply instantaneous or once-for-all events. The human being, both individually and socially, is not only temporally stretched out over time but complexly constructed with multiple layers of woundedness, trauma, deep prejudices, even cruelties. Hence, healing and the liberation of the human being can be greatly assisted by subjecting layer after layer to the insights, profound wisdom, metaphors, and negations of the narratives and traditions of the community. And this is just what contemplation, both as a determined discipline and an occasional activity, can do.

Finally, there is a seventh concept we dare not omit: *totality*.[21] The term, taken from the works of Emmanuel Levinas, joins the apophatic and practice in naming a different dimension. It is the anti-concept, the competitor and alternative (even as a practice) to all of them. In Farley's works, totality means a way of thinking, a worldview, a way of being in and having the world, and a societal power. Because it is a way of thinking which reduces knowing and language to systems, quantities, and causalities, its effect is to obscure or deny the desire that keeps things open and flowing. Because it finds expressions in words, concepts, and even narratives to further its self-serving aims, it perpetuates illusion and deceit. Because it is invariably in service of social and institutional powers oriented only to the various kinds of domination, its effect is to counter and erase love and compassion. Totality and domination are thus closely

20. Practice can be found in many passages of these works. At the same time, it is the assumption, primary thesis, and tone throughout the (non)project. But see *Wounding and Healing*, Preface, chapter 7, on contemplative practice. See also *Gathering Those Driven Away*, chapter 3, on truth and practice, chapter 6.

21. This motif appears in Farley's first book as part of the discussion of deceit and illusion (*Tragic Vision*, 44–45). Especially important is the analysis of the concept in Levinas, and Farley's elaboration of that in *Eros for the Other*, 18–26, 54–60, and chapter 2. See also *Gathering Those Driven Away*, chapter 4.

linked. When we turn our attention back to the recurrent themes that constitute Christian history, worship, and community, we quickly see the results of Farley's contemplations as she poetically rethinks each theme. *God* names not a principle or structure but an unfathomable creative *activity* in all things.[22] Neither a law court figure nor a vengeful omni-causality, God is the generative, compassionate source and constant re-shaper of nature, history, peoples, and individuals. In the old narrative, human beings are fallen and guilty, worthy of eternal punishment; they suffer and face mortality as payments for their sins. For Farley, human beings, like all created things, are victims of tragic structures that come with life, change, particularity, and creativity itself. In this ambiguous condition, they are both pitiful victims and responsible actors. Thus, their redemptive transformation is not a change of legal status but a healing, a restoration of their deepest structure (desire). The emotive tone of this coming to freedom is not relief over a legal pardon, but joyful freedom. *Christ* names the eternal, creative Wisdom of God embodied (incarnate) in human history, which in the Christian strand of history is encountered and remembered as Jesus.[23] This means that in a specific space, time, and language of history, compassion and love have a distinctive display and embodiment. Yet totality as a worldview, a hermeneutic, and a societal power ever lures the past and present to obscure these themes of mystery and incarnate presence. When totality is dominant, mystery, love, and in-carnation are traded for self-absolutizing, oppressive powers that entrap human beings in a metaphysics of causal power, forensics, and violence.

Does anything tie all of this together? Do we have in these works a unifying vision of things? The answer appears to be affirmative. Farley's writings confront us with a variety of concepts and theological themes that apply to the world itself under the divine mystery, concepts that express how the world works, the human condition, and the divine en-ergy. Together, these powerful metaphors constitute a kind of genre that the religious and the theological quickly recognize. The project voices a theodicy: a vision of God, world, suffering, and evil.[24] But to use the term "theodicy" to unify this project gives the impression that the author has

22. On God as "beyond being," see *Gathering Those Driven Away*, chapter 5. On God as desire or creative and compassionate Eros, see *Tragic Vision*, chapter 4; and *Wounding and Healing*, chapter 6.

23. On Christ and incarnation, see especially *Wounding and Healing*, chapter 6; and *Gathering Those Driven Away*, chapters 3, 5 (on the emanation of divine Wisdom).

24. See *Tragic Vision*, chapter 1 and 123–33.

revived an old intellectual puzzle, reconciling the existence of suffering and evil with an all-powerful and loving deity. There is no such problem in these works. Theodicy can mean something broader and deeper than the solving of that puzzle. Here we remind ourselves that every problem taken up in these writings, every criticism, every metaphor and concept, is useful—not just in the sense of revealing an insight, but as an invitation to a journey. The textual face of these works is the path all human beings walk, especially the excluded and the marginalized, the suffering and the oppressed. This path is the task and opportunity to exist in freedom, relate to others, and be part of institutions in the ongoing situation of suffering, temptation, and transformation. There is a vision here, but it is not so much a general metaphysical scheme as a glimpse of the elements of a life-transforming struggle. Hints of Buddhist ways of thinking shadow these writings. Farley is also haunted by ghosts of Pascal, Kierkegaard, Levinas, and many medieval women contemplatives. This is why the coherent vision of interrelated concepts and dimensions is taken away as soon as it is offered. It is not so much offered to intellects as to human beings who would be transformed in their ways of experiencing their pitiful fragility, suffering, afflictions, self-absolutizing desire, and even their cruelties. We human beings need a theodicy as we walk paths of shadow and light; we need insights into what blocks, tempts, and empowers us on the journey.

How does this happen? How does one walk these paths in freedom, empowerment, and joy? The author suggests an answer to this question, a theme that occurs throughout her writings. A powerful—perhaps *the* powerful—means of empowering insight for people on the way is a disciplined "poetic thinking" or *contemplation*.[25] Here the author is drawing on figures, traditions, and texts from various faiths that offer ways in which human beings can come to insight. It is at this point that Farley's (non)project seems to conflict with the prevailing cultural, political, and even religious moods of the postmodern era. Certain moods and styles of life prevail in the brave new world of industrialized postmodern societies. Can we take up contemplation in the inescapable presence of ten thousand visual and auditory advertisements a day, pressured busyness at work, and anxious pursuit of adult toys, games, causes, and relations? The communities, rituals, and pieties of religious groups seem to have

---

25. On contemplation, see *Wounding and Healing*, chapter 7; and *Gathering Those Driven Away*, 99ff., 104ff. Note especially how contemplation relates to the apophatic, practice, compassion, and how it faces built-in obstacles (darkness).

little effect on the everyday lives of postmoderns. But contemplation may be the one thing we can do, the one thing that momentarily shuts down the noise and the chatter.

Bibliography

Farley, Wendy. *Eros for the Other: Retaining Truth in a Pluralistic World.* University Park, PA: Penn State University Press, 1996.

———. *Gathering Those Driven Away: A Theology of Incarnation.* Louisville, KY: Westminster John Knox, 2011.

———. *Tragic Vision and Divine Compassion: A Contemporary Theodicy.* Louisville, KY: Wesminster John Knox, 1990.

———. *The Wounding and Healing of Desire: Weaving Heaven and Earth.* Louisville, KY: Westminster John Knox, 2005.

ONE

Gathering Victims, Allowing No Villains: The Challenge of Wendy Farley's Theology

Monica A. Coleman

WENDY FARLEY'S WORKS ALWAYS make me cry. I read *Tragic Vision and Divine Compassion* in the year after I was raped.[1] The urge to take seriously the compassionate presence of God was illumined for me then and became entrenched in my core understanding of the gospel. Even if my theology changes with the encounter of new experiences, deeper spirituality, and greater conflict, I remain convinced that I will center myself on the kind of present God that expresses itself as Emmanuel: God with us.

I needed go no further than the preface of *The Wounding and Healing of Desire* to admire the depths from which Farley writes, the challenges she mitigates, and the courage of her confessional witness.[2] In the days when parts of my life align with the experiences she recounts, I am not only assured that desire itself is meaningful, but that there may be theological value in the depths of paralysis. I cannot name where my tears began in *Gathering Those Driven Away.*[3] I suspect it is in the sheer beauty of how Farley constructs theology. Here is one example. Nearly a decade ago, Karen Torjesen and I were talking about Origen and

1. Farley, *Tragic Vision and Divine Compassion: A Contemporary Theodicy.*
2. Farley, *The Wounding and Healing of Desire: Weaving Heaven and Earth.*
3. Farley, *Gathering Those Driven Away: A Theology of Incarnation.*

Augustine when she made what might have seemed like a throwaway comment: "Heresy is the shadow-side of orthodoxy."[4]

That orthodoxy is constructed from a negation of the other seems clear. That heresy is dragged alongside it was revelatory to me. I embrace the proposition that heretics are as Christian as the rest, losing less because of theological inadequacies and more by the political power struggles of their day. I love that heresy is not hard to find; that it hides around the corner, in hushed arbors, and in house churches and theology pubs; that it asserts itself in the daily lives of individuals and communities. In *Gathering*, Farley not only considers so-called heretics—the losers and victims of Christendom's past—alongside thinkers accepted in the Western Christian scholarly tradition, she also reveals the sinister acts by which they were deemed heretics in the first place. In so doing, she gathers in those who were driven away, modeling her thesis with her method.

Farley also exhibits a radical engagement for the Western Christian tradition, despite its exclusionary traits. As she moves in and through various thinkers, calling forth the teachings that gather people in, she does so with a compassionate heart for all. For instance, the average feminist religious scholar would see it as shameful to affirm an atonement theory of salvation. With the multitude of convincing work on their deficits, atonement theories have become the persona non grata in feminist theological spheres. Yet Farley is able to see the divine even there: "Perhaps the idea of atonement, as well as serving to justify suffering and uphold patriarchal structures, also speaks to the delusions of guilt and punishment in ways that bring news of a gracious love. We might cling to this imaginary love until we are strong enough to accept the reality of an infinite tenderness that had never let us go."[5] How easy it is for us theologians and people of faith to become so emboldened by our convictions that we are unable, unwilling, or blinded to the value of what grasps others in theories we may personally eschew. Here, Farley's own scholarly compassion mirrors the divine compassion she purports and also serves as a characteristic of good constructive theology. As one weaves together a courageous and emboldened view of our most liberative, inclusive life

---

4. Karen Jo Torjesen is the Professor Emerita of Religion at Claremont Graduate University, where she served for several years as dean of the School of Religion. She is best known for her book *When Women Were Priests: Women's Leadership in the Early Church and the Scandal of their Subordination in the Rise of Christianity*.

5. Farley, *Gathering Those Driven Away*, 158–59.

with the divine, it is easy to highlight the shortcomings of others without compassionately recognizing the deep motivations of perspectives we might never embrace.

In a marketplace where ideas are readily commodified and codified, *Gathering Those Driven Away* defies easy classification. While this may be a result of negotiating savvy and embodiment, I believe that it is the result of an amazing range of conversation partners. While the theology in *Gathering* gains its fortitude from Irenaeus, Marguerite Porete, Pelagius, the mindfulness of Buddhism, the practice of mothering, liberationists, postcolonialists, and faithful engagement with the Bible (to name just a few), the work manages to exhibit the characteristics of them all. It is feminist, liberation, classical, heretical, comparative, queer, poetic, embodied, concerned, joyful, and mysterious. By conversing in print with those who have been driven away and those who are concerned with those who are driven away, *Gathering* brings forth the multiplicity of the voices that sing the same song of joyful concern (or, more aptly, "concerned joy") in our world. Taking them into her own theology, incorporating rather than transcending, Farley calls us towards a theological position that fits poorly in the names wherein many of us find our homes.

But I still suspect that it is not this beauty that evokes my tears. Over 25 years ago, I began speaking out against sexual violence. My activism was rooted in well-meaning, yet often destructive churches that unintentionally drive away those who deeply need to be embraced by a communal embodiment of God's grace and presence. Through education, structures, programs, and a book, I wanted to show churches how to stop evicting their own.[6] This work was and continues to be motivated by my own experience as a survivor of sexual violence. It was and is rooted in compassionate solidarity with those who loved me, who also underwent a psychological and theological crisis in the face of intimate violence and intense suffering. I have insisted on the terminology "those who have experienced sexual violence" to try to highlight the fact that sexual violence affects communities. The obvious victims are those who are violated, but so are the people who love them, as well as the violators and the people who love them—and, given the patterns of abuse, it is not always easy to distinguish victim and violator. I have eschewed language of "the rapist" to remind myself that an individual is more than a single act. That is where I have been able to locate forgiveness.

6. Coleman, *The Dinah Project: A Congregational Response to Sexual Violence.*

As the years have progressed, I find myself speaking more often to groups of male clergy who ask about my ideas and programs for violators. I have none. My ministry around churches and sexual violence does not include a ministry to and for those who violate. I admit that my heart is not that large. My forgiveness is not that deep. Farley lays my entire faith on the threshold. Will I open the door? she asks. How wide? Like Farley, I believe that sexuality and pleasure and embodiment unnerve Christian theologies. And yet I am unable or unwilling to minister to those I see as villains. *Gathering* challenges me by asking if my passion for justice drives others away.

As much as it challenges, *Gathering* also guides me toward a response. Farley convinces me of the need to walk the path between naming and negation, between victim and villain. Farley's theology pushes me to release my grip on certainty. I have generally been convinced that "mystery" is another name for "uncertainty" and preferred the image of a God and world that can be described in a philosophical metaphysic.[7] I have preferred the process of change, dimensions of immortality, and a God who is more like me than not, to the claims of apophatic theologies.

But Farley shows how slippery the slide to idolatry is and how easily we all become commandment breakers, "using the name of God as cover for the idols of our hearts." Thus, I am persuaded that the necessary balance between certainty and mystery, metaphysical explanation and apophatic theology, and orthodoxy and heresy is a wordlessness and imagelessness. The ability to encounter God without the comfort of words and pictures can draw me to see the divine in new ways. I can see the divine both in myself and in the violator-victim—who I also may be. In reading Farley, I have been won over to the value of divine mystery because I understand that "protecting divine mystery is, in this sense, not only a prophylactic against idolatry, but intrinsic to the practice of love."[8]

Likewise, I cling more closely to an epistemological understanding of the gospel. What amazes me—both metaphysically and personally— about God and the witness of saviors is not only that God is with us, but that God knows us. This corresponds to what Farley identifies as the kind of optics that Jesus illustrates, an optics that may indeed be the core of the gospel. Like Farley, I come to an awe of God through the incarnation. While my own soteriology emphasizes the unexpected embodiment

7. I am referring to my identification as a process theologian who works with the metaphysics of Alfred North Whitehead.

8. Farley, *Gathering Those Driven Away*, 69.

of salvation and names it as the process by which we amble, with starts and falls, towards justice in community, I have assumed the incarnation.[9] That we are emboldened, empowered by, and exhibiting the divinity that is deeply within us is necessary to my own understanding of that which saves us. Farley names this more directly than I have. She is clear that divinization itself, incarnation, not only begins God's intimacy with us and our understanding of the gospel and daily right action, but it is the central feature of our faith.

In the past, I also felt that there are more exciting things to say about God than God is love. That God is present, compassionate, and intimately knowing impresses me much more than love. I may hold an anemic view of love, but I remain compelled by God's presence. Yet Farley's assertion that "love is this emptying, connecting energy that in its power originates new connections and new life" shows me that I have simply called love by another name: creativity.[10]

In Whiteheadian process metaphysics, creativity is widely considered an ultimate (along with God and the world) that describes the activity by which the many become one and are increased by one. This is the animating activity of God and the world. As the changing and becoming power of the universe, creativity leads me towards the contemplative practices that Farley knowledgeably describes. Indeed, it is in cooking and cycling that I am the most contemplative, the most in-tune, the most calm, the most human, and the most divine.[11]

To return to the violator-victim issue that I struggle with in ministry, Farley says it plainly: "Great compassion not only calls us to practices of social justice, it also challenges us to inhabit this quest through practices that help us to recognize the humanity of those we identify as opponents."[12] What I hear is this: We must embrace a view that gathers the victims but allows no villains. This is not easy, so it must be practiced. For those like me who find contemplation in cooking and cycling, it reminds me that I must ride with those who differ greatly or even offend me; I must prepare a meal for them at my table. This is not only an act of

9. Coleman, *Making a Way Out of No Way: A Womanist Theology.*

10. Farley, *Gathering Those Driven Away*, 66.

11. Coleman, "On Baking and Biking: The Theological and Neurological Value of Non-Contemplative Spiritual Disciplines as Spiritual Practice in the Context of Depressive Conditions."

12. Farley, *Gathering Those Driven Away*, 220.

justice or Eucharist. It is an act of incarnation, divinization, and forgive-ness—which is, of course, salvation.

There is theology that intrigues, theology that remarks, theology that deepens, and theology that constructs. Farley's theology challenges. It challenges me to be more divine. It also acknowledges that the incar-nation is the presence with us as "we rise to awareness of our spiritual nature."[13] It reminds us that we need not be good at it; we need only to practice it.

What baffles me about Farley's theology is her inclusion of Trini-tarian Wisdom in her conception of God. While Jesus embodies and reveals divine incarnation, why the need for Wisdom? Must there be a primordial aspect of the divine moving throughout creation? How is this Wisdom so different from the Love (God) that Farley so poignantly describes? Is this attachment to Trinitarian thinking any healthier than the atonement theory, with which Farley can sympathize while naming as provisional? Despite the move to engage with non-theistic traditions and swinging wider the door for comparative theological work, I find that the use of Wisdom as the incarnating force—affiliated in any way with a Trinity—reduces, if not truncates, the kind of respect, parity, and engagement with non-Christian traditions (or even just low Christologi-cal Christians like myself) that the principles of love, contemplation, and joy so deeply evoke.

These questions, however, are relatively minor and do nothing to abate my tears. In short, I believe I am so deeply moved by Farley's the-ology for its ability to lovingly challenge while holding the theological family of God together.

Bibliography

Coleman, Monica A. *Making a Way Out of No Way: A Womanist Theology.* Minneapolis, MN. Fortress Press, 2008.

———. "On Baking and Biking: The Theological and Neurological Value of Non-Contemplative Spiritual Disciplines as Spiritual Practice in the Context of Depressive Conditions." Paper presented at Neuroscience and Spiritual Practice: Transforming the Embodied Mind, Claremont School of Theology, Claremont, CA, October 2008.

———. *The Dinah Project: A Congregational Response to Sexual Violence.* Eugene, OR Wipf & Stock Publishers, 2010.

13. Farley, *Gathering Those Driven Away*, 152.

Farley, Wendy. *Gathering Those Driving Away: A Theology of Incarnation.* Louisville, KY: Westminster John Knox, 2011.

———. *Tragic Vision and Divine Compassion: A Contemporary Theodicy.* Louisville, KY: Westminster/John Knox, 1990.

———. *The Wounding and Healing of Desire: Weaving Heaven and Earth.* Louisville, KY: Westminster John Knox, 2005.

Torjesen, Karen Jo. *When Women Were Priests: Women's Leadership in the Early Church and the Scandal of their Subordination in the Rise of Christianity.* San Francisco, CA. Harper San Francisco, 1995.

TWO

Mindful Desire:
Contemplation and the Practice of Theology in
Wendy Farley

Ian Curran

IN THE SPRING OF 2001 I took a seminar at Emory University with Wendy Farley on theological anthropology. At that time, I was locked into a vision of theology as a purely intellectual enterprise, and I was expecting to be fed a steady diet of systematic theologians. While Farley had us read some traditional theological fare, much of the seminar was devoted to contemplative writings like Athanasius' *The Life of St. Antony*, Dorotheus of Gaza's *Discourses and Sayings*, Pseudo-Macarius' *Fifty Spiritual Homilies*, and Julian of Norwich's *Revelations of Divine Love*. Farley also played a good bit of spiritually evocative folk music. I simply did not get what was going on. What had contemplation to do with theology?

Christian theology since the twelfth century has been plagued by a division between the conceptual articulation of the faith and the lived experience of God.[1] While theological learning in the early medieval period was centered in a monastic environment that held together intellectual reflection and prayer, the rise of the university system and the development of scholasticism in the later Middle Ages privileged logical, propositional methods of theological inquiry and divorced them from the contemplative practices, affective dispositions, and unitive end of the

---

1. The historical decoupling of theology and spirituality has been admirably traced by Sheldrake in *Spirituality and Theology*, 33–64. See also Farley, *Theologia*.

spiritual life. Although this division has been exacerbated by the Enlightenment and its valorization of reason, some recent theological writing has sought to recover the ancient sense of theology as a practice that orients the whole person—body, mind, heart and soul—towards God.[2]

Wendy Farley is well-known for her profound explorations of theodicy, her theological epistemology, her original conception of suffering as the fundamental human problem rather than sin, her critiques of atonement theory, her construction of a Christology from the margins, and her erotic theology of God, all of which make original contributions and pose incisive challenges to the discipline of theology. In this essay, however, I will focus on Farley's contributions to a rapprochement between theology and spirituality, first delineating the features of her understanding of contemplation and then exploring a radical implication of this understanding, that theology is itself a contemplative practice, an act that makes us mindful of God.

Farley on Contemplation

In *The Wounding and Healing of Desire* and *Gathering Those Who Are Driven Away*, Farley devotes chapters to discussing the nature of contemplation and its significance for the process by which we are healed of the wounds which life gives us. In the former book, Farley advances a theological anthropology built around the centrality of desire in human life, the woundedness of desire that occurs through suffering, and the healing of desire through contemplative practices, formation in virtues, and our living out of the divine glory that is manifest within us. In the latter book, Farley develops a Christology intended to speak to those who live at the margins of church and society, particularly the sexually marginalized. She writes several preliminary chapters addressing the issues of monotheism and idolatry, negative theology, and contemplation in the context of the incarnation. The subsequent chapters construct a wisdom Christology, an account of the union of divinity and humanity in Jesus, an exploration of the passion as Christ's intimacy and solidarity

2. In addition to the works by Sheldrake and Farley, see LeClerq, *The Love of Learning*; Leech, *Experiencing God*; and McIntosh, *Mystical Theology*. Hadot explores how both ancient philosophy and theology were transformative contemplative practices in his *Philosophy as a Way of Life* and *What is Ancient Philosophy?* The essays in Ferrer and Sherman, *The Participatory Turn*, suggest that the wider field of religious studies is a spiritually self-involving discipline.

with humanity in its brokenness, a soteriology rooted in a theology of incarnation and divinization, and a study of the gospel narratives and their practical implications for Christian life. The two accounts of contemplation that Farley provides, while contributing to theological anthropology, on the one hand, and Christology, on the other, are similar enough that a number of motifs in her view of contemplation can be identified.

In the broadest sense, Farley defines contemplation as "a conscious desire to enter more deeply into the Divine Eros that flows through all things as delighting, compassionate love, together with processes and practices that nurture that desire."[3] Because the Divine Eros is nondualistic, contemplative desire is a desire to open our awareness to the noncognitive, non-imagistic, depth dimensions of reality. Contemplative desire is a given of our experience—we are desiring beings—but Farley associates this desire with an awareness of a love for God and neighbor present in us without having been perfected. Desire is the mode of our intimacy with God, who is also desire, or Eros. Sin (which is caused by our woundedness) is simply the distance between our desire for the good and the reality of it in God, the Good beyond being. Contemplation strengthens and transforms our desire so that it may gradually release us from our habitual egocentrism. The ego is not itself bad; the problem is when our consciousness becomes centered on it. As human beings, we are prey to passions or negative emotions that serve as obstacles to the realization of our deepest desire to be in communion with the divine love that pervades the world. Thus Farley writes that "contemplation dislocates the ego, rerouting the flow of energy from the pains and pleasures of the ego to the river of Eros that bathes all of reality."[4] The process by which contemplative desire dislocates the ego and leads to an encounter with the Divine Eros, moreover, points to a number of other features of contemplation: the contemplative life is a path; it involves specific, embodied practices; it entails an apophatic theology of the self; it is woven into the fabric of everyday life; it supports work for social justice and the cause of the marginalized; and it is therapeutic, relational, salvific, and theological in nature.

Because contemplation is directed toward the Divine Eros, which is infinite, contemplation can never be a final achievement but only a path on which we continually journey toward union with God (in Christianity)

---

3. Farley, *Wounding and Healing*, 116.
4. Farley, *Wounding and Healing*, 116.

or enlightenment (in Buddhism). Christian theologians have historically described the three stages of the contemplative path as purgation, illumination, and union, although some recent writers, in honoring a creation spirituality, place illumination as the first stage.[5] The contemplative path, however, inevitably involves us in a process of purification, where we have to struggle with obstacles to union within us that need to be healed. The path involves moments of darkness that are necessary for our healing, though Farley carefully distinguishes between the healing potential of the dark night and the darkness of egregious suffering. Although we are in movement on the path, Farley also emphasizes that we need to attend to the present moment in which we find ourselves. There is no absolute norm of where we should be on the path, or what the path will exactly look like, so discernment is appropriate for each person to decide which way is right in her given context. The contemplative path, as we will see, overlaps significantly with therapeutic models of human development.

The chief means by which we progress along the path are through contemplative practices. While contemplative awareness is possible in people who are not religious, we typically need contemplative practices to transform us into deeper devotees of God. Since the contemplative practitioner is a unity of body and soul, contemplative practices are embodied acts. They are means by which we let go of the control of the ego and discipline our awareness to be open to the divine. They are "techniques or tools that assist us in calming the chatter of our consciousness so that silence, the first language of the divine, can speak."[6] She also considers ostensibly secular pursuits, such as gardening, to be means of contemplation. Contemplative practices are not inordinately difficult, but rather are possible for all human beings.

Contemplative practices draw our attention to dimensions of reality that exceed the grasp of concepts and images. This includes the depths of the Divine Eros and the depths of the human being. A contemplative approach therefore entails an apophatic theology of the self. As Farley notes, discursive reasoning is only one part of the human being and contemplative practices are "one way to move belief more deeply into the recesses of heart and mind."[7] Contemplation moves us to the place within where

5. This is the position of Dorothy Soelle, and it resonates with Farley's commitment to describe the human condition as wounded love rather than sin. See Soelle, *The Silent Cry*.

6. Farley, *Wounding and Healing*, 120.

7. Farley, *Gathering Those Driven Away*, 91.

the self meets "the visceral reality of apophatic divinity."[8] In this place, we come to see that we are not only images but indeed carriers of the Divine Eros. Contemplation is therefore "a journey of self-knowledge in which we come to know ourselves and all other beings as God-bearers."[9]

Despite the apophatic depths of our humanity to which we are called by contemplation, contemplation is not an esoteric activity, but rather is woven into the fabric of ordinary life. It is an awakening to a call that God has already proclaimed in creation. Contemplation "does not generate divine love but is a response to the love that is already being showered on us."[10] Contemplative practices turn our attention to the reality of divine love in the midst of life and in our very own souls. In this respect, they also transform how we see the world around us. As Farley explains, "when what we mostly do is look at a computer screen, fight traffic, metabolize stress, these things dominate our identity. Practices that interrupt the domination of daily tasks rehabituate our experience of who we are."[11]

The capacity of contemplative practices to transform us in everyday life illustrates their intersection with therapy. Contemplative practices can heal us psychologically by releasing us from neurotic fear and guilt (often resulting from belief in a punitive deity), by giving us a hope that frees us from painful memories and experiences, and by enabling us to work through the various wounds and traumas that have accumulated in the unconscious. The psychological progress that often accompanies contemplative practice is rendered traditionally as the stage of purgation in the spiritual life. For Farley, however, the language of purgation is too often bound up with notions of sin and she prefers to re-describe this stage in terms of woundedness.

The therapeutic, personally transformative dimensions of contemplation are relevant for Christians concerned about social justice as well. Contemplation puts us in touch with our true identity as bearers of the divine and thus enables a critical distance from the selves imposed on us by the world. As Farley explains, for those who are marginalized or living in conditions of oppression, this identity liberates them from the identity provided by the oppressor or the dominant power structures of church

---

8. Farley, *Gathering Those Driven Away*, 91.

9. Farley, *Gathering Those Driven Away*, 91.

10. Farley, *Gathering Those Driven Away*, 93.

11. Farley, *Gathering Those Driven Away*, 95.

and society.[12] The healing provided by contemplation also includes liberation from internalized oppression. As Farley explains, "the purgation of internalized oppressions, of debilitating shame, of submission to prevaricating church authorities is an essential therapy of the spirit."[13] She also emphasizes the importance of feminist, womanist, and queer theologies which contribute to contemplation by emphasizing the full humanity of everyone and the place of the erotic in Christian devotion. Contemplation and social action are thoroughly interdependent.

Thus, while contemplation is not immune from the danger of collapsing into an egocentric spirituality, its transformative energy is both personal and relational, impacting the development of persons and the larger communities to which they belong by moving us toward the love of God and neighbor. "Love is our deepest identity, and healing the wounds of the ego frees us for love, even as love tends to the wounds of the ego. Contemplation is one way to move more deeply into this circulation of justice and compassion."[14] Contemplation can sometimes be distorted into narcissistic self-absorption, or masochistic self-sacrifice, but its authentic expression is a love for others that preserves self-care.

The personally and relationally transformative dimensions of contemplation provide evidence of its salvific nature. Farley follows the Eastern church and interprets salvation, embodied in and effected by the person of Christ, as *theosis*, or divinization. Divinization, which Farley defines as "the path by which humanity returns to the Divine Eros," is one of the primary aims of contemplation.[15] Contemplative practices are also "practices of divinization," and they can lead us to a unitive vision of the divine light.[16]

Farley's use of the language of divinization to describe the effects of contemplation exemplifies her insistence that secular language (such

12. Farley, *Gathering Those Driven Away*, 95.

13. Farley, *Gathering Those Driven Away*, 99.

14. Farley, *Gathering Those Driven Away*, 103.

15. Farley, *Gathering Those Driven Away*, 170.

16. In her chapter on salvation in *Gathering Those Who Are Driven Away*, Farley discusses the contemplative practice of meditating upon the face of Christ, who is present in all created faces, as a way of transforming our perceptions of the visible and invisible world. She writes that "the contemplative movement from visible to invisible light is a practice that deepens the capacity to perceive the invisible in the visible. Seeking the 'face of faces' breaks up the attachments of the ego. The blaze of Divinity burns away the ego-mind and frees us for truer vision." Farley, *Gathering Those Driven Away*, 184.

as that of therapy) "does not displace a theological account of what happens in contemplative practice."[17] Contemplation is not merely a form of self-improvement or well-being, but is "a way to connect to our identity as bearers of the divine image."[18] Contemplation, furthermore, aims to connect us to the divine reality, the object of theological reflection.[19] Theology is needed to provide a full account of contemplation and, as we will see, contemplation is needed to provide a full account of theology.

Contemplation and the Practice of Theology

Contemplation is central to Farley's understanding of the human person and the work of Christ in human bodies and souls. She also suggests, at certain points in her writing, that contemplation is crucial to the work of theology. In this section, I will explore what Farley writes about theology in relationship to the practice of contemplation, and then note some implications of her writing for re-imagining theology as a contemplative practice.

Farley principally characterizes theology as wisdom. She recognizes it as an academic discipline that consists in the intellectual reflection upon doctrine but emphasizes that theology is also *sapientia*.[20] She thus follows Edward Farley's recovery of *theologia* as "a practical, salvation-oriented (existential-personal) knowledge of God."[21] As she writes, theology "is longing for wisdom: pain seeking understanding."[22]

Theological judgments do not depend only on the mind, but also draw upon our emotional life, our experience of suffering, and our desire for God. "Theology is a practice," she continues, "that uses words and ideas, books and concepts to throw one's mind and heart toward the eternally erotic Abyss that is our heart's desire. Theology lingers at the margin of concepts, passing back and forth between the womb of Divinity and the discipline of thought."[23] As a sapiential discipline, therefore, it both uses concepts and also moves beyond them into sacred dimensions of

17. Farley, *Gathering Those Driven Away*, 99.
18. Farley, *Gathering Those Driven Away*, 99.
19. Farley, *Gathering Those Driven Away*, 100.
20. Farley, *Gathering Those Driven Away*, 1.
21. Edward Farley, *Theologia*, 36.
22. Farley, *Gathering Those Driven Away*, 1.
23. Farley, *Gathering Those Driven Away*, 1–2.

our experience—the abode of the divine—that transcend what the human mind can grasp on its own. Theology is conceptual and experiential. Moreover, Farley's Christology re-imagines Christ as the eternal Wisdom emanating from the Good Beyond Being.[24] Just as the divine Wisdom descends from the transcendent reality of God into the immanence of creation and the human body, so theological wisdom ascends from the upper limits of embodied human thought towards the mystery of the divine. Farley also conceives of theological wisdom as existing in the space between contemplation and action. "Wisdom is like the movement from a yogini's direct perception of reality to manifestation in words and action"[25] Wisdom, human and divine, lives at the margins.

Farley's emphasis on the sapiential character of theology, moreover, tends to overlap with a consideration of its contemplative dimensions. Farley, for example, notes the historical unity of theology and contemplation and refuses to separate them. She both addresses the subject of contemplation as the content of her theological reflection and also writes theology as someone who is a contemplative herself. Thus, she can acknowledge that her focus on contemplation makes her writing similar to ancient theologians "for whom theology was not only thinking but 'tasting . . . a practice that carried [men and women] into the womb of God and back into the world with an intensified compassion."[26] Her description of the practice of theology here is close to how monastic communities have regarded sacred reading or study as a contemplative practice whose purpose is spiritual formation. In the context of monastic and contemplative communities, theology cannot be understood as an academic discipline separate from the spiritual aspirations of the contemplative theologian. Farley's self-understanding as a theologian and as a contemplative entails that theology is both a "thinking" and a "tasting" of the divine. Farley also notes that both the intellect and the will are parts of the contemplative path. "It is not that thinking and willing are irrelevant to the contemplative path," she explains. "The great metaphysicians of the religions were also contemplatives, and contemplatives generally write and live out of rigorous and profound intellectual positions. It is not an accident that the women contemplatives whose writings survive the

---

24. Farley, *Gathering Those Driven Away*, 117.

25. Farley, *Gathering Those Driven Away*, 119.

26. Farley, *Gathering Those Driven Away*, 30.

upheavals of history are brilliant and creative theologians."[27] Theological reflection might therefore be described as endemic to the contemplative life. It is a discursive, cognitive activity that aids the contemplative in moving beyond discourse and cognition. In this respect, theology is a contemplative practice.

Within the framework of her erotic theology of God, theological inquiry is driven by the same desire that motivates the contemplative on the path to spiritual enlightenment or union with God. Since divine desire (and desire for the divine) is the energy that moves through all of creation and human experience, that same energy animates the work of theology. Theology, even as it professes to be systematic and conceptually rigorous, incorporates non-cognitive ways of thinking, perceiving, and relating to the divine. Theology, as the intellectual dimension of contemplation, is driven by eroticism.

The desire of the theologian, like the contemplative, is to experience the reality of God. Both theologian and contemplative are motivated by love to seek the source of all love. "Reality is beyond being, beyond word and concept, but we pursue it with mind and emotion, with word and concept, and in communities that are flawed and limited."[28] Theology is therefore a practice that draws both our minds and our whole spiritual selves into contact with the Divine Eros. The pursuit of divine reality is a way both of understanding and of experiencing God. Whenever we think about God, the Divine Eros, we are seeking Her.

Farley's writing on theology and contemplation has a number of important consequences for a consideration of the nature of theology. First, theology is a holistic, desiring activity, encompassing mind, heart, and spirit. The academic study of theology tends to overlook the emotional dynamics and spiritual yearnings of its practitioners, in favor of an Enlightenment-based style of rationality that prizes systematic completeness, conceptual rigor, logical consistency, and linguistic precision. Theology in a contemplative mode, however, makes use of our cognitive apparatus while also opening itself to the wild stirrings of the heart, the insights gained through intuition, the vagaries of poetic language, the perception of the divine at play in the natural world, and the cumulative effects on consciousness of such other contemplative practices as prayer, meditation, *lectio divina*, yoga, retreat, solitude and silence (to name a

27. Farley, *Wounding and Healing*, 130.
28. Farley, *Gathering Those Driven Away*, 14.

few). These contemplative practices are valuable sources of theological wisdom alongside arguments produced from systematic texts. Theology, too, cannot fully intellectually grasp the object of its desire, and its conceptual trappings must inevitably direct it beyond itself to reach the truth of which it seeks.

Second, theology is a practice that is integral to the spiritual life. Many contemporary books on spirituality list a number of common contemplative practices for their readers to explore without paying attention to theology or theological study. The academic theological world ghettoizes spirituality, and popular writing on spirituality does not respect theology as an essential spiritual practice. Yet, at least since the time of Evagrius, theology for a contemplative is part of the three-stage process, including asceticism, natural contemplation, and theology, by which the contemplative ascends to God. Theological attention to our doctrines, symbols, and images for God opens our consciousness to the deeper reality of the Divine Eros. The dialectical movement in theology between speaking of God and recognizing that God lies beyond all speech "gives way to the contemplation of the Divine Emptiness in which the transformation of mind opens upon 'vision beyond negation . . . this objectless contemplation allows the soul to drop into the Divine Abyss, no longer tyrannized by images and attachment to images."[29] Theology is the mind's involvement in the contemplative movement toward God, and how we interpret basic theological questions can either advance or derail our progress toward union with the divine. Theology matters for our spiritual progress.

In addition to expanding our awareness of the divine, theology expands our awareness of ourselves. By reflecting upon God and engaging in other contemplative practices that focus our mind on God, we come to see ourselves as creatures who are made in the image of the divine. Farley notes that "contemplation stills thoughts and emotions so that we can become more conscious of dimensions of mind beneath the grunge and distraction of everyday life."[30] These dimensions of mind lie beneath our surface egocentrism and show us where the divine is located within ourselves. Hence, Farley can write that "contemplation is a journey of

29. Farley, *Gathering Those Driven Away*, 91.
30. Farley *Wounding and Healing*, 125.

self-knowledge in which we come to know ourselves and all other beings as God-bearers."[31] Theological work is work on ourselves.

Third, theology is an everyday, not an esoteric, activity. Like all contemplative practice, it "is an ordinary practice that turns our attention to the nearness of the Divine, a nearness that is always present but to which our attention is less often turned."[32] Theology occurs in the midst of ordinary life, with its work, busyness, daily stressors, family responsibilities, church commitments, and the demands of social justice. For the marginalized, theology is done within the concrete realities of power, oppression, and extreme suffering. Theology is thus not a matter for idle speculation, but a matter for how we live out our love for God and neighbor as persons, communities, and participants in larger social structures. Theology is inseparable from activism. Contemplation, by distancing the prayerful person from the world, establishes a critical distance on the world as it is. In *The Silent Cry*, her classic work on the political implications of mysticism, Dorothy Soelle contends that mystical experience and radical social action are interdependent. The rapturous experience of God's love necessarily requires that the mystic see the gap between the joy of that love and the suffering and oppression of the world which fails to realize it: "Whether it be withdrawal, renunciation, disagreement, divergence, dissent, reform, resistance, rebellion or revolution, in all of these forms there is a No! to the world as it exists now."[33] Farley notes that, for those who are marginalized or living in conditions of oppression, contemplation provides a different identity than the one provided by the oppressor or the dominant power structures of church and society.[34] For both the marginalized and those given the power to act on behalf of them, "one can not think what one does not do . . . I can see God's love only when I become part of it myself."[35] An authentic experience of God is proven by the work one does for the reign of God in history.

Fourth, theology has a therapeutic dimension. As Farley argues, for example, punitive models of the atonement and constructions of human beings as fundamentally sinners can distort our self-understanding so that we think that we are objects of divine wrath rather than beloved

31. Farley, *Gathering Those Driven Away*, 91.

32. Farley, *Gathering Those Driven Away*, 94.

33. Soelle, *The Silent Cry*, 3.

34. Farley, *Gathering Those Who Are Driven Away*, 95.

35. Soelle, *The Silent Cry*, 5–6.

in the sight of God. This distorted self-understanding can produce or reinforce already existing feelings of neurotic fear, guilt, and self-hatred in a person. Theology at its best, by teaching us that we live under divine grace and love, can aid in the psychological healing of persons damaged by harmful images of God and self.

Finally, theology is negative, critical, and pluralistic. The contemplative path requires us to travel through experiences of darkness as well as light. In the experience of purgation, or what St. John of the Cross termed "the dark night of the soul," images and concepts lose their capacity for guiding us along the spiritual path and we are thrown into a darkness of pure faith. Contemplative theology therefore always supplements its positive statements about God with a negative qualification that such statements point to a reality beyond language and understanding. The possibility of self-deception is also a peril for anyone on the spiritual road. As Farley writes, "contemplation is desire and a path, but it is not certainty. Nothing in particular guarantees that we are not being led astray by the self-deceptions, that we are truly being gentle with ourselves, or that what we believe to be the face of Christ is not really a destructive image projected by our ego, eager to avoid being displaced."[36] This awareness of the possibility of self-deception means that the theologian must maintain a relentlessly critical perspective on her own claims as well as the claims of church and society.

The negative and critical character of theology produced within a contemplative framework means that the particular doctrines, categories, and schools of thought which we bring to theological reflection are necessarily limited by God's transcendence of our language and concepts. No theological system can claim exclusive access to the divine. As David Tracy argues in *Blessed Rage For Order*, this pluralism in theology "allows each theologian to learn incomparably more about reality by disclosing really different ways of viewing both our common humanity and Christianity"[37] As Farley's work demonstrates, great contemplatives, both past and present, often work from the margins, so we cannot assume that the dominant, orthodox stream of Christian theology is the only one that can reveal insights about God. We need a more expansive, pluralistic theology that is open to the diversity of voices that make up the present. We should pay close attention to those voices who have been marginalized

36. Farley, *Wounding and Healing*, 128.
37. Tracy, *Blessed Rage for Order*, 3.

in the past as well, if we would draw close to the God whom we name in speech and encounter in silence.

Theology is a mindful activity in the sense that it requires the fullness of mind, the complete attention of the intellect, to comprehend the Christian tradition's proclamation about Christ. But it is also mindful in the sense in which this word is used by contemplatives, an act of "keeping one's consciousness alive to the present reality."[38] Theology invites us to be attentive to the divine reality that is present in our experience but mostly escapes our awareness. Theology, viewed as a contemplative practice, is keeping one's consciousness alive to the present reality of God. It is a holistic, desiring activity of the mind as well as the will, heart, and spirit that opens us to a transformative awareness of the Divine Eros. It is no small part of Farley's interpretation of contemplation that it forces a reconsideration of what it is that we are doing when we practice theology.

Bibliography

Farley, Edward, *Theologia: The Fragmentation and Unity of Theological Education.* Minneapolis: Fortress, 1994.

Farley, Wendy. *The Wounding and Healing of Desire: Weaving Heaven and Earth.* Louisville: Westminster John Knox, 2005.

———. *Gathering Those Who Are Driven Away: A Theology of Incarnation.* Louisville: Westminster John Knox, 2011.

Ferrer, Jorge N., and Jacob N. Sherman, eds. *The Participatory Turn: Spirituality, Mysticism, Religious Studies.* Albany, New York: State University of New York Press, 2008.

Hadot, Pierre. *Philosophy as a Way of Life: Spiritual Exercises from Socrates to Foucault.* Edited by Arnold Davidson. Translated by Michael Chase. Oxford: Blackwell, 1995.

———. *What is Ancient Philosophy?* Translated by Michael Chase. Cambridge, Mass.: Harvard University Press, 2002.

LeClerq, Jean. *The Love of Learning and the Desire for God: A Study of Monastic Culture.* Translated by Catherine Misrahi. New York: Fordham University Press, 1961.

Leech, Kenneth. *Experiencing God: Theology as Spirituality.* San Francisco: Harper and Row, 1985.

McIntosh, Mark. *Mystical Theology: The Integrity of Theology and Spirituality.* Oxford: Blackwell, 1998.

Sheldrake, Philip. *Spirituality and Theology: Christian Living and the Doctrine of God.* Maryknoll, New York: Orbis, 1998.

Soelle, Dorothy. *The Silent Cry: Mysticism and Resistance.* Minneapolis: Fortress, 2001.

38. Thich Naht Hanh, *The Miracle of Mindfulness*, 11.

Thich Nhat Hanh. *The Miracle of Mindfulness*. Translated by Mobi Ho. Boston: Beacon, 1975.

Tracy, David. *Blessed Rage for Order: The New Pluralism in Theology*. Chicago: University of Chicago Press, 1996.

THREE

Theology That Breaks Your Heart

Kristen Daley Mosier

"It is true that, of all things with form, nothing is closer to the formless than earth and the abyss. It is true that you made not only whatever is created and endowed with form but also whatever is capable of being created and receiving form."[1]

THEOLOGY IS ENCOUNTERING AND growing into new sensibilities of intimacy as old boundaries give way to permeability. The overall shift away from the impassible, rational, impenetrable, invulnerable researcher is one that is familiar to a multitude of academic disciplines. It follows the Kantian subjective turn, and subsequent postmodern turnabouts, that has fully infiltrated the humanities and—through anthropology especially—is impinging itself upon the sciences. Contrary to the objection that such a turn relativizes all knowledge (thus trivializing it), by bringing the researcher into the frame, so to speak, knowledge becomes more fully recognizable as an ongoing work of construction, deconstruction, and reconstruction. It becomes locatable, accountable to others, conversational even. Such knowledge comes from somewhere and is developed under particular sets of temporal circumstances. It is knowledge with heart.

The following reflections look at recent breakdowns in related fields. Beginning with anthropology, always on the brink of the humanities and the sciences, authors have begun to confess that they can no longer

---

1. Augustine, *Confessions* XII.xix.28.

36

remain aloof, to the point that "the field enters the researcher."[2] Next, theology, in a similar predicament, is having not only to rearticulate its relations with others but also, as we see in Wendy Farley's work, *Gathering Those Driven Away*, to reformulate humanity's connection with the Divine. Thirdly, with new insights from the "hard" sciences emerging daily about the planet, galaxies, and an ever-expanding cosmos, the old divisions between human self and creaturely other require ongoing and significant revision. The eradication of division appears to be forming something new, but this requires first a journey of not knowing, of being laid bare, of abandoning *self* to enter formlessness born of particularities. And it will quite possibly cost the researcher/theologian her life.

Of Vulnerability

"As a mode of knowing that depends on the particular relationship formed by a particular anthropologist with a particular set of people in a particular time and place, anthropology has always been vexed about the question of vulnerability."[3]

Ruth Behar's evocative work, *The Vulnerable Observer*, describes through a series of essays the paradigmatic shift occurring within the field of anthropology from invisible observer to that of a researcher in place. This new situated researcher is described as fallible, affected by her surroundings, no longer objective and all-knowing. The shift follows suit with what some might describe as the emasculation of the field as more women and people of color—particularly those who were once considered "subjects"—take up the work of field research, bringing their bodies and histories with them. These new voices turn tables on the classical models of knowledge-construction about the Other and, in doing so, have developed a significant body of critique that forces the anthropologist's hand to reveal its own role in the process. Not satisfied with mere revelation and curtains flung wide to the world, then, the critiques push into the realm of (true) praxis toward a dynamic model of knowledge construction wherein the researcher is held accountable to her research subjects.

2. See Avella-Castro, "Critical Reflections."
3. Behar, *The Vulnerable Observer*, 5.

Knowledge, in this regard, is attuned to people, place, and time. In the case of anthropology, the implications for this situated knowledge-gathering include a shift to more collaborative, more open-ended textual constructions. It becomes more self-reflective. The anthropologist "come[s] to know others by knowing herself and . . . come[s] to know herself by knowing others."[4] It is affective. And it is rooted in the person as anthropologist herself—her history, her family, her biography. Dare we say, it is incarnational.

In *The Vulnerable Observer*, Behar describes an event—the annual meeting of American Ethnological Society—where she is tasked with responding to a panel of writers commenting on Renato Rosaldo's essay "Grief and a Headhunter's Rage" published twelve years prior. For Behar, the essay is a masterwork demonstrating the significant turn toward reflexivity. In a sense, the essay is sacred ground. Rosaldo's essay was born from the death of his wife while they were together conducting fieldwork in the Philippines, and it is filled with mourning. The writing is remarkable for demonstrating the unusual move whereby a researcher writes himself into his piece, rather than maintaining the traditional posture of an aloof notetaker. How could anyone remain aloof in the face of immense grief and loss? As she describes, Rosaldo the anthropologist "only came to fully understand the meaning of the rage in grief, which characterizes Ilongot head-hunting in the Philippines,"[5] after the sudden death of his wife. Only through a horrific loss of his own was the researcher opened to (re)construct ritualistic meaning in relation to these particular Others he had been studying. In becoming vulnerable, new knowledge emerged.

Faced with significant human suffering, particularly in the twentieth century, the social sciences are finding new voices. The "field" of anthropology has moved and shifted away from the exotic and wholly unknown, to more familiar spaces—as close as one's own grief and loss. The world is increasingly seen through power structures and dialectical relations, even as familiar places take on an aura of alienation. Norman Denzin begins an essay on alternate forms of ethnographic writing with the acknowledgement, "Writing is not an innocent practice."[6] In light of the kind of writing that begins with researchers' own experiences—particularly in cases of

4. Behar, *The Vulnerable Observer*, 33.

5. Behar, *The Vulnerable Observer*, 167.

6. Denzin, "Two-Stepping," 568.

grief, loss, and mourning—Denzin proposes that vulnerable writing take on an ethical stance, that it perform as a "moral ethnography." "A new ethics of writing is advocated. This is an ethics of narrative that demands that writers put their empirical materials in a form that readers can use in their own lives."[7] No longer abstracted beyond recognition, reflexive ethnography identifies the power and politics of the person who is in control of the writing. The researcher is revealed to come from somewhere, to reside in a time and place, with access to certain privileges and a body of knowledge that takes priority over other (and Otherized) bodies. In light of the interrelational realities of self and Other, the researcher can no longer write off the suffering of others. Their grief is hers; her grief is theirs. The researcher recognizes that she is granted access to the deep intimacies of others, whom she faces as fellow subjects, and that this work, this knowledge-production, is more than "just research." Life and death, grief and loss, suffering are all present. Behar ends, "I say that anthropology that doesn't break your heart just isn't worth doing anymore."[8]

Anthropology that breaks your heart is affective and vulnerable when the distance between interviewer and interviewee, or researcher and "subject," is as close as your own breath; when you realize just how intricately linked your lives are—not regardless of background, but precisely in terms of socioeconomic class, race, nationality, and religion. The connection is not simply that both persons are human, but that shared humanity implies responsibility (response-ability) to the Other, beginning with how the researcher renders the other in writing, and for whose benefit. Our hearts are broken when we see how an/other's fullness of life is somehow truncated or systemically foreclosed, and all we can do is write.

As Intimate as Your Own Breath

"Contemplation is a journey of self-knowledge in which we come to know ourselves and all other beings as God-bearers, luminous through connection to all creation."[9]

---

7. Denzin, "Two-Stepping," 568.
8. Behar, *The Vulnerable Observer*, 177.
9. Farley, *Gathering Those Driven Away*, 91.

In Wendy Farley's essay "And What Is a Merciful Heart?" she describes an occasion when her family was denied communion by the priest at the funeral for her partner's mother. The sentiment expressed liturgically in the hymn, "All Are Welcome in This Place," was in reality reserved for certain types of people, selected according to traditional forms of dualistic theology. She observes, "For me this funeral was emblematic of the incapacities of the Christian church to witness to radically inclusive love and to drive away its own by intolerance and actual and spiritual violence."[10] The priest prioritized one category of being, queer, over that of "beloved of God" in making the decision to deny Eucharistic participation in the body of Christ to Farley's family. But is this a true example of the way of Love? The way to the Erotic Abyss cannot/does not solely pass through gatekeepers who close the gate as they see fit, subjecting some persons (and not others) to the experience of getting shut out. Rather, she argues, "The deep root of great compassion is awareness of the ungrounded reality through which all beings remain interconnected."[11]

Dualistic theology conceives of God in contradistinction to that which is not-God, following a long tradition of binary logics used to construct theological models and methods. The result often entails one dominant form of theology winning out over others. A prime example she takes to task in her work *Gathering Those Driven Away* is Athanasius' formulation of the incarnation of Christ, and the Arian controversy. As she demonstrates the means by which Athanasius employed a logic of domination to construct theological heresies within his writing, she also highlights just how he went about consolidating dominance for material gain, noting, "The construction of heresy could be lucrative in a situation that allowed bishops to acquire significant benefits from a line between true and false belief."[12] Thus, the attack was twofold: Athanasius promoted a soteriological narrative that foreclosed redemption apart from the hierarchical church, as mediated through clergy, and effectively removed, or had church property removed from, those clergy who did not fully agree with his narrative. This early move toward magisterial messaging effectively overshadows more generous and decentralized readings of the incarnation event and more narrowly aligns God's presence with ecclesial power. The plurality of the gospels, with visions of indiscriminate divine

10. Farley, "And What is a Merciful Heart?," 405.

11. Farley, "And What is a Merciful Heart?," 406.

12. Farley, *Gathering Those Driven Away*, 26.

visitation and gratitude expressed for men and women engaged in the work of serving God and the world, all begins to shrink under the weight of councils. So, too, early communitarian and democratic power-sharing models evaporate as simpler forms of power take precedence. When it comes to articulating the mystery of the incarnation, Divinity is reduced to male and mediated solely through the ecclesial leadership.

For Farley, the critique of theological knowledge (construction) is linked to material impacts and this provides an impetus for seeking a deeper truth. Akin to Behar's dissatisfaction with the invulnerability of "traditional" anthropology, Farley is keenly aware of and has experienced the exclusionary practices of "traditional" theology that establish barriers between persons and God. And so she has sought to learn from others, mystics and misfits of the faith who have traversed the way of unknowing. Following her method of "pain seeking understanding," Farley invites those who would to sit, to meditate on incarnation, to face Divine Emptiness, beginning with the *via negativa*. "The relationship between naming and negation is at the core of Trinitarian and incarnational theology . . . The *via negativa* acts as a solvent that dissolves both what and how we think about the Divine Eros."[13] Demonstrating theology as sapiential wisdom, she guides the reader to the kind of work necessary to construct theologies rooted and grounded in love, in Divine Eros.

The apophatic journey to construct theology born of intimacy calls for such guidance. As with the intersubjectivity of vulnerable writing about self and other, the theologian who traverses the *via negativa* will find herself in unexpected company. "The *via negativa* takes another step by proposing a practice that dismantles ideas about the Beloved, allowing the living love of Divinity to flow more unrestrainedly. Contemplation of the Divine Emptiness prepares us for the radical and universal love to which the gospel calls us."[14] Radical intersubjectivity opens an invitation to seek out those who have fallen to the "underside" of authoritarian impulses throughout Christianity's doctrinal history and to revisit the immense diversity of thought and metaphor within the faith.

Through contemplation (as praxis) Farley describes how it is that the ordinary theologian can begin to move the mind and heart beyond dualistic thought by entering into Divine Emptiness. "This objectless contemplation allows the soul to drop into the Divine Abyss . . . Through

13. Farley, *Gathering Those Driven Away*, 65.
14. Farley, *Gathering Those Driven Away*, 69.

contemplation, ineffability is not an infinite qualitative difference but a flame that connects Beloved and lover. Desire is a medium through which nonduality and duality dwell together."[15] The suffering of fellow humanity draws us into relationship with such potency as to break barriers between self and Other. For connection with the Divine, it is desire that works through the cracks of self-perception like water on rock to draw our gaze followed by our soul into the embrace of the Beloved.

Planetarity and Divine Eros

> "Correlative immanence problematizes the autonomous notion
> of Self and Other that the Western imaginary has espoused and
> the straight dividing line that has kept the two separated."[16]

Farley's theology of incarnation grounded in nonduality takes a leap of faith similar to Behar's insistence on reflexivity and vulnerability in the face of an/other. This leads us to consider the possibility of breaking down barriers between human self and creaturely Other. The rest of creation appears to be peeking out from under the robe of incarnation as particularly expressed through Christ in Farley's text. While focused on humanity's relationship with Divine Eros, creation itself largely remains in the backdrop as the material matter of incarnation and as the stage setting for humanity. Yet, Farley invites her reader to follow Wisdom into the world to encounter divine beauty and presence. "Wisdom is the divine ground of creation and its impulses toward joyous embrace. Love of the earth and of our bodily nature is rooted in love of incarnate Wisdom."[17] Following Farley's guidance, we may come to know the rest of creation through contemplation.

The Erotic Abyss is the womb from which all that is created emerges, thus it is through the apophatic journey and facing Divine Emptiness that we human creatures may encounter the cosmos. All that is created is made intelligible, material, apprehensible, through Wisdom because Divine Eros desires to be made material and concrete. Love expressed through Wisdom/Sophia is always already seeking to exist *with* its other, which is creation. "Wisdom is the hinge between the fathomless depths

---

15. Farley, *Gathering Those Driven Away*, 91.
16. Kwok, "What Has Love," 38–39.
17. Farley, *Gathering Those Driven Away*, 127.

of the Divine Eros and the utter concreteness and uniqueness of a human body. Wisdom renders the Abyss into concrete form."[18] For Farley, it is Sophia/Christ, firstborn of all creation, who is the "hinge" between humanity and Divinity.

The nondualistic reality of Divine Eros described by Farley holds resonance with the work of Gayatri Spivak, particularly as it is rendered by theologian Kwok Pui-lan as she engages with Spivak in her chapter in *Planetary Loves*.[19] For Spivak and Farley, the rest of creation is already and always connected to the Divine. In Spivak's work, it is the notion of "planetarity" that describes a kind of underlying formlessness, an abyssal connectivity across creation. "The use of planetarity allows Spivak to move beyond the discourses of the nation, gender, class, culture, and colonialism to edge toward species talk and an animist liberation theology ... She invites us to imagine the complexity and pluralization of planetary systems, and not be confined by narrow identity politics or superficial binary thinking. Planetarity signifies an alterity that does not derive from us, a system that is beyond us, and yet we inhabit in it."[20] Kwok describes a similar dynamic, "correlative immanence," which offers an opening to encounter planetary love, and a means to bypass entrenched dichotomies so as to make intersubjectivity an essential characteristic over and above traditional categories.

Radical intersubjectivity does not and cannot find its terminus solely within humanity. The reason for this is twofold. First, returning to the field of anthropology, the vulnerability that opens the researcher up to an/other person and another way of being in/with the world discovers that the nature/culture divide is highly subjective and contrived. Secondly, within the Christian tradition there are examples of ancient ecological sensibilities which, like dandelions and thistles in the northern hemisphere, will find cracks through which to emerge in the most inhospitable surroundings. Hildegard of Bingen, with her verdant references and songs of creation, is one such dandelion saint frequently cited in ecotheology. The praxis of contemplation sends us into the open embrace of the Erotic Abyss which, beyond all else, is Love. Faced with an overabundance of love that reveals itself concretely through incarnate Wisdom, the im/possibility of interacting with creation as though it is always already

18. Farley, *Gathering Those Driven Away*, 116.
19. Kwok, "What Has Love," 31–45.
20. Kwok, "What Has Love," 33.

connected to the Divine becomes a natural impulse. As Farley observes, "The cosmos is by its nature a spiritual entity, imbued with divinity. Or, to put it the other way, the creation of the cosmos by Erotic Wisdom saturates it with a spiritual dimension. Devotion to the Word, to Christ, requires veneration of her body in creation."[21]

The beginning of a planetary ethic is radical compassion that comes from encountering the Erotic Abyss. Seeing the face of Christ/Sophia in an/other points toward seeing Christ in the creaturely Other. And we have experienced such glimpses in recent years. In 2018 a Southern Resident Orca mother, J35 Tahlequah, riveted viewers around the world during her seventeen-day-long saga of loss, lifting up her dead calf as she traversed the Salish Sea. Orca, along with dolphins and others in the family of cetaceans, are known to carry their deceased on occasion. The motion is congruous with the initial push to the surface that encourages a newborn to begin breathing on its own. In this instance, however, the prolonged duration of her tour of grief was (and still is) beyond explanation—though not beyond comprehension for anyone who has encountered intense grief and loss. J35 Tahlequah impressed upon the human world radical com-passion in the form of an invitation to *suffer with* her, allowing our hearts to break open wider with each passing mile. As the days multiplied, and the news story traveled further afield, we found ourselves to be witnesses to an *Orcinus orca* pietà. When she finally let go and let her dead calf sink to the depths of the sea floor, the sense of relief was trailed by a shadow of mourning.

Attending to this one unique population of orca on the verge of extinction is a path of contemplation amidst creation that can draw us closer to the Divine source. Faced with the suffering of J35 Tahlequah, we sink into the Abyss, into Love's dissolution of (human) self and (creaturely) Other where we can begin to glimpse the *Logos* of Wisdom. "At the same time, contemplation of the Logos does not raise us out of creation *but drives us more deeply into it.*"[22] The praxis of contemplation moves us to suffer with creation, then also to rejoice with creation—as many are with the September 2020 announcement of two calves born to J-pod orcas: J41 Eclipse and our beloved J35 Tahlequah. In this moment, we sing with the psalmist, "Praise the Lord from the earth, you sea monsters and all deeps" (Psalm 148:7). But until and unless we continue to encounter the Erotic

---

21. Farley, *Gathering Those Driven Away*, 128–9.

22. Farley, *Gathering Those Driven Away*, 126 (emphasis added).

Abyss out of which we might recognize the light and life of the *Logos* of Wisdom, until and unless we pursue an ethical singularity of planetary responsibility, we will grieve with J35 Tahlequah again.

Theology that Breaks Your Heart[23]

> But ask the animals, and they will teach you;
> the birds of the air, and they will tell you;
> ask the plants of the earth, and they will teach you;
> and the fish of the sea will declare to you.
> Who among all these does not know
> that the hand of the Lord has done this?
> In [God's] hand is the life of every living thing
> and the breath of every human being. (Job 12:7–10)

"The genesis of theology is pain." Wendy Farley attributes her need to construct a theology of the incarnation to the wounds of exclusion regarding sexual minorities in the church. Such exclusion does not demonstrate the radical compassion and love to which the gospel accounts of Jesus' life and ministry call disciples and Christians.[24] Nor, as she illustrates, does it follow the example set by the early church before a logic of domination took hold. And so we are left with the pain of deep woundings in the church, by the church. For Farley, this pain requires the praxis of contemplation in order to move toward healing. This is theology that will break your heart.

The *via negativa* is the beginning of the search for Wisdom. The cloud of unknowing sends us to the Abyss, to *tehomic* depths in search of the Beloved. Faced with exclusions and annihilations of all kinds in the twenty-first century, we return again to our divine root and source, to examine our hearts and transform our minds, to break with old patterns and ever so slowly move toward nonduality. Theology that doesn't break our hearts just isn't worth doing anymore because we are no longer facing or faced with an impassible God. We *know* better. We can no longer know ourselves in the ways that we used to, with the same old categorizations and dichotomies that separated and divided—saved/unsaved, male/female, human/animal.

---

23. I am indebted to my colleague, Paul Blankenship, PhD, for mentioning this phrase in conversation.

24. Farley, *Gathering Those Driven Away*, 1.

Theology that doesn't break our hearts is theology that maintains a destructive and immoral status quo. When the focus is on keeping theological categories intact and unquestioned, remaining impermeable in the face of new (planetary) dangers, it is virtually impossible to engage in a more intimate form of knowledge. Until and unless we are willing to lose ourselves to the world around us, to creation, we cannot know ourselves as creatures awaiting to be carried into the Erotic Abyss. Unless we are willing to have our hearts broken through the journey of naming and negation, encountering nonduality as revealed by Wisdom, then barriers and blockades remain in the form of categorical differences between humans and the rest of creation, and we are cut off from the pain of the cosmos.

Theology that breaks your heart is theology that willingly undertakes apophatic journeys through the heart's deep woundings in order to descend with others into their hell. "Practices of radical compassion deepen our capacities to live as if the earth were the garment of Wisdom, diaphanous with beauty; and to live as if each person was Christ, precious and lovely."[25] Without traversing the way through our own vulnerability and receiving the grace and love of Divine Eros, it is near impossible to encounter the suffering of any others with radical compassion. Like the ethnographer who takes her subjects/interviewees seriously, at their word, so as to collaborate in building truth together, the brokenhearted theologian will seek wisdom in unusual places; she will even go so far as to meditate upon the decaying flesh of an orca calf raised toward the sky by its mother, discovering that her grief is the mother's grief. Theology as *sapientia*, as Farley envisions, will guide us into the dark corners of ourselves and the world around us at this very critical time of need. When we pay close attention, the Erotic Abyss can free us from ourselves to better see and hear the Other before us—the human other, the Divine other, the creaturely other.

---

25. Farley, *Gathering Those Driven Away*, 221.

Bibliography

Augustine, *Confessions*. Translated by Henry Chadwick. Oxford World's Classics. Oxford: Oxford University Press, 2008.

Avella-Castro, Douglas. "Critical Reflections on and in 'the Field': The Study of 'Religion' and the Methodology of True (Reflexive) Praxis in Puerto Rico." Master's thesis, University of Washington, 2014. http://hdl.handle.net/1773/27379.

Behar, Ruth. *The Vulnerable Observer: Anthropology that Breaks Your Heart*. Boston, MA: Beacon, 1996.

Denzin, Norman. "Two-Stepping in the '90s." *Qualitative Inquiry* 5, no. 4 (1999): 568–72.

Farley, Wendy. *Gathering Those Driven Away: A Theology of Incarnation*. Louisville, KY: Westminster John Knox, 2011. Kindle.

———. "And What is a Merciful Heart? Apophatic Theology and Christian Ethics." *Theology Today* 67 (2011): 405–18.

Kwok, Pui-lan. " What Has Love to Do with It? Planetarity, Feminism, and Theology." In *Planetary Loves: Spivak, Postcoloniality, and Theology*, edited by Stephen D. Moore and Mayra Rivera, 31–45. New York: Fordham University Press, 2011. www.jstor. org/stable/j.ctt13x099k.6.

Spivak, Gayatri Chakravorty. *A Critique of Postcolonial Reason: Toward a History of the Vanishing Present*. Cambridge, MA: Harvard University Press, 1999.

FOUR

Unauthorized Writing:
Feminist Theology as Apophasis

Emily A. Holmes

"When you are writing, it feels like you are bleeding.
I mean, your soul just rolls out and it is a good bleeding,
like a transfusion."
—Leroy,
member of the Door of Hope Writers Group[1]

Writing Decreation

IN HER MEDITATION ON the writings of three women, poet Anne Carson describes the decentering of the self that each writer evokes in her text: Sappho's dream of distance from her beloved, Marguerite Porete's annihilation of the soul, and what Simone Weil calls "decreation," which Carson adopts as the title for her own book.[2] Decreation, as Carson describes it, involves negating, absenting, or annihilating the self, so that desire for the beloved—the lover, the goddess, Lady Love, or God's creation— might take center stage. The seemingly dark and self-destructive images found in each of these writers are, however, hard to reconcile with the audacious act of writing undertaken by all three women:

1. Quoted in Bryson, "Writers Come to Memphis' Defense," B1.

2. Carson, *Decreation*.

48

When Sappho tells us that she is "all but dead," when Marguerite
Porete tells us she wants to become an "annihilated soul," when
Simone Weil tells us that "we participate in the creation of the
world by decreating ourselves," how are we to square these dark
ideas with the brilliant self-assertiveness of the writerly project
shared by all three of them, the project of telling the world the
truth about God, love and reality? The answer is we can't. It is no
accident that Marguerite Porete calls her book a *Mirror*. To be a
writer is to construct a big, loud, shiny centre of self from which
the writing is given voice and any claim to be intent on annihilating this self while still continuing to write must involve the
writer in some important acts of subterfuge or contradiction.[3]

To many readers of these brilliant women, images of decreating or annihilating the self invite feminist concern for the self-destructive impulses
of the author.[4] They also appear to be directly contradicted by the self-as-
sertive fact of their writing. How can the "decreated" self or "annihilated
soul" author a book, where authorship demands intellect, ego, and the
will to create? Marguerite Porete, for instance, claims that the soul's annihilating encounter with divine Love "takes away absolutely the practice of
telling."[5] If annihilation takes away the soul's ability to "tell," Carson asks,
"We might at this point be moved to question what Marguerite Porete
thinks she is doing in the remaining chapters of her book . . . . We might
wonder what all this telling is about. But . . . to leave us in wonder is just
what such a writer feels compelled to do."[6]

It would be a mistake to think that any of these women is naively
unaware of the apparent contradiction in which she entangles herself by
writing erotic poetry, essays, and aphorisms, or an allegorical dialogue
of the soul's annihilation in love—all the while claiming a lack of self.
Such paradoxes stem from the nature of desire and its effect on writing:
desire for the beloved is ecstatic; to move more fully toward the other
entails getting oneself out of the way, through decreation, annihilation,
or absence from the romantic scene. What each of these writers faces
in her description of ecstatic desire is also a basic problem of theology:

3. Carson, *Decreation*, 171.

4. On the problematics of "annihilation" for feminist theology, see Engel et al.,
"Roundtable Discussion," 143–87; see also Hollywood, "'Who Does She Think She
Is?'"; and Webb, "Writing Hunger on the Body."

5. Carson, *Decreation*, 173. Carson's translation is of Porete, *Le Mirouer des
Simples Ames*, published as *Corpus Christianorum, Continuatio Medievalis 69*, 72–74.

6. Carson, *Decreation*, 173.

How to deploy the written word to point beyond itself, to the ineffable mystery that transcends the limitations of human language? How to get one's own loud and shiny ego out of the way so that the Beloved might appear in the mirror of one's writing? The problem is twofold. Theology strives to say that God's transcendence exceeds the capacity of human language to bear it. But in those very efforts, the divine transcendence recedes behind the all-too-human attempt—through intellect, ego, and will—to grasp it in the form of writing. The solution, as Sappho, Porete, and Weil discovered, requires some rather drastic transformations—of oneself and one's writing practices. "God's absence," Carson writes, and here "absence" includes transcendence, or mystery, "is something tricky, perhaps impossible, to tell. This writer will have to invoke a God who arrives bringing her own absence with her—a God whose Farness is the more Near. It is an impossible motion possible only in writing."[7] As Carson hints, what appears as contradiction may also be subterfuge: a form of writing that presents absence, that annihilates the self so that desire for the Beloved might appear.

The Death of the Author

One way of understanding Carson's literary conundrum is through Roland Barthes' description of the death of the author.[8] Arguing against modern forms of literary criticism that seek to explain a work with reference to its "Author"—his biography, his illness, his passions, and intentions—Barthes claims that the Author is the product of modernity and its emphasis on the prestige of the individual. Writing, and in particular fiction and poetry, however, severs the link of a work to its supposed origins: "Writing is the destruction of every voice, of every point of origin. Writing is that neutral, composite, oblique space where our subject slips away, the negative where all identity is lost, starting with the very identity of the body writing."[9] With reference to trends in twentieth-century literature, Barthes introduces the "scriptor" or writer in the place of the deceased Author. Whereas the Author was "believed in" as the authority, past, and father of his book, "the modern scriptor is born simultaneously with the text, is in no way equipped with a being preceding or exceeding

7. Carson, *Decreation*, 179.
8. Barthes, "The Death of the Author."
9. Barthes, "Death," 142.

the writing, is not the subject with the book as predicate; there is no other time than that of the enunciation and every text is eternally written *here and now*."[10] The scriptor lacks both originality and authority because the source on which writing draws is not the genius of the Author. Rather it is the entire field of language that pre-exists the writer: writing is but the assemblage and recombination of words, quotations, and ideas of others, and the writer herself a mere placeholder of performative enunciation.[11]

Like Barthes and his subjects, the women writers invoked by Carson have little interest in the self as Author, that is, in the self as a figure of authority whose genius or ego is the source of writing. Their sensibility is more theologically driven, but they arrive at the same conclusion as Barthes, namely, that writing is not dependent upon the "self"—the author or ego—who writes. Writing can register the decreation, annihilation, and absence of the self without contradiction because it isn't dependent upon a self, individual, or author in the first place. The field of writing is larger than the individual as source or origin. We can call Sappho, Porete, and Weil writers or "scriptors" because they deliberately call into question their status as authors, refusing all authority over their words.

Unauthorized Writing

Something similar happened to Wendy Farley when the authorizing props of academia fell away. In the preface to *The Wounding and Healing of Desire* and in the conclusion to *Women, Writing, Theology*, Farley describes how she lost the ability to read for six years beginning with an eighteen-month migraine. This profoundly debilitating but ultimately temporary disability forced her to engage with traditional texts in a nontraditional and disorienting way, at least for modern scholars: exclusively through memory rather than through the standard academic practices of rereading and citation.

> When I wrote this book, I still could not read. Whatever was not in my head and immediately available to my memory could not be a part of my writing. As you might imagine, this felt like a terrible handicap, and the absence of all my would-be conversation partners will no doubt be as keenly felt by my readers as it has

10. Barthes, "Death," 145. Emphasis in original.
11. Barthes, "Death," 145–6.

been felt by me. I have written this book in a style at variance
with the customs of the academic world, not out of disrespect
for those customs but because I found myself exiled from that
world by the conditions of my life.[12]

This disability radically undercut her sense of herself as scholar and
author by taking away the foundation of her authority, which she describes in "Wounded Writing, Healing Writing":

> I was accustomed to a style familiar to readers of this volume:
> going to the library, checking out as many books as I could car-
> ry, reading them, and then exchanging them for another pile of
> books. My footnotes were more copious than my text. But this
> writing is impossible for someone who cannot read. Without
> other scholars, without the props and insights of male writing to
> underwrite my own, it seemed absurd to write. It was excruciat-
> ing to give up my understanding of myself as a scholar, to give
> up the authorizing methods that permitted me some small place
> at the table. I had to proceed with no real hope that I would be
> able to return to scholarly writing. I had to rely only on what
> was already in my head, as if I had journeyed into the wilderness
> and there was no resource beyond what I could carry with me.[13]

Despite debilitating illness, without the props of scholarship by
which authority is established, without even the ability to read, Farley
continued to write. How is this possible? What notion of writing is this?
"But I did write. I wrote as my self-understanding, my resources, my intellectual home—as essential to me as my own breath—were burned to
ash. I wrote without the approval of my authorizing voices, without even
my own approval. But I did keep writing. It burned my skin. It authorized
itself."[14]

"It authorized itself." Scholarly authority, the product of institutional
and guild approval granted on the basis of books read, cited, and written,

---

12. Farley, *Wounding and Healing*, ix. See also Farley, "Wounded Writing," 254: "My
own writing has been mutilated by the efficiencies of gentle and less gentle violence.
It entered a tomb—or perhaps it was a womb—when I found myself unable to read
for several years, a symptom of traumatic stress disorder. It was demoralizing—a weak
word!—it was devastating to think that my life as a scholar was over and that writing
had become impossible for me."

13. Farley, "Wounded Writing," 254–5. The gendered nature of Farley's experience
echoes Beverly Lanzetta's description of "the dark night of the feminine," in *Radical
Wisdom*, 119–36.

14. Farley, "Wounded Writing," 255.

was dismantled, the Author dead. But writing persisted, indifferent to external means of authorization, indifferent to Farley's own approval. I read
Farley's inability to read as an apophasis of the self, an "unsaying" or annihilation of the academic Author, brought on by affliction. Her disability
undercut her own authority as Theologian and Author where authority is
established through the ability to underwrite one's own words with reference to greater authorities. That self, the Author, disintegrated. Instead of
impeding Farley's ability to write, however, this apophatic disability liberated her writing from its ties to Authorship, with all that that implies, so
that *writing* can be born, and with it, the writer. Writing in the absence of
reading—unauthorized writing—emerges from that space identified by
Anne Carson: the decreated, annihilated, absent self, engaged in written
acts of subterfuge and contradiction.

Apophatic Theology, Apophatic Anthropology

The apophatic tradition deploys both subterfuge and contradiction to
write God's transcendence into Christian theology. This lineage, typically
associated with Pseudo-Dionysius and his followers, points to God's unknowability "against the background of human ignorance of the nature
of God."[15] Because God exceeds the human capacity to know, grasp, or
speak, "we do not know what kind of being God is."[16] Theology itself
becomes a "strategy and practice of unknowing," issuing in a distinctive
form of theological discourse: "speech about God which is the failure of
speech."[17]

The writings of the apophatic tradition convey the mystery and
transcendence of God through both affirmation (cataphasis) and negation (apophasis), and the further negation of negation as each statement
said about God must be "un-said" or negated in turn.[18] While it is true, for

15. Turner, *Darkness of God*, 19.

16. Aquinas, *Summa Theologiae*, I, q.12, a.13, ad 1.

17. Turner, *Darkness of God*, 19–20. See also Sells, *Mystical Languages*, 2–4 and
9–10.

18. See Turner, *Darkness of God*, 252; and Sells, *Mystical Languages*, 2: "The formal
denial that the transcendent can be named must in some sense be valid, otherwise ineffability would not become an issue. Insofar as it is valid, however, the formal statement
of ineffability turns back upon itself, and undoes itself. To say 'X is beyond names,'
if true, entails that it cannot then be called by the name 'X.' In turn, the statement 'it
cannot then be called X' becomes suspect, since the 'it,' as a pronoun, substitutes for

instance, to say that God is like a rock or a lion, or is Love or Being, it is in some sense truer to say that God is not a rock or a lion, nor our human conception of love, and certainly not a being like other beings; truer still to leave both affirmation and negation behind (negating the opposition between affirmation and negation) and to unite "to the completely unknown by an inactivity of all knowledge . . . [to know] beyond the mind by knowing nothing."[19] This mystical union of the unknown with the unknown by means of unknowing takes place, according to Pseudo-Dionysius, beyond language in the "brilliant darkness" of a "hidden silence."[20] But something like it is conveyed in writing through a distinctive form of apophatic discourse characterized by the "self-subverting utterance,"[21] paradox, the coincidence of opposites, and the collapse of spatiotemporal and subject-object distinctions. In other words, apophasis proceeds not only through negative statements (what God is not), but through the performance of negation that doubles back upon itself in an unending motion, as in Meister Eckhart's prayer: "let us pray to God that we may be free of 'God.'"[22]

This dialectical movement between affirmation, negation, and negation of negation rests upon a deeper dialectical movement, typically associated with Neoplatonism, of process and return. God desires the other and pours forth in procession through creation; the created soul in turn desires to return to her origin in God. Writing apophatic theology takes place in this gap of desire: between self and God, between decreation and negation, between immanence and transcendence, language and reality.[23] In a footnote in *Eros for the Other*, Farley observes how "Anne Carson describes the gap present in all knowledge." Carson writes, "Neither reader nor writer nor lover achieves such consummation. The words we read and the words we write never say exactly what we mean. The people we love are never just as we desire them. The two *symbola* never perfectly match. Eros is in between."[24] This lack of consummation, this

---

a name, but the transcendent is beyond all names. As I attempt to state the aporia of transcendence, I am caught in a linguistic regress."

19. Pseudo-Dionysius, *Mystical Theology*, 137.

20. Pseudo-Dionysius, *Mystical Theology*, 135.

21. Turner, *Darkness of God*, 21.

22. Eckhart, "Sermon 52: *Beati Pauperes Spiritu*," 200.

23. On the relationship between eros and apophasis, see Brintnall, "Transcribing Desire," 59–80.

24. Carson, *Eros the Bittersweet*, 109, quoted in Farley, *Eros for the Other*, 190.

gap in all knowledge, is not the tragedy of writing, but rather its gift. Like music, writing can convey the desire that moves through the gap between concept and reality, self and other, lover and Beloved. Reality is never perfectly reflected in language; this is the basic point of apophatic theology. But writing can convey something of the eros that lies in between through a distinctive form of discourse, straining beyond its capacity to the point of breaking into fractured, paradoxical, disordered utterances.

Apophatic theology finds its mirror in apophatic anthropology. Just as we do not know who God is, we do not know who we are. The best we can do is to strip away our false self-conceptions as we peel back the layers of our idolatry, like a sculptor chipping away at stone.[25] In the process, we discover our masks and idols: our passions, our cravings, our attachments, our investments in our own ego, the props of our own authority.[26] Marguerite Porete provides a particularly fine example of apophatic anthropology as she describes how the love of God brings the self to "nothing" through the relentless annihilation of reason and the will. Even her ecstatic love of God must be burned away as the soul is transformed by love completely into God: "But this Soul, thus pure and illumined, sees neither God nor herself, but God sees himself of himself in her, for her, without her, who—that is, God—shows to her that there is nothing except him."[27]

Both apophatic theology and apophatic anthropology fracture writing. Apophatic discourse, in its strictest delineation, is "collapsed, disordered language."[28] Acts of subterfuge, contradiction, paradox, and self-subversion proliferate in this form of writing that performs what it asserts.[29] Apophatic theology is at the heart of Farley's theological thinking, but her writing does not mirror the "disordered language" or "self-subverting utterances" of apophatic discourse. Her first books, *Tragic Vision and Divine Compassion* and *Eros for the Other*, reflect what Michael Sells identifies as "apophatic theory as opposed to apophatic discourse. Apophatic theory affirms the ultimate ineffability of the transcendent; but as opposed to apophatic discourse, it affirms ineffability without turning

---

25. Pseudo-Dionysius, *Mystical Theology*, 138.

26. See Farley, *Wounding and Healing*, 35–69.

27. Porete, *Mirror of Simple Souls*, 145–6.

28. Turner, *Darkness of God*, 22.

29. See Sells, *Mystical Languages*, 3.

back upon the naming used in its own affirmation of ineffability."[30] Farley typically uses the term "apophatic" to indicate God's transcendence and unknowability, and the provisional character of theological language that results, rather than particular strategies of "unsaying" of the sort examined by Michael Sells.[31] Hence, her frequent reference to "apophatic depths" indicates the mysterious abyss of divinity without dwelling on self-subversive ways of writing that work to convey those depths.

If anything, Farley's early books evince a fairly utilitarian view of writing, in part because she shares Plato's distrust in the ability of writing adequately to reflect reality.[32] In accord with her interpretation of apophatic theology, she argues that truth is better understood as an activity, a practice, and a relationship than as a set of propositions. Structurally, reality is in a similar position to God with respect to our language and concepts for it. Just as God ultimately transcends all our divine names, reality exceeds our attempts to grasp it.[33] Because all writing is subject to

30. Michael Sells reserves "the term *apophasis* for those writings in which unnameability is not only asserted but performed" (*Mystical Languages*, 3). In my reflection on Farley's work, however, here I follow her usage to retain the broader sense of apophatic theology as affirming God's transcendence and unknowability, without necessarily performing ineffability at the level of writing.

31. The apophatic theological tradition appears in Farley's references to the limitations of the theological project itself and particularly the ability of words and concepts to convey God's transcendence. These comments typically arise in the methodological reflections opening a book, for instance, in *Tragic Vision and Divine Compassion*: "I have what still seems even to me the shocking temerity to bring up God in the following discussion. In attempting the absurd task of relating transcendent power to historical evil, I have been most dependent on the dialectic between affirmative and negative theology inaugurated by Pseudo-Dionysius the Areopagite. Negation qualifies every symbol, statement, or experience concerning divine being. No method or authority assuages the radical and unsurpassable alterity of God. But the logic of causality provides a basis for affirmative theology." Farley, *Tragic Vision*, 14.

32. In *Eros for the Other*, 186, Farley writes, "I interpret truth as something available through ongoing effort, undertaken as a practice, in dialogue with others and in relationship to the unceasingly changing and infinitely complex concreteness of existence. But to capture this *in writing* remains paradoxical. It is not only that writing is a practice undertaken in solitude; writing exhibits a static quality that is already a distortion of the livingness of reality. Writing is at best a moment of a conversation that has achieved an artificial stasis, rather like a butterfly that has been pinned to a board." Emphasis in original.

33. Farley writes, "The static and abstract nature of thoughts and ideas, especially communicated in writing, is already a distortion of the living quality of reality. . . . The reality of beings, which is the proper concern of truth, is plural, living, changing. This reality can be lived, acted toward responsibly; it can be harmed and destroyed. But it

these limitations, writing functions for Farley, at least in her early books, primarily as a "heuristic device," a tool for participating in a longer and more complex dialogue through scholarship, books, study.[34] Writing may be at best a pale reflection of the living dialogue where truth can emerge, but it is also a tool available to those who know how to wield it with authority. Instead of silencing her speech or limiting her writing to tentative, second-order statements, Pseudo-Dionysius and the apophatic tradition seem, if anything, to embolden Farley. Contrary to current academic trends, she doesn't shy away from general claims about human nature or hesitate to write as "we." Because all language for God is at best symbolic and subject to negation, we therefore proceed in our affirmations as best we can, confident that others will correct us in the on-going dialogue of tradition.[35] This way of writing can be unsettling to those steeped in postmodern thought, but it is also rhetorically powerful, persuading the reader to see God, the world, and human beings in all their beauty, complexity, and vulnerability from her theological perspective.

But something shifts during Farley's experience of disability and consequent apophasis of the academic self. Her writing moves in a different direction, bereft of the props of scholarship.[36] As "unauthorized writing," *The Wounding and Healing of Desire* exemplifies a different kind of apophasis, what Denys Turner calls an "excess of affirmations."[37] This way of writing, which he identifies with Bonaventure and Julian of

---

cannot be adequately captured in words, texts, concepts, and theories. A mystery and exteriority always remains that is not properly accounted for when truth is identified as correct ideas or propositions." Farley, *Eros for the Other*, 189.

34. Farley describes writing and books in this way: "As a heuristic device for participating in one of the practices by which truth may emerge, namely, dialogue and study, they can have a powerful effect. But when truth is understood as identical with theory, words, arguments, texts, then something important has gone wrong. A tool has displaced the work it was to assist." *Eros for the Other*, 189.

35. See, for example, Farley, *Tragic Vision*, 14.

36. Whereas earlier works describe the status of theological claims as "symbolic" with reference to Tillich, Schleiermacher, and Pseudo-Dionysius, in *Wounding and Healing*, Farley appeals to poetry: "What follows is no more an attempt at a universal claim for Christianity or human experience than a poem is. If, in its extremely particular and idiosyncratic unfolding, anything resonates with a reader, it can do so because sometimes particular expressions of a point of view can have this connecting effect. . . . Each of us can see things and say things in ways no one else would, and this shared insightfulness is part of the sweetness of our interdependence." Farley, *Wounding and Healing*, xii–xiii.

37. Turner, *Darkness of God*, 257.

Norwich, reaches toward apophasis and "bursts its own bounds in a kind of self-negating prolixity" through sheer cataphatic multiplicity. In Farley's case, cataphasis topples over into apophasis in the form of an astonishing variety of multivocal sources woven together and grounded in her own contemplative practices.

Writing Cataphasis

The shift in Farley's writing is traceable to her temporary disability, a transition from writing as author to writing as scriptor. In both *Wounding and Healing* and her subsequent book, *Gathering Those Driven Away*, she assembles the voices of others and lets them speak without censorship or concern for approval.[38] And what others they are! Anonymous folk musicians, the heroines of fairy tales, polar bear kings from children's videos, poets, spiritual guides living and dead. Heretics, gay men, lesbians, trans and non-binary folks, post-colonials, womanists, feminists, contemplatives, Buddhists. It is as if the inability to read closed a door, leaving barely a crack through which only the narrowest stream of folk music could enter;[39] when reading returned, the door opened wide, and all manner of people marched in, theologian and non-theologian alike, bringing their friends from the margins and underside of Christianity to take center stage with them. Interweaving these diverse and non-traditional sources (at least for what typically counts as academic theology) gives Farley's writing a vibrant prolixity, a rich excess of cataphatic voices.[40]

This form of writing, interweaving such diverse sources, is equally grounded in her own embodied contemplative practices. Both *Wounding and Healing* and *Gathering Those Driven Away* include chapters on the effects of practices such as chant, yoga, centering prayer, and insight meditation. Contemplation creates a kind of stillness and stability in the mind beneath the comings and goings of thoughts, emotions, pains and pleasures. A similar stillness appears in both *Wounding and Healing*

38. Wendy Farley, *Gathering Those Driven Away*.

39. See Farley, *Wounding and Healing*, ix, xiii, and 3, along with references to music throughout.

40. Her book *Wounding and Healing* "weaves theology together with one of its crucial sources: the wisdom and experience of people who are not themselves academics. If theology cuts off its roots from practices, stories, and song, from the accumulated experiences of the ages, then how can we pretend that what we say has anything to do with human life?" Farley, *Wounding and Healing*, xi–xii.

and *Gathering Those Driven Away* in the gaps and silences beneath the multiple voices that can be heard in the text. Contemplative practice in the absence of the ability to read redefined for Farley the nature of theology: "Deprived of the usual access to philosophical theology, I have been reminded that theology is not primarily texts but a kind of desire that employs thought as a religious practice."[41] This insight was the gift of disability, the apophasis of academic authority:

> Yet I am also aware of the great gift not-reading has been to me. . . . I found . . . that an act of integration and synthesis was occurring and that my mind was carried from the words and arguments to the matter of the text itself. . . . [T]he subject matter of theology is a reality beyond any word or argument. The words and arguments on the page of even the most brilliant theologian's work are only rough attempts to carry mind toward that reality. Having trained my whole life in reading texts, notreading gave me a different kind of access to these same texts.[42]

The combination of deep contemplative practice with a multiplicity of other voices turns Farley's cataphatic theology into apophasis: gesturing toward the reality beyond the page through writing that is multivocal, open-ended, self-authorizing, written from "the wilderness" without the author's own approval. The writer is born with the text.

Because I am interested here in the effect of Farley's experience on her writing, it is necessary to differentiate the two. The experience of disability, of affliction and dark night, is personal and it is painful: "It was excruciating to give up my understanding of myself as a scholar, to give up the authorizing methods that permitted me some small place at the table."[43] This experience (or, insofar as it is a symptom of trauma, a non-

41. Farley, *Wounding and Healing*, xii. Metaphysics in her view is not systembuilding but a religious practice with soteriological significance: "That Buddhist and Christian metaphysics are efforts to move back and forth across the line between cataphatic (naming God) and apophatic (negating names) experiences that arise out of practice had not really occurred to me. The soteriological significance of metaphysics collapsed into system building when the only access I had to the texts was through reading them." *Wounding and Healing*, x–xi.

42. Farley, *Wounding and Healing*, x.

43. After making a careful distinction between affliction and the dark night of the soul (*Wounding and Healing*, 134–42), Farley goes on to acknowledge, "But this simple, clear demarcation becomes confused in the actual living of life. These two kinds of darkness can be neatly distinguished in thought, but we who live do not fall neatly into the categories of contemplative or afflicted. We may be neither, or both, or move from one to the other or back again." *Wounding and Healing*, 142. Whether in dark night or affliction, she argues, Christ is there with us.

experience)[44] is anterior to what happens *in* the text, but it leaves its traces on her writing. After such an encounter with affliction, Farley might have re-affirmed herself as Author (through a return to the props of scholarship to shore up her authority). Alternatively, the apophasis of the self might have been written into or mirrored by apophatic discourse—in the fashion of Marguerite Porete, Simone Weil, and Sappho, who write their own annihilation or decreation. Farley's writing takes a third approach, neither writing her own annihilation into the text nor shoring up her authority in new ways. With reference to music, folk tales, contemplatives, and the wisdom of her teachers in *Wounding and Healing*, and later, in *Gathering Those Driven Away*, to the theologies of heretics, African-Americans, gays and lesbians, all those on the underside of official Christianity, Farley gives voice to others in a way that releases her claims to authority and enlarges the field of writing.[45] Gathering these texts, images, and melodies, interweaving them into an astonishing profusion of ideas, results in a form of writing closer to Barthes' "scriptor" than any traditional "authorship":

> We know now that text is not a line of words releasing a single "theological" meaning (the "message" of the Author-God) but a multidimensional space in which a variety of writings, none of them original, blend and clash. The text is a tissue of quotations drawn from the innumerable centers of culture. . . . the writer can only imitate a gesture that is always anterior, never original. His [sic] only power is to mix writings, to counter the ones with the others, in such a way as never to rest on any one of them.[46]

Cataphasis topples over into apophasis through prolixity, subverting the authority of the academic theologian in order to point to what lies beyond words.

44. Farley describes her disability as "a symptom of traumatic stress disorder." "Wounded Writing," 254. On trauma and experience, see also Cathy Caruth, *Unclaimed Experience*.

45. Consider Farley's description of her theological conversation partners: "I could have written nothing without them . . . because they compose the background music of my mind." Farley, *Wounding and Healing*, x.

46. Barthes, "Death," 146.

Conclusion

Barthes would no doubt disparage my attempt to read Farley's writing in light of her affliction. Do I not risk falling prey to the cult of the Author—"victory to the critic"—in interpreting her writing through the lens of her experience?[47] But that event, what I have been calling the apophasis of academic authority, now forms part of her published writing. The self-described inability to read is itself a moment narrated through the text, which the reader bears in mind while reading all that follows. Although I do not share the impulse to sever a written text completely from experience (as if writing isn't an embodied practice that emerges from the context of our lives[48]), I take Barthes' point to be that when we pry loose that connection, we open up the text and set free interpretive possibilities for the reader:

> Once the Author is removed, the claim to decipher a text becomes quite futile. To give a text an Author is to impose a limit on that text, to furnish it with a final signified, to close the writing. . . . In the multiplicity of writing, everything is to be disentangled, nothing deciphered; the structure can be followed . . . but there is nothing beneath. . . . In precisely this way literature (it would be better from now on to say writing), by refusing to assign a 'secret', an ultimate meaning, to the text (and to the world as text), liberates what may be called an anti-theological activity, an activity that is truly revolutionary since to refuse to fix meaning is, in the end, to refuse God and his hypostases—reason, science, law.[49]

Barthes identifies this shift as anti-theological, the death of God the Author posited as the origin and master of the text/world. In my reading, however, I see the same movement precisely *as* theological, in the best apophatic tradition: the death of God the Author is the removal of one more idol, out of whose destruction writing, the voices of others, and glimpses of the divine abyss beyond all words and concepts might appear.

This apophatic theological move places the meaning of a text in the hands of the reader. "A text is made of multiple writings," Barthes writes,

47. Barthes mocks this reductive form of literary criticism: "when the Author has been found, the text is 'explained'—victory to the critic." Barthes, "Death," 147.

48. See Paulsell, "Writing as a Spiritual Discipline," in Jones and Paulsell, *The Scope of Our Art*, 17–31.

49. Barthes, "Death," 147.

drawn from many cultures and entering into mutual relations of dialogue, parody, contestation, but there is one place where this multiplicity is focused and that place is the reader, not, as was hitherto said, the author. The reader is the space on which all the quotations that make up a writing are inscribed without any of them being lost; a text's unity lies not in its origin but in its destination.[50]

The reader of Farley's books holds this cataphatic multiplicity of voices together—along with her awareness of the author's affliction. The empowerment of the reader might seem ironic in the case of a writer who cannot herself read.[51] But even when incapable of reading the books of others, Farley wrote. "But I did keep writing. It burned my skin." The position of Author dismantled, the writer/scriptor emerged: assembling the voices of others, their music, their folk wisdom, their longing, and letting them speak for themselves. In this fashion, Farley returned to reading, not, this time, as author, but as writer. Perhaps writers are best understood as readers of their own texts, discovering the connection between their writings and their lives as readers rather than authors.[52]

Bibliography

Barthes, Roland. "The Death of the Author." In *Image, Music, Text*, translated by Stephen Heath. Hill and Wang, 1977.

Brintnall, Kent L. "Transcribing Desire: Mystical Theology in Dennis Cooper's *The Sluts*." In *The Poetics of Transcendence*, edited by Elisa Heinämäki, Päivi Mehtonen, and Antti Salminen, 59–80. Amsterdam: Rodopi, 2015.

Bryson, Samantha. "Writers Come to Memphis' Defense Over Negative Forbes Magazine Article." *Commercial Appeal*. July 17, 2011, sec. B.

Carson, Anne. *Decreation: Poetry, Essays, Opera*. New York: Knopf, 2005.

———. *Eros the Bittersweet: An Essay*. Princeton, NJ: Princeton University Press, 1986.

Caruth, Cathy. *Unclaimed Experience: Trauma, Narrative, and History*. Baltimore, MD: Johns Hopkins University Press, 1996.

50. Barthes, "Death," 148.

51. Farley describes how her writing aims to awaken the reader's desire: "I am hoping that the poor words I write here might help to stir up others to remember the power of their desire and find the resources, communities, teachers, and traditions that will feed it in their own lives. But because words fail, I have included references to music that carries a longing that may reconnect you with your own." *Wounding and Healing*, xiii.

52. I would like to thank Kent L. Brintnall for reading and discussing an earlier draft of this essay.

Eckhart, Meister. "Sermon 52: *Beati pauperes spiritu, quoniam ipsorum est regnum caelorum (Mt. 5:3)*." In *Meister Eckhart: The Essential Sermons, Commentaries, Treatises, and Defense*, translated by Edmund Colledge and Bernard McGinn, 199–203. New York: Paulist, 1981.

Engel, Mary Potter, Carol P. Christ, M. Shawn Copeland, Wonhee Anne Joh, Julie B. Miller, Nancy Pineda-Madrid, and Masako Kuroki. "Roundtable Discussion: Mysticism and Feminist Spirituality." *Journal of Feminist Studies in Religion* 24, no. 2 (Fall 2008): 143–87.

Farley, Wendy. *Eros for the Other: Retaining Truth in a Pluralistic World*. University Park, PA: Pennsylvania State University Press, 1996.

———. *Gathering Those Driven Away: A Theology of Incarnation*. Louisville, KY: Westminster John Knox, 2011.

———. *Tragic Vision and Divine Compassion: A Contemporary Theodicy*. Louisville, KY: Wesminster John Knox, 1990.

———. "Wounded Writing, Healing Writing." In *Women, Writing, Theology: Transforming a Tradition of Exclusion*, edited by Emily A. Holmes and Wendy Farley, 253–57. Waco, TX: Baylor University Press, 2011.

———. *The Wounding and Healing of Desire: Weaving Heaven and Earth*. Louisville, KY: Westminster John Knox, 2005.

Hollywood, Amy. "'Who Does She Think She Is?' Christian Women's Mysticism." *Theology Today* 60, no. 1 (April 2003): 5–15.

Holmes, Emily A., and Wendy Farley, eds. *Women, Writing, Theology: Transforming a Tradition of Exclusion*. Waco, TX: Baylor University Press, 2011.

Lanzetta, Beverly. *Radical Wisdom: A Feminist Mystical Theology*. Minneapolis, MN: Fortress, 2005.

Paulsell, Stephanie. In *The Scope of Our Art: The Vocation of the Theological Teacher*, edited by L. Gregory Jones and Stephanie Paulsell, 17–31. Grand Rapids, MI: Eerdmans, 2002.

Porete, Marguerite. "Speculum Simplicium Animarum; Le Mirouer Des Simples Ames," *Corpus Christianorum, Continuatio Medievalis*, Vol. 69. Edited by P. Verdeyen and R. Guarnieri. Turnholt, Belgium: Brepols, 1986.

———. *The Mirror of Simple Souls*. Translated by Edmund Colledge, J. C. Marler, and Judith Grant. Notre Dame, IN: University of Notre Dame Press, 1999.

Pseudo-Dionysius. "The Mystical Theology." In *Pseudo-Dionysius: The Complete Works*, translated by Colm Luibhéid. New York: Paulist, 1987.

Sells, Michael Anthony. *Mystical Languages of Unsaying*. Chicago: University of Chicago Press, 1994.

Turner, Denys. *The Darkness of God: Negativity in Christian Mysticism*. Cambridge, UK: Cambridge University Press, 1995.

Webb, Elizabeth A. "Writing Hunger on the Body: Simone Weil's Ethic of Hunger and Eucharistic Practice." In *Women, Writing, Theology: Transforming a Tradition of Exclusion*, edited by Emily A. Holmes and Wendy Farley, 159–82. Waco, TX: Baylor University Press, 2011.

FIVE

Attentive to the Ordinary:
Eros and Apophasis in Practical Theology

Kendra G. Hotz

MEMPHIS, TENNESSEE, HAS BEEN dubbed both the hunger capital of the United States and its most obese city.[1] The city offers an abundance of cheap calories, but expensive nutrition. We have miles of food deserts and high infant mortality rates. Memphis is a city with a rich cultural heritage that enriches our common life, but also with enormous disparities that write themselves into our bodies. My work as a practical theologian has brought me into conversation with administrators and healthcare workers at a major hospital system and at a community-based healthcare provider, both of which work to redress these inequities. This work has also brought me into relationships with congregational health promoters, lay members of area congregations who undertake special training to initiate health ministries in their communities.[2]

The vast majority of health promoters are women from black church traditions, and they represent the wide diversity of those traditions. But in the midst of their differing theological convictions, liturgical sensibilities, and social mores, the health promoters also display a remarkable consistency in their language about bodies and community and in their readiness to push back against polite acceptance of disparities with sassy

1. Sayle, "Unjust Desserts," 19–23.
2. The Congregational Health Promoter program is offered through the Church Health Center's office of Faith Community Outreach.

demands for justice. I find embedded in their language of embodiment rich resources for a lived theology that might begin to transform our city, but I also harbor profound misgivings about mining those resources. In fact, the metaphor I've chosen here of mining resources is at the crux of the problem with its suggestion of a colonial power graciously offering to extract raw materials for a native population that doesn't know how to value them. Does a practical theologian from another Christian tradition and a different ethnic heritage have anything to offer here, and is there any way to offer it without the usual colonial condescension?

My contention is that if I am to continue this work with integrity, then I need a new metaphor for practical theology. This essay is an effort to find that metaphor. I begin my search by turning for help to two unexpected sources: an anonymous sixth-century Syrian monk, the Pseudo-Dionysius, and a contemporary apophatic theologian, Wendy Farley. These sources are unexpected because they are so foreign to the thought worlds inhabited by the Congregational Health Promoters. But their foreign character—and my own—is precisely where I find both the challenge and the promise for a new approach to cross-traditional practical theology.

Reading Pseudo-Dionysius and Wendy Farley Together

In the face of increasingly confident, technical, and vitriolic squabbles between Chalcedonian and Monophysite theologians, a sixth-century Syrian Christian could be forgiven for fearing to speak a word of faith. That same Christian might also look with wonder to the virtuoso self-denials of the stylites on their pillars and imagine the *practice* of faith also beyond reach. In both their language and their practices ordinary Christians in that time and place were likely to feel inadequate and somehow marginal to the community of faith. In the midst of this world, the Pseudo-Dionysius (Denys) spun a vision of the cosmos alive with desire for a God beyond knowing. In the midst of disputes about heresy where lives depended on precision, Denys spoke in deliberately fractured language. In a world of spectacular ascetical practices that ordinary Christians could never hope to emulate, Denys located the heart of the Christian life in the ordinary practices of prayer and sacraments, baptisms and funerals. In a world where paganism was dying and pagan practices outlawed, Denys drew deeply on the riches of ordinary pagan theurgical practices.

The interplay of wanting and not-knowing, of always reaching and never grasping, led Ps-Dionysius to a theology that valued the ordinary. God was found not in the precision of theological formulations, nor atop pillars, but on the ground in ordinary ways of speaking and keeping silence. God was not found by the solitary desert dweller, but by the community, in the fragrance of incense, in the taste of bread and wine, and in the soothing luxury of anointing oil. A methodological focus on the apophatic and a substantive emphasis on the erotic drove Dionysian theology toward the ordinary.

This essay proposes that we find the same dynamic in the theology of Wendy Farley.[3] In her sustained meditations on the theological function of eros, we find deep humility about the limits of human knowing and a wide appreciation for the everyday—for the haunting melodies of traditional folk music and for the narratives of women and queer Christians. Farley's theology of desire deliberately employs language that violates the conventions of academic theology and that circles around a mystery she refuses to domesticate. Farley's work, moreover, supplements and corrects the Ps-Dionysius in at least two ways. First, Farley brings special attention to the witness of those ignored and driven away by the norming powers of institutional Christianity. Second, her attention to those on the margins also grants her a more nuanced vision of how our erotic core can be distorted. Where Denys understood sin primarily as a fragmentation or misdirection of desire, Farley knows that desire can be wounded.

A conversation between Denys and Farley, then, gestures toward a new, erotic and apophatic method for theologies of the ordinary—that is, for practical theology. By practical theology, I mean the discipline of interpreting theologically the practices of living communities of faith. By practical theology I also mean the practice of theology that intends to be taken up and used in an immediate way by those communities. Simply put, it is theology that aims to be helpful for church folk. Although practical theology has often focused on practices such as preaching and pastoral care, things that pastors do,[4] an erotic and apophatic approach to the ordinary will also attend to the practices of those not invested with institutional authority.[5]

---

3. In this essay I will focus on Farley's theology as it is expressed in *The Wounding and Healing of Desire: Weaving Heaven and Earth*.

4. Edward Farley explores this "professionalist approach" in *Practicing Gospel*, 24–28.

5. Stephanie Mitchem uses the term "ordinary theologies" to describe the way

Practical theology can also be understood as the discipline that names and analyzes beliefs and values that are embedded within practices, making visible what is assumed by practitioners. An apophatic and erotic theology of the ordinary will do this, but it will also allow the language of the community to shape, supplement, and correct its own discursive preferences. When practical theology is methodologically erotic and apophatic, I contend, it can draw on the primary discourse of living religious communities without the risk of colonizing that language. The risk of colonialism is subverted in part because the practical theologian engages the ordinary not as an impartial observer, but as an attentive lover. After describing the dynamic of eros and the apophatic, this essay experiments with it through use of a case study focused on the language and practices of health promoters in African-American congregations in Memphis, Tennessee.

Pseudo-Dionysius

Let's begin with a brief review of the relationship between the erotic and the apophatic in the Pseudo-Dionysius. In 532 at a council in Constantinople, the Monophysite Severus appealed to the sub-apostolic authority of Dionysius, the companion of Paul, whose conversion had been recorded in the book of Acts, to affirm his view that the union of God and human in the Incarnation was so complete as to effect a fusion so that only one nature remained. But the texts of this Dionysius—now Pseudo-Dionysius—resisted confinement to such a precise, technical matter. Instead, the texts burst into that divisive debate with breathtaking descriptions of a cosmos alive with beauty and dancing with delight before a God whose beauty infused everything with a deep yearning for the splendor of God and the harmony of creation. "God," according to the Pseudo-Dionysius, "is a movement of yearning," and the divine desire is mirrored in human life and finds expression in the worship practices of the Christian community.[6] Denys offered a vision of the Christian life

---

womanism roots itself in the ordinary practices of black women's lives. See Mitchem, *Introducing Womanist Theology*, 46–49.

6. Suchla, *De Divinis Nominibus*, 4.14 (I, 160). Translations of the Pseudo-Dionysius throughout this essay are my own, based on the critical edition of the Greek. Subsequent citations indicate the treatise title followed by the chapter and section numbers from the corpus. For convenience of reference, I have also included in parentheses the volume and page number from the critical edition of the Greek text.

lived out within a community of common yearning and embedded in an unspeakably beautiful world.

Denys offered as many definitions of God as there are words to describe God. Every name by which the worshiping community can call God simultaneously lifts it toward the light of divine truth and plunges it ever deeper into the darkness of divine mystery. The names appropriate to designate a God who generates and orders everything are as many as the multiplicity of every instance of being that has ever come into or vanished from existence and as few as the singular One who is the source of each of those instances of being. God both is and is not drunken, jealous, angry, life, power, and zeal; but one complex of names seems to course beneath the eddies and currents of the other divine names. "God is," Denys explained, "a movement of yearning, simple, self-moved, self-acting, pre-existent in the good and gushing out from the good to things existing, and returning to the good."[7] In Denys's theology Good, Beauty, and Yearning serve as key concepts for approaching the God who transcends all of our efforts at conceptualization. A divine yearning which is deeply connected to goodness and beauty "gushes" out from the transcendent simplicity of divine reality to created reality and, bringing creation with it, returns to God as the source of goodness. Divine yearning "coils" through God's reality in an eternal dynamic of proceeding, abiding, and returning.[8]

Creation issues from a divine yearning after God's own goodness and beauty, and that yearning becomes the characteristic activity of everything that exists. God's being, then, is a dynamic, eros-driven one, but it is also productive. God's way of being as goodness and beauty *wants* to be communicated. "One must even venture," he insisted,

> beyond truth, to say this: that the cause of all itself, by the beautiful and good yearning for all, through an exceedingly good yearning, comes providentially out of itself into all things, and is, as it were, beguiled by goodness, by love, and by yearning, and is led out of its exalted place above all things toward being in all things in accordance with an ecstatic, supernatural power that [nevertheless] does not roam outside of itself.[9]

7. Suchla, *De Divinis Nominibus*, 4.14 (I, 160).
8. Suchla, *De Divinis Nominibus*, 4.14 (I, 160).
9. Suchla, *De Divinis Nominibus*, 4.13 (I, 159).

Here Denys employs yearning as a category to interpret God's creative activity. That activity is, first, impelled by a yearning for beauty. It is a "being in all things," a coming to abide with, that serves as the source of the essentially relational character of beautiful being. This divine yearning is, second, an "ecstatic" capacity that calls the lover (in this case, God) outside of the self. But, third, the yearning that characterizes God's creative activity is also a unifying power that maintains the lover's ontological integrity so that, in the end, God's ecstatic eros does not "roam outside of itself." Denys's God is seduced out of the sublime beauty of divine transcendence by God's own yearning for beauty. Divine ecstasy, rooted in a wondrous beguilement, lures God into a frenzy of creative activity that generates, orders, sustains, and attracts everything.

It is God's erotic communication of goodness that accounts for why creatures are always reaching for a God they never grasp. That God is beguiled, but never roaming, means that all of the words used to praise God are simultaneously true and not true, that they both reveal and hide God. Theologians, quite literally, do not know what they are talking about, and their more or less inadequate words shape religious subjectivity with a profound sense of mystery, ambiguity, and humility.

Because the creation is derived from goodness and beauty, and because its continued existence depends on participating in that goodness and beauty, it longs for return to the same. Because God "sets the whole [cosmos] in place, firmly founds it, holds it together, and completes it in himself . . . he is that lovely being eagerly desired by all."[10] This longing becomes the definitive activity of being. "Their longing [for the good]," Denys explained, "holds them fast in both being and well-being . . . and they are stamped with the impression of [the good] they strive after."[11] The activity of yearning for the good makes a thing what it is. Existing means participating in the unified beauty and goodness of divine reality. It means exerting an effort toward order. Being, according to Denys, signifies an activity—the activity of yearning. Hence, particular beings, one might say, are individualized activities of yearning whose modes of being consist in distinctive ways of expressing that yearning. "The irrepressible cause of all yearning," as Denys put it, "rules and has primacy over all [these yearnings] and [is that] toward which the whole yearning

---

10. Suchla, *De Divinis Nominibus*, 10.1 (I, 214–5).

11. Suchla, *De Divinis Nominibus*, 4.1 (I, 144).

of everything everywhere attempts, in the way natural to each, to be lifted up."[12]

A creature made for yearning, Denys argued, would sin through a misdirection of desire. And because nothing but the beguiling beauty of God can fully satisfy our longing, misdirected desire always multiplies itself, seeking out satisfaction in every corner of the creation. Other creatures are reduced from subjects in community with whom we express our erotic drive for the divine to objects of our avaricious gaze. Because we are made in the image of what we desire, our misdirected and multiplied desiring writes itself into our souls as fragmentation. Our inward fragmentation, a lack of coherence in the structure of our egos, gushes out into the world damaging relationships and shattering communities. Sin fragments the hierarchies at the heart of Denys's worldview, leading inferiors to grasp at power and superiors to exercise power coercively, and disrupting the mutuality of relationships between equals.

Only in the practices of the worshipping community did Denys find the balm for souls in such pain. Because we are creatures of the senses, it is through the sensible that God attracts our longing gaze and redirects our eros. It is in the taste of the bread and wine, in the sweetness of the kiss of peace, in the cool comfort of the waters of baptism, in the fragrance of the incense that we find ourselves looking for what we cannot see, hearing what is just out of earshot. It is in these practices that we "taste and see that the Lord is good" with the result that our lives are knit back together, our relationships are restored to harmony, and our communities become again reflections of God's beauty.

Farley

Like Denys, Farley's theology turns on an erotic axis. It is desire that thrums through reality, giving it its most basic structure and flowing through humanity, giving us the shape of a self. In *The Wounding and Healing of Desire,* Farley draws the reader into a sustained meditation on the longing that coils around the core of human subjectivity, not by first offering a discourse on the history of eros in philosophical thought, but through reflection on the lyrics and melodies of traditional folk music. The songs remind us that we long for what we do not possess. Folk singers draw us into their own ache for home, for the particularity of place

---

12. Suchla, *De Divinis Nominibus,* 4.16 (I, 161).

"where the birch and the pine and the bonnie rowan tree, they are all blooming fair."[13] And Farley draws us into awareness of the insatiability of our longing. Return to the place of the birch and the pine may temporarily sate our appetite, but finally it too will leave us hungry for something else. It is the nature of desire itself, Farley explains, to want, and to want is not to have. We are creatures who always reach, but never grasp, and we are defined by that constant hunger, that endless longing. And so, despairing of any finite thing that can satisfy, we grant the name "God" to that vast emptiness, that great no-thing, that promises us rest from never-ending seeking and satisfaction for our bottomless wanting.[14]

When Farley turns to a diagnosis of how this wanting can go wrong, she departs from Denys for whom sin is primarily misdirected desire that results in fragmentation. That description is helpful, she grants, but only to a point, for it—along with so many other Christian theologies that name our wrongness "sin"—constricts our perspective, binding our diagnoses of our wrongness to guilt. "The problem with desire," she insists, "is not that it desires the wrong objects: the problem is that it relinquishes its erotic structure for the economy of possession."[15] When we surrender wanting for having, our longing is truncated, betrayed, wounded. But Farley does not name this betrayal "sin" because to do so would bind our description of our wound to guilt, and not all forms of the wound incur guilt. Instead, Farley describes the wrongness as "an addiction to the causes of evil and suffering, [and] as bondage arising out of the deep woundedness of existence."[16]

Farley describes a wide variety of ways in which that addiction manifests itself: as a stubborn egocentrism that lives in the illusion of autonomy, as addiction to caring for others that surrenders the self, and as immersion in the pleasures of the world that, like a painkiller, masks the symptoms of our wounded desire.[17] All of these twist and distort the longing that draws us toward the immense no-thing that heals us until that longing takes on the shape of terror that makes us so sensitive to the possibility of danger that we become paralyzed, or rage that protects the ego from those dangers by preemptively harming others, or addiction

13. Farley, *Wounding and Healing*, 4.

14. Farley, *Wounding and Healing*, 13.

15. Farley, *Wounding and Healing*, 15.

16. Farley, *Wounding and Healing*, 25.

17. Farley, *Wounding and Healing*, 34, 24, 36, 41.

that reduces the subjects that might delight us to objects that we hope will satisfy us.[18]

Farley's attention to the multiple ways in which our longing core is distorted arises in part from her attunement to the narratives of those outside the structures of institutional power and those marginalized from the norming center of the dominant culture. In the effort to push back against the elitism of the ascetics and exclusivism of the orthodox, Denys turned to the ordinary practices of the Christian community; but for all his careful descriptions of the ordinary movements of Christian worship, Denys spends little time with the penitents, demoniacs, and catechumens who are excluded from the Eucharist. But this is where Farley's theology begins, in the outer chamber, with those who can see, but are not invited to taste that the Lord is good. Regarding the exclusion of women's voices from the history of theology, for instance, Farley laments "what a terrible defrauding of our understanding of what theology is and of the beauty of the Christian faith this exclusion has been. There is also a terrible diminishment of theology when the oral tradition of these communities is not integrated with the study of a textual tradition."[19] In the traditional curricula of theology schools, it seems that when women write or are written about the works are always regarded as "mysticism" or "spirituality," and not as theology proper. In *Gathering Those Driven Away*, Farley reminds us that we need to listen to those whom the institutional church has driven away, and that a healthy dose of apophatic humility can act as an antidote to the poison of hegemony.[20]

Like Denys, Farley offers a path toward healing, and this is a path that is both ecstatic and embodied. For Farley, contemplative practices help us to relinquish the passions that block our eros and cultivate virtues that open the flow of eros so that we might become more loving.[21] These practices are ecstatic because they call us out of our ego-centrism; they are embodied because they root us in our true selves.

18. Farley, *Wounding and Healing*, 58, 60, 64.

19. Farley, *Wounding and Healing*, xi.

20. Farley, *Gathering Those Driven Away*.

21. Farley, *Wounding and Healing*, see especially chapters 7 and 8.

An Erotic and Apophatic Approach to Practical Theology

In both Denys and Farley we find that the dynamic of the erotic and the apophatic results in a theology that is unusually attentive to the ordinary, especially to embodied practices. These theologies suggest that attending to our deepest longings leaves us nearly speechless and with a heightened awareness of the ordinary practices of living religious communities. Implicit in these theologies is the conviction that the practices of living religious communities express our deepest longings and encode values and beliefs that escape the capacity of traditional theological language to name or describe. If practical theology aims to employ and explore the ordinary language and embodied practices of living religious communities, then it must be always self-consciously apophatic.

But their erotic and apophatic theologies also suggest that the practical theologian, the theologian of the ordinary, cannot function as an anthropologist who observes these practices while bracketing out her own normative commitments. Practical theology wells up from within faith communities as a practice of self-clarification, as a longing for the well-being of the beloved, and as a desire for the mutual delight that bubbles up in the interplay of seeing and speaking, veiling and keeping silence. The practical theologian is not the disinterested scholar of the Enlightenment, but an attentive lover who delights in the movements and words of the beloved.

Theologians of the ordinary to seek to thematize what is taken for granted and left implicit in practices. The lover seeks to name those deep longings, which practice leaves unnamed, and to do so for the sake of clarifying and enriching practice. This means that the practical theologian must speak as a lover whose life is bound to the community, who makes its language and its practices her own, who can say with Ruth, "Your people shall be my people, and your God my God" (Ruth 1:16). But just as the lover and the beloved are united by love without being a single person, and just as Ruth, who is bound to Israel by a vow of faithfulness, always remains "the Moabitess," so too the practical theologian is not absorbed into the community without remainder, and cannot, with her words, exhaust the full meaning of communal practices.

Lover and beloved delight one another, serve each other as faithful companions, and help one another; but lover and beloved also question each other and sometimes misunderstand and are misunderstood by each other. There is between lovers a dynamic of listening and speaking, of reaching out and of holding back. Practical theology, then, is embedded in the primary religious discourse of a faith community, but is often explicated in terms foreign to its home. An apophatic practical theologian will always remember that she is the lover, not the beloved, that she is always a Moabitess. But only when that apophatic impulse is wed to erotic attentiveness does the practical theologian begin to understand and join with the community in its particular way of longing. Only the attentive lover can manage to avoid the devil of patronizing faith communities and the deep blue sea of simply colonizing their language.

Case Study: Medical Fatalism

Let me experiment with this erotic and apophatic method by considering one instance of how the health promoters speak of embodiment and healthcare. Healthcare practices encode deeply held beliefs about and longings for our bodies, and when a community experiences the beliefs and desires of the medical community as being at odds with its own bodily longings, the results can be tragic. Healthcare workers in Memphis and the congregational health promoters alike report a pervasive and seemingly intractable fatalism with respect to illness and disease among African Americans, especially among the poor. One health promoter explained that a common attitude about diabetes among many members of her church is that "big momma had sugar, I'm a have sugar too."[22] In neighborhoods where fresh produce is rare and expensive and fast food chains and liquor stores abundant and affordable, where streets and parks are unsafe places for outdoor exercise, and where residents return exhausted in the evenings from long days at distant jobs that do not pay a living wage, it is no mystery why many come to believe that they have little control over their lives or their health.[23] Diabetes, hypertension, obesity, asthma, and depression seem natural and stoic acceptance of the easiest path.[24]

22. All quotations from Congregational Health Promoters come from an interview I conducted at the Church Health Center on March 7, 2011.

23. For a fascinating account of how racism produces the neighborhood disadvantage that results in health disparities see Baltimore and Fullilove, "The Destruction of Aunt Ester's House," 111–27.

24. William Cockerham offers a helpful explanation of how the stress associated with social class can contribute to poor health and fatalism. See Cockerham, "Class and Health," 114–37, and "Living Conditions," 164–80.

Fatalism is complex, but we can trace it to at least two sources. First, there is a well-warranted distrust of the medical community among poor African Americans throughout the South. One of the health promoters reports a reluctance among members of her community to visit the hospital because "that's where black people go to die," or because "they experiment on people there." The word "Tuskegee" is spoken in a hushed, horrified whisper, but the Tuskegee experiments are only one instance in a long list of gross atrocities and subtle slights that generate distrust.[25] Here we see plainly a painful and living example of how wounded desire can turn to terror that is so attuned to possible dangers that it becomes paralyzed.

A second source for the fatalism can be traced to atonement language especially popular in some black church traditions that emphasizes Christ's passive suffering on the cross. He received injustice in his own body and "never said a mumblin' word." This sense that undeserved bodily suffering should be met with a stoic willingness to endure without complaint gets replicated in expectations about the suffering of our own bodies. If we imitate a savior who passively accepted injustice at the expense of his own bodily integrity, then how do we warrant any response to ill health other than uncomplaining acceptance? One health promoter expressed exasperation with a member of her community whose blood glucose reading at a health fair was far too high. The woman calmly explained, "I get dizzy sometimes, but I just sit down and it passes after a time." "What that woman needs," the health promoter insisted, "is less Bible and more insulin." What she needs is to believe that her health matters. But atonement theology can act as a powerful, addicting painkiller that masks our true wound. And pairing atonement theology with language of guilt and sin only exacerbates the problem by suggesting not only that we should accept our suffering, but also that we somehow deserve it.

Early in my conversations with these health promoters, it occurred to me that their own language of "being sassy," language picked up by womanist theologians in other contexts, offers a remedy that invites the community into alternate views of the atonement and moves it in the direction of provocative suffering and bold somebodiness.[26] When

25. See White, *Seeing Patients*.

26. Stephanie Mitchem makes a powerful case that "agency . . . stands against the internalized self-hatred found among some African Americans. Self-hatred becomes embedded into a group through its adoption of prevailing negative images." Mitchem, *Introducing Womanist Theology*, 21.

the health promoters speak of the life of Jesus they speak of someone on the margins whose sassy defiance of the authorities provoked a violent response. In his parables and sermons he called out the corruption of those in power, and in his healing ministry he lifted up the value of those cast out and driven away. In their language about the life of Christ they acknowledge that his words and actions provoked the violence that cost him his life and that, in imitation of Christ, Christians should never shrink back from demanding justice.[27] In other words, when the health promoters speak of Jesus's life, they speak of provocative suffering, not of passive acceptance of injustice.

The notion of a sassy Jesus whose suffering is provocative suggests a model of atonement far different from the conventional one, and certainly this model of atonement has been explored in black and womanist theology.[28] Should the poor of Memphis allow such a view of the life of Jesus to change their ideas about the death of Jesus, it could dramatically reshape attitudes toward bodily suffering and begin to reverse the damaging effects of medical fatalism.

These are the resources of the communities of the health promoters themselves, and they are ripe for use in reinterpreting bodily longing and bodily well-being. But this is where the essay began, with a question about whether it is possible for a relative outsider to suggest this language and to connect it to health equity without the taint of colonialism. The practical theologian who approaches the community as attentive lover, and not as colonial power, may be able to join in the longing of the beloved, reaching for but never grasping the beloved. In the metaphor of the attentive lover, the practical theologian may find both the apophatic restraint to be the Moabitess and the erotic freedom to say, "Your God is my God, and your people are my people."

Bibliography

Baltimore, Terri, and Mindy Thompson Fullilove. "The Destruction of Aunt Ester's House: Faith, Health, and Healing in the African American Community." In *Faith,*

27. James Cone likens the cross to a lynching tree, which those with social power use to try to silence those who question the reigning hierarchy. Suffering caused by injustice should not be embraced as redemptive, Cone argues, but suffering that emerges from resisting injustice may be. See Cone, *The Cross and the Lynching Tree.*

28. For an excellent treatment of embodiment, race, and atonement language, see Copeland, *Enfleshing Freedom.*

Health, and Healing in African American Life, edited by Stephanie Y. Mitchem and Emilie Maureen Townes, 111–27. Religion, Health and Healing. Westport, CT: Praeger, 2008.

Cockerham, William C. "Class and Health: Explaining the Relationship." In *Social Causes of Health and Disease*, 2nd ed., 114–37. Malden, MA: Polity, 2013.

———. "Living Conditions and Neighborhood Disadvantage." In *Social Causes of Health and Disease*, 2nd ed., 164–80. Malden, MA: Polity, 2013.

Cone, James. *The Cross and the Lynching Tree*. Maryknoll, NY: Orbis, 2011.

Copeland, M. Shawn. *Enfleshing Freedom: Body, Race, and Being*. Innovations, African American Religious Thought. Minneapolis: Fortress, 2010.

Farley, Edward. *Practicing Gospel: Unconventional Thoughts on the Church's Ministry*. 1st ed. Louisville, KY: Westminster John Knox, 2003.

Farley, Wendy. *Gathering Those Driven Away: A Theology of Incarnation*. Louisville, KY: Westminster John Knox, 2011.

———. *The Wounding and Healing of Desire: Weaving Heaven and Earth*. Louisville, KY: Westminster John Knox, 2005.

Mitchem, Stephanie Y. *Introducing Womanist Theology*. Maryknoll, NY: Orbis, 2002.

Sayle, Hannah. "Unjust Deserts." *Memphis Flyer*, September 26, 2010.

Suchla, Beate Regina, ed. *Corpus Dionysiacum. Band 1 Pseudo-Dionysius Areopagita. De Divinis Nominibus*. Vol. 33. Patristische Texte und Studien. Berlin: De Gruyter, 1991.

White, Augustus A., and David Chanoff. *Seeing Patients: Unconscious Bias in Health Care*. Cambridge, MA: 2011.

SIX

On Erotic Faithfulness:
Or How Eve Earned Her Name

Mari Kim

CONTEMPORARY NORTH AMERICAN THEOLOGIAN Wendy Farley develops eros as a symbol descriptive of divine power. Her work on Divine Eros responds to traditional philosophical and theological arguments that insist that the nature of divine perfection is idealized as desireless, self-sufficient unity. While acknowledging that such formulations of divine perfection "protect divine being from emotional or ontological entanglements with creation . . . [and preserve] the majesty and integrity of transcendent divinity," Farley nevertheless finds their correlative metaphysical implications theologically troubling.[1] If "self-enclosed identity is the ideal of perfection," then what logically follows is the suggestion that "difference and relationship diminish perfection."[2] Farley further laments the dichotomy established when "the goodness of ultimate reality" is pitted "in direct opposition to the perfection of creation," such that there emerges a "radical disjunction between the perfection of God and the striving for perfection in human beings."[3] She recognizes that this fundamentally undermines the efficacy of analogies attempting to establish a logically consistent and viable description of how God and the world,

1. Farley, *Tragic Vision*, 104.
2. Farley, *Tragic Vision*, 104–5.
3. Farley, *Tragic Vision*, 105.

despite being essentially different, can be said to be relationally involved, whether as Creator and Created, or Redeemer and Redeemed. [4]

Indeed, where undifferentiated unity and solipsistic contemplation represent divine perfection, the presence of Creation—as a structure of existence differentiated from that of the divine—introduces correlative philosophical problems, chief among which has traditionally been the challenge of formulating how monadic divine perfection would or could relate to that which is not identically perfect like itself. In response, Farley rightly resists an ideal of divine perfection as only able or required to relate to that which is perfect like itself. Framing both her discontent with, and her solution to, this theological problem, Farley reasons, "if God is said to be causally connected to human beings as the power of creation and redemption, and if both creation and redemption are constituted by relationship, *then a relational symbol for divine perfection may be more appropriate.*"[5]

Divine Eros: Oriented by Benevolent Hospitality

Divine Eros is the symbol for divine power that Farley introduces as most suitable for overcoming this problematic disconnect between the existence of Creation and its Source. The perfection of divine loving emerges through her understanding of Creation. Farley describes Divine Eros as being manifest in a dynamic of ecstatic communication of—that is, an outward (*ek-*) movement of—its relational nature. Creation models, she points out, this divine acting in order to transcend itself. Indeed, in transcending itself to share existence with Otherness, Divine Eros dynamically shatters the emptiness of its solitude to graciously usher in the presence of a differentiated Other. Farley sees the loving nature of Divine Eros epitomized as a generative hospitality that transcends itself to share existence in, with, and through a vast and differentiated plurality. Through the diversity of existence manifested in Creation, it becomes clear that Divine Eros imparts value to that which is unlike the Divine.

Underscoring Creation's theological identity as the Other, and in particular that Other called into existence for loving relationship with the Divine, Farley's work on Divine Eros empowers, rather than undermines, a prophetic valuing of the differentiated plurality of Creation and affirms

4. Farley, *Tragic Vision*, 105.

5. Farley, *Tragic Vision*, 105. Italics mine.

the necessity of benevolence towards forms of existence that are deemed Other-than-Divine. If Divine Eros is a symbol for divine power, Farley's description of Creation also helps us cultivate the further awareness that when Divine Eros acts—whether to share existence with that which is not itself or to generate those conditions necessary for the fulfillment of its nature as loving—it is oriented by a quality of what I will call *benevolent hospitality*.

While *benevolent hospitality* is not a term Farley uses, it is introduced here to describe in greater detail the character of the energy of Divine Eros—that quality of acting to embrace the flourishing of an existence that is Other-than-itself. Theologically, the concept names a dynamic of mutual honoring and appreciation capable of empowering the *tov* (the good, the beautiful, the right) in partnership with an Other. Building on Farley's awareness that the erotic perfection of love is manifest through the relational hospitality of Creation, *benevolent hospitality* is an energy recognizable by its intention as well as its effects.

Significantly, Farley's description of Divine Eros as expressing the perfection of its loving nature through Creation challenges traditional philosophical and theological formulations that suggest the existence of Creation represents the existence of something that is a diminution of divine nature. She resists a tradition obsessed with monolithic perfection and refuses to frame the kenotic sharing of existence that is Creation as somehow diminishing of divine nature in any way. In Farley's paradigm, Creation as an expression of divine activity not only generates an abundance of existence, such that existence is not diminished, but of existence that is not like itself. It therefore manifests the fulfillment of Divine Eros as a relational energy expressing *benevolent hospitality* towards that which is unlike itself. This clarity offers us the vital discernment that as the perfection of love welcomes the flourishing of the Other in Creation, there is no loss, hindrance, or diminishment of divine nature. The divine in no way neglects the fulfillment of its own nature, nor fails to honor the thriving of its whole goodness as it extends the *benevolent hospitality* of existence to Creation.

As Farley makes it clear that the divine moves wholly and fully in harmony with the *tov* of its own nature, it becomes possible to understand how the benevolence enacted by Divine Eros is a hospitality that does not separate out or sacrifice the good of itself in seeking partnership with the good of another. Creation as an act of hospitality welcoming the *tov* of Otherness into existence shows Divine Eros to be fulfilling its most original and primary nature as loving. Therefore, *benevolent hospitality* describes the energy of Divine Eros as desire shaped as an intentionality that honors the fulfillment of one's own nature in empowering the flourishing of Otherness and the *tov* of hospitable relationship with the same. Thus, *benevolent hospitality* emerges as grounded in realizing the *tov* of its own nature while oriented to relationships that promote the flourishing of Others.

Given that Creation is declared (seven times) to be wholly and perfectly *tov*—that is to say, perfect in goodness—this quality of *benevolent hospitality* shapes Creation and mediates all relationships therein. Furthermore, examining Creation through the lens of *benevolent hospitality* cultivates our awareness of the profound interdependence structuring the nature of *tov* or that perfect goodness throughout Creation. Thus, *benevolent creation* describes the experience of an existence that has been imprinted with an awareness that the benevolence towards existence which birthed Creation persists in the ontological structure of existence, in how Creation is hospitably oriented to the flourishing and fulfillment of an ever-increasing multiplicity of *tov*.

Conceptualized this way, there is an existential benevolence inherent in Creation that recognizes how Divine Eros structures all *tov*, sharing existence, including its own, with and through a necessarily mutual dynamic of edification. How? As a profound and radical interdependence that is reflected in the structure of all existence. This radical interdependence inevitably shapes Creation as an experience of existence in which the honoring and fulfillment of one's own nature likewise cultivates and brings to flourishing the *tov* of that which is Other in Creation. Any rudimentary examination of ecological structures readily reveals this. Conversely, this also introduces the clarity that a failure to honor the flourishing and fulfillment of one's own *tov* becomes occasion for a subsequent inability to offer genuine hospitality to the *tov* of an Other. Where we cannot or do not embrace the flourishing of our own *tov*, the partnerships we cultivate not only suffer from the inadequacy of that lack of inclusion but become unable to generate the genuine hospitality of appreciation capable of energizing delight in truth of the Other's *tov*. Indeed, in the absence of our ability to have our own *tov* realized, we become vulnerable to the sense of incompleteness and inadequacy associated with not recognizing our own goodness, perfection, or *tov*.

Subsequently, when faced with the prospect of encountering the Other with whom we are in partnership, and encountering the power of their tov goodness and beauty, it becomes difficult, if not impossible, to avoid the envy and jealousy, as well as the fear and doubt, of self-inadequacy that fundamentally cripples our relational capacity to genuinely offer the hospitality of appreciation to the *tov* of Others. Relationships cultivated in this state of lack become distorted by the desire to secure what we need through the Other, or to extract it from the partnership, as if such external sources could provide what we have failed to embrace and realize for ourselves.

In the absence of honoring the fulfillment of our own *tov*, what appreciation of the Other we can manage to muster remains prisoner to fear of inadequacy and therefore self-seeking gain. The fear and doubt generated by the experience of doubting our own *tov* deprives our partnerships, or more specifically our capacity to be in partnership, of the power of genuine hospitality. In this state of feeling inadequate, any opportunity to appreciate the *tov* of Others cultivates fearful envy and jealousy rather than the freedom of delight that empowers us to embrace the flourishing of the Other. Troubled by this perceived lack, conflicted competition rather than hospitality distorts and diminishes our capacity for partnership. The mutuality of relationship is thus distorted, undermined by ambiguity and ambivalence; as a consequence, engagements with cultural hybridity accentuate the experience of alienation rather than a mutual enhancement of *tov*.

Blessedness, Erotic Faith, and Erotic Faithfulness

Acknowledging that we inhabit a condition that is essentially characterized by ambiguity and ambivalence, it is the experience of our desires that both attests to a persistent lack of clarity and continually conflicting desires and gifts us with the awareness that we seek a fuller *tov* than what we may know. In such a context, we are not saved from this condition by obedience or by clarity but by the desire for the good. Schleiermacher is helpful here, as he illumines an understanding of human beatitude or blessedness in conflict. Schleiermacher's conviction echoes the hope of Christian faith as declared in Romans 8:38–39: that nothing in our experience functions to impede the intention of Divine Benevolence towards us, "neither height nor depth, nor things past, nor things present." If indeed nothing in our lived experience separates us from the love of God, then even our most distressing, disorienting, debilitating struggles with the Otherness of cultural hybridity can be recognized as participating in that structure of benevolent creation invested with the capacity to mediate "immediate God-consciousness."

In a context of cultural hybridity, Schleiermacher's understanding of blessedness invites consideration of how the challenging confusion generated by cultural hybridity can encapsulate the perfection of *tov*, of the great beauty and rightness inherent in God's creative genius. Focusing on whether and what kind of virtue can be discerned as emerging from within contexts of cultural hybridity, this most basic trust in the providence of God's gracious and loving design suggests that it was entirely possible for experiences of cultural hybridity to cultivate and manifest particular virtues appropriate to the context and, in doing so, to mediate the truth of our belovedness. Meditatively, what compelled my attention were the kinds of desires that could be discerned through those same experiences. Invited to another level of attention, the particular experiences of cultural hybridity that compelled my desire became the unintentional focus of an opened attentiveness.

As expressed by Julian of Norwich in her conviction "that all will be well, and all will be well, and every kind of thing will be well,"[6] blessedness emerges as the audacious courage of trust that stands in defiance of suggestions that anything less than the hospitality of Divine Benevolence is at work in our lives. Schleiermacher's profoundly compelling understanding of benevolence suggests, theologically, that our experiences of frustration and confusion, and of the hardship, suffering, and struggle generated by conflict, nevertheless sharpen the longing of our hunger to know the truth of *benevolent hospitality* and awaken us to our identity as bearers of the Divine image.

A Theological Anthropology of Contemplative Desire

The theological anthropology that emerges from such an understanding of *blessedness* primarily affirms that humanity, as formed in God's likeness to bear the image of God, is imbued with a profound capacity for what Farley calls "erotic faith." At its heart, erotic faith emerges as an orientation towards the Divine. Still further developed through Farley's analysis of contemplative eros, erotic faith emerges as a practice of trust oriented by the contemplative hope of union with the Divine. We draw upon her understanding of contemplative eros to discern a theological

6. Julian of Norwich, *Showings*, 225.

anthropology capable of illumining our vocation as "God-bearers." As Farley describes contemplation, it is a practice of desire expressing our longing to be connected to the Divine image in us:

> As contemplative desire is aroused, the desire for genuine free-dom from the passions intensifies. Our longing to connect to the Divine Image in us, to live more completely out of the "one-ing" of our soul with Holy *Eros*, and to radiate this love to other beings becomes increasingly, painfully urgent.[7]

This description of contemplative desire as a painful urgency to inhabit an existence that is more "oned" with ourselves—intended by the One who created us to need such connection—resonates with the description of the desire for existential integrity that emerges through our earlier theological analysis of cultural hybridity. Farley's analysis illumines that when desire for existential integrity is examined through a contemplative lens, the experience of cultural hybridity, as the experience of a human condition defined by finitude, cultivates a fundamental desire for contemplative freedom.

As Farley presents it, this freedom is ill-conceived as either the absence of constraints or as residing in some form of ungrounded omnipotence that falsely suggests we have power to do anything or be anyone—that seductive delusion of modern North American myths of personal freedom. Instead, the "genuine freedom" that Farley conceives as emerging through contemplative attentiveness is grounded in an ontological context that takes a sober account of the vulnerabilities of an existence situated in a context of finitude, and the blessings and curses found therein. Teleologically oriented by the concern to inhabit an existence with integrity, the freedom of contemplative eros is fundamentally associated with that which empowers in each of us an experience able to concretely authenticate the potential goodness embedded in our being. For this reason, contemplative freedom is concerned with overcoming those obstacles that hinder the concrete expression of the goodness of existence embedded in one's being. Borrowing the ancient monastic il-luminations about the passions to discuss those dispositions we assent to, trained by habits, in ignorance, Farley's description of darkness helps us recognize that opening ourselves to new understandings of reality en-counters a resistance. This process involves the reluctance of the ego to be dislodged: "The ego maintains its centrality by habituation, skepticism,

---

7. Farley, *Wounding and Healing*, 119.

and fear. The habit of egocentrism is so deeply ingrained that it seems to be existence itself."[8]

> The ego is not amused by the possibility of dislocation, for the egological structure of mind is intimately tied to the habit of egocentrisms. This intimacy is so thorough that it feels as if there were no difference between mind and ego at all. We feel as if the dislocation of the habit of egocentricity would be tantamount to ceasing to be a person altogether. We rightly resist images of humiliation or annihilation that imply personal existence has no place in contemplative desire.[9]

Yet freedom from the ego is of ultimate value to us, according to Farley, because "love breaks free in us as we disarm and dislocate egocentrism."[10] Centered by her conviction about God's enduring desire for union with us, Farley suggests contemplative eros cultivates in us the endurance necessary for us to seek the Divine, even when the appeal of good and evil tempt and distract us. Acknowledging that the struggles we experience sometimes coax us into settling idolatrously for preemptive satisfactions, or other times compel us to succumb to being overcome by the despair of hopelessness, Farley reminds us to be sober-minded about how fraught the path of contemplative faith is with the demons of doubt, fear, anxiety, insecurity, etc.

Yet even in the midst of such struggles, Farley affirms that the path of contemplative eros has the ability to inspire hope because the pain and struggle of such challenging experiences are, in fact, verily the path of faith, rather than the result of falling away from it. With this clarity, she offers a corrective to misunderstandings that falsely suggest that the path of faithfulness is without doubt, fear, anxiety, insecurity, discouragement, or despair.

Her understanding of the challenges confronted by a contemplative faith link Farley to the anthropological tradition epitomized by the ancient monastics, whose contemplative existence allowed them to recognize how our passions—those distortions and destructive habits capable of deceiving us about the truth of who we are and of impeding our ability to manifest the goodness of our particular existence—could disempower any experience of blessedness. Thus, taking freedom to be primarily a release from the fictions of our passions that liberates a person to know

8. Farley, *Wounding and Healing*, 130.
9. Farley, *Wounding and Healing*, 130.
10. Farley, *Wounding and Healing*, 130.

who s/he really is, Farley conceptualizes "genuine freedom" as nothing less than being empowered to embody who you are, without falling prey to distortions or self-deceptions from within.

Thus liberated by the freedom wrought by a contemplative faith, Farley describes us as able to discover that Divine Eros ultimately flows through us, ecstatically expressed in an appreciative hospitality towards the goodness manifest in the existence of others. The theological anthropology that emerges from such an understanding of contemplative eros presents humanity, first and foremost, as an expression and embodiment of the loving presence of Divine Eros. Furthermore, Farley, like Augustine, insists that the manifold and increasing variety of existence arrayed in Creation, inclusive of human diversity, contributes to the divine perfection manifested by Creation. Indeed, just as Creation's hospitality to the endless variety in existence reflects the conviction that divine perfection is enhanced and expanded, rather than diminished or distorted, by each variation of human uniqueness, it likewise follows that with each unique instance of cultural hybridity created through intercultural convergence, the truth of Divine Beauty is increased.

Her understanding of Divine Beauty as increasingly embodied in a universe still birthing creation in endlessly increasing perfection allows Farley to see divine goodness being multiplied rather than diminished, negated, or in any way diluted and weakened. Just as Farley recognizes in *Tragic Vision* that a traditional philosophical understanding of perfection might insist that divine perfection is only manifest as that which is unchanging and invulnerable to the imperfection of change and transformation, in *Eros for the Other,* she also further criticizes the metaphysics generated by this philosophical suggestion of divine perfection. Engaging those concrete or political practices generated when that-which-is-Other-than-God is categorically defined as defiantly defiling divine perfection, Farley reveals how such an understanding of perfection can translate, politically, into a practice of totalitarian-like dominance that generates an ethic of hate and violence contrary to orthodox convictions about the loving benevolence of the Divine.[11]

11. Working with Hannah Arendt's criticism of totalitarianism, Farley exposes how perfection, defined as similarity, generates an ethic of violence toward difference— punishing deviations from the norm in a destructive policy of monolithic conformity that upholds replication as expressing the truest "loyalty" to the ideal of Divine Perfection. Politically embodied as totalitarianism, the logic of this philosophical perfection calls for imitation, or cloned replication, not merely as the highest compliment, but as the only and mandatory form of existence tolerated. However, interpretations of

ON EROTIC FAITHFULNESS 87

Farley also draws upon Levinas's ethical necessity of the Other to empower a theological embrace of divine hospitality towards alterity, or the Other, as expressing the truth of Divine Eros for the greater perfection of relationship.[12] Thus understood, Farleyan eros reinvigorates an orthodox valuing of the generative aspect of Creation and redeems traditional interpretations of the alterity that is core to the existence of the Other from being demonized as that which separates Creation from the Creator. The otherness inherent in Creation is redeemed as expressive of imitating the Divine; and, in particular, the necessary capacity of humanity to reproduce life by introducing only uniquely original variations of human being (rather than cloned replicas of any progenitor) is recognized as expressing the ongoing fulfillment of Farleyan eros.

Indeed, the valuing of alterity allows for hybrid expressions of variety in human *being* that emerge—whether expressing a biological or cultural syncretism or both—to be signified in Farley's theology of eros for the Other as a concrete instance of Divine beauty being manifest in existence. And as such, expressions of hybrid diversity emerge, symbolizing an increase in Divine goodness capable of adding to the existing perfection that has already been manifest in Creation.

Farley's understanding of Divine Eros allows her anthropology (summarized as *human beings are created with the capacity to enjoy relationship with the Divine*) to intersect with the ontological recognition

creation dependent upon a philosophical paradigm of Divine Perfection that aligns perfection with similarity (and, conversely, understands degrees of difference to express degrees of imperfection) struggle to articulate an organic relationship between Creation and Creator that preserves the perfection of the Divine while allowing that which is unlike the Divine to have been generated by the Divine. Where Divine Perfection excludes that which was not the same, how can perfection be understood to relate to, much less be caused by, that which is not Divine?

12. The understanding of Divine hospitality highlighted here most interestingly approximates a theological understanding of beauty developed by eighteenth-century American theologian Jonathan Edwards. Edward Farley's historical investigation of the conceptualization of Beauty reveals that Edwards' essay "The Nature of True Virtue" (1703) articulates an understanding of primary beauty expressed as a "disposition of benevolence" to whatever exists. In this definition, Edwards anticipates my own definition of beauty as a praxis manifesting an orientation of hospitality towards the good in existence. By applying Wendy Farley's understanding of Creation (as an act of Divine love sharing the goodness of existence with other beings) to the struggles core to experiences of cultural hybridity, I conceptualized an understanding of beauty as expressed in a hospitality (by God and ourselves) whose Love created space and affirmed the goodness of those distinctions expressed through the existence of cultural hybrids. This will be discussed in further detail below, in our reading of Genesis 3 and the woman's praxis of beauty.

that humanity's capacity to enjoy relationship with the Divine both mediates and is mediated by a relational structure of interdependence through which the clarity and fullness of experiencing God's love rests through our relationships with Others. *Eros for the Other* offers a compelling argument for why it is critical to our healing and theo-ethical empowerment to accept and further forge ways of appreciating and integrating, whenever possible, those expressions of our interior otherness, that is, the otherness within ourselves. It is at this intersection of theological anthropology and ontology that Farley's reflections on Divine Eros permit a very helpful analysis of contemplation as that praxis of desire most appropriate to our nature as "God-bearers."

For us as "God-bearers," desire emerges as the practice most appropriate to imitate as we seek to realize our embodiment as creatures designed with the capacity to long—a desire akin to thirst for water—until the truth of God's love is realized fully in us. Contemplation is an analogous awakening of desire. With this awakening, awareness dawns of how little we are able to love, how bound we are to our fears. This is why great saints describe themselves as such terrible "sinners." They become more and more aware of this infinity of love within us and available to us, just as knowledge of that single word, "water," made Helen Keller know that a universe of connection was available to her. From the tiniest taste of Holy *Eros*, the infinity of love manifest in every soul and spiraling through the endlessness of our own soul is apprehended. The thirst of contemplation lives in the gap between that single taste and the infinity of the cosmos.[13]

It is a taste of the infinite that awakens our yearning for the infinite. Thus, Farley's work on contemplation insists that we must practice the spiritual discipline of seeking in order to recognize how appropriate and akin to our divine nature it is to embrace a contemplative faith. The practice of contemplative desire begins with the conviction that human beings, having been created to bear the image of God, need and hunger for greater intimacy with God. This fragile tension between human freedom and responsibility is one that Farley wants to maintain in the "tragic vision" that she finds offering the most compelling theological ontology. That we continue to be capable of exercising power to make decisions in contexts where we have little or no control of the outcomes remains no less than an ethical mandate despite the undeniable vulnerability we experience as human beings.[14] However limited the ability to determine

---

13. Farley, *Wounding and Healing*, 122.

14. When Dietrich Bonhoeffer was imprisoned in a Nazi concentration camp,

one's path, and however deprived of that crucial glimpse of a larger reality that would compel a different choosing, Farley maintains that the true genius of the anthropology of desire preserved in ancient Greek tragedies remains the fundamental recognition that human freedom is not merely a matter of *action* but more primarily a freedom of *disposition* to pursue and embrace the truth of one's being.

Human freedom remains the key to related notions of resistance that Farley admires in the ancient tragedies that tell the stories of virtuous Greeks, such as Prometheus and Antigone. The lives of these tragic heroes are not marked by passive or despairing acquiescence to the Fates but rather by the defiant exercise of freedom, determined to pursue the integrity of the good desired in the face of downfall.[15] Through Farley, we learn that the manner in which tragic heroes embrace (or fail to embrace) their imminent demise helps to confirm the outcomes of the heroes' choices. Farley reminds us of this critical insight: because human life is ontologically structured for relationality, that which confirms the truth of who we know ourselves to be can no less empower transformations in who we are called to be, our community relationships, and our relationship with those god-like or divinely ordained contingencies of our existence, such as our need for food, water, and sleep, the economic constraints that effect professional performance, and the educational and recreational spheres.

Most significantly, Farley suggests that if these tragic heroes could have managed to avoid their failing—figuring out, instead, how to save their lives—in a very real sense, they would have violated who they were, and in doing so, become imprisoned in an existence ill-fitting them. Therefore, she interprets the freedom of being human as never being entirely violated, even while it becomes the case that the various contingencies of a finite existence extinguish the availability of choices. Moreover, unwilling to deny the freedom implicit in human experiences of desire,

---

despite being stripped of manifold freedoms and necessary conditions for thriving, Bonhoeffer neither insisted he was without the capacity to act according to his faith or conscience, nor desired to do so. As Farley maintains, no doctrine of predestination or fatalistic philosophy of determinism is able to absolve humanity of having responsibility for our actions.

15. Interesting to note, in such instances the heroes' downfalls do not reflect a violation of who they are; rather, their choices empower the fulfillment of the truth of their being, even as their destinies are sealed. Their virtue—embedded in the virtue of *who they are* and the *kind of beings they are*, as well as their *particular way of expressing human existence*—is not diminished by even the loss of existence as they know it.

Farley insists there is an existential integrity in the ancient Greek refusal to interpret human suffering as either necessarily deserved or resulting from a transgression of the divine. Influenced alternatively by the compassionate anthropology of Greek tragedies, Farley suggests that human struggle and suffering are often inexplicable and best appreciated as the tragic consequences of inhabiting an existence inscribed by profound and persistent limitations, unalleviated even by the truth of human agency. In her analysis of contemplative experiences, Farley develops this tragic sensibility in her theological anthropology, insisting that the tragic dimension of the human condition is not merely introduced by the constraints of finitude but augmented by a vocational longing for intimacy with God that is fated, in this lifetime, to secure only our contact with persistent struggle and suffering.

Despite this, Farley's anthropology refuses to absolve humanity either of the freedom to desire God or of accountability for the limited outcome resulting from those limited choices we can make (often with no greater "freedom" than desiring the good in the face of our, or another's, harm and hurt). The influence of the Greek tragedian's brilliance persists, as Farley's contemplative anthropology presents us with an entirely knowable humanity whose desire to seek truth-in-being through intimacy with God brings on a plague of struggle and suffering that invites our compassion.

Even as we read of humanity seeking to embrace its destiny to "become like God, knowing good and evil" in Genesis 3, in the spirit of the Greek tragedian, Farley's anthropology invites us to refuse assigning any guilt or blame to the "hero." Rather, learning the compassion of the tragedian, Farley calls us to reject practices of condemnation (whether towards ourselves or others), as contemplative practices invariably expose our lack and inability, as well as our doubt and uncertainty. Instead, Farley's anthropology invites us to embrace all tenderness while we struggle and suffer. Internalizing the truth of ourselves as beloved of God, Farley describes contemplative desire as growing in us the courage to recognize our vocation as designed for union with the Divine. In the freedom to be faithful to our vocation as "God-bearers," we will discover that Farley gives us grounds to reject the inadequacy of rote or unreflective obedience that lacks in an internal moral process. Mere obedience does not require the discernment of a mature faithfulness, which is characterized by delighting in a choice for the sake of its virtue. By allowing contemplative *eros* to interpret how we experience desire as we seek to hear the Divine in the Edenic narrative, we are looking to discern the truth of blessedness emerging through the text.

Genesis 3: Erotic Faithfulness in Eden

As we read Genesis 3 and examine the function of the woman's desire, the significance of conceptualizing an understanding of faithfulness as mediated by desire is crystallized. The biblical narrative reveals how eros inspires the enlightening of consciousness in the woman. We see that this consciousness in turn empowers an intentioned desire for the good, an eros for *tov*. By her contemplative attentiveness to the serpent's suggestion, the woman is awakened to the truth of the desirable *tov* inherent within creation. We are told that with the help of the serpent's strategic knowing (*'arum*) the woman's contemplative gaze does not merely make her aware of the beauty of the tree but in fact enables her to discern the particular *tov* of wisdom mediated by the fruit of the tree. She understands that by embracing relationship with the Other-in-creation, the tree, its fruit will make her wise. And when faithfulness to her eros for the good becomes *an intention* that is exercised as a choice, the woman is able to manifest fulfillment of the *tov* of wisdom intended for humanity via the blessing of the tree.

It is important to recognize in all this how eros stimulates greater awareness in multiple directions simultaneously. We learn that desire is oriented toward expansion: even while drawn to the beauty and goodness of something concrete, eros as love of *tov* also effortlessly expands towards the horizon of that *tov* which lies beyond what is within reach. Farley's insight, that "the economy of desire is not toward possession,"[16] takes on further clarity, therefore, as we discover the double-edged gift of erotic struggle. Embedded in the woman's experience of eros we discern that what has been traditionally misinterpreted as the "curse" of her desiring is the very blessing that has served to awaken in her the awareness of the *tov* or beauty and goodness that is worth loving. Through her desire, we discover that the "gift" of suffering lack is able to impart a

16. Farley, *Wounding and Healing of Desire*, 123. She introduces this concept earlier on, stating, "The economy of proportionality, correlation, of *possession* is not the economy of desire." She clarifies, "Desire, precisely by *not* possessing what it desires, is infinitely more connected to its beloved." This is because "desire carries us beyond the objects that can be possessed to an intimacy that is possible when this structure of object and possession has been left behind." Farley, *Wounding and Healing of Desire*, 16–17.

keen awareness of discontent that helps awaken a longing to experience the wholeness of a fuller goodness in our lives. Thus, via the faithful attentiveness of *eros,* the woman allows the power of discontent to stir in her a contemplative expansion of awareness.

In refutation of traditional interpretations of Genesis 3 that suggest both the woman's desiring and her decision are expressions of transgression against the Divine and the good intended for humanity, indeed, in contrast to arguments that insist the vice of the woman's desire precipitated her disobedience and consummated humanity's fall, the perspective of *erotic faithfulness* insists the woman's dedication to her desire is not a reflection of sinful disobedience but the fulfillment of a divine orientation in her that is drawn towards the *tov* that she rightly discerns is part of a benevolent creation. The goodness that she discerns as being inherent in the fruit of the tree is necessary to make her wise, and in her desiring of it, she must be seen as expressing a most appropriate faithfulness, dedicated to pursuing the fulfillment of humanity's intended capacity for wisdom.

On one level, to assert that the woman acts with *erotic faithfulness* is simply to suggest the woman acts from faithfulness to her desire. Yet desiring, or the act of being faithful to one's desiring, does not, in and of itself, indicate that virtue is present. Indeed, as exemplified by Cain's acquiescence to his desire in the very next chapter, it can represent the fulfillment of the most basic, most reprehensible capacities that shadow humanity's potential for virtue. However, when understood as manifesting benevolent creation's desire to fulfill the *tov* of existence—hers and that of the fruit of the tree—*erotic faithfulness* gives us the eyes to see that Eve's longing is in fact oriented towards that which is Divine. By virtue of her desiring the *tov* of the fruit of the tree and the wisdom it actualizes in her, *erotic faithfulness* becomes the energy of the woman's vindication, as the narrative reveals the consequence of acting on her desire to be a blessing of clarity. The knowledge of good and evil, that is, the recognition of the profound vulnerability em-bodied goodness that the woman, and then her partner, experience from eating of the fruit, is in fact what makes them like the Divine: knowing that which is good and the vulnerability of that good, which becomes experienced as an evil to be avoided.

Through faithful wrestling to discern a fuller wholeness of *tov,* the woman's consciousness is born and she emerges as embracing the freedom of conscious choice. With freedom and desire acting together, the woman is able to choose to love that which she sees as *tov,* in fulfillment of humanity's vocation to be wise. Consciously choosing from, with, and through faithful attentiveness to what she desires—from *erotic faithfulness*—the woman cultivates that freedom in decision-making that constitutes conscious, creative choice. And consequentially, the woman's faithfulness towards that which she sees as good and beautiful—that which is *tov*—results in the mutual fulfillment of the highest *tov* available to both the tree and humanity. In this way, the woman's decision to eat of the fruit of the tree represents virtue, not vice, as it brings her into an appropriate relationship with another goodness of creation, a relationship of hospitality that activates the fullest *tov* available for each.

We are told the tree's fruit serves humanity by opening their eyes and making them wise, begetting in them the vulnerable knowledge of good and evil, just as humanity's appreciation of the goodness of the fruit serves the tree by empowering its fullest capacity for goodness. The woman's practice of *erotic faithfulness* emerges potently enough to empower the manifesting of what is *tov* for the tree, herself, and her partner and ultimately enables the woman to fulfill her calling as *mother of all living*.

Reading Genesis 3 through lens of Farleyan contemplation makes clear that the *erotic faithfulness* which characterizes the fullest expression of human virtue in the Edenic narrative manifests an essential quality of conscious intention without which we cannot act to empower the *tov* of divine potential that waits patiently in us. It is *erotic faithfulness* that empowers the woman's act with the capacity to actualize, or make real, the truth of the *tov* she rightly desired. Thus, *erotic faithfulness* is not merely an expression of faithfulness because it is oriented by desire to be faithful, but it emerges in Genesis 3 as a practice of truth—imbued with the attentive power of conscious intention—capable of actualizing, that is, making known and bringing into existence, the desired goodness and beauty being called forth in love.

Thus, the lens of Farley's understanding of erotic faith allows us to see how the woman models a powerfully creative *erotic faithfulness* in Eden. From this perspective of *erotic faithfulness*, we recognize how the woman in Genesis 3 ultimately acts to fulfill humanity's vocation to be "God-bearers"—those who consciously create from nothing less than freedom and desire, in imitation of the Divine. The woman is not wrestling against God, or what God deemed *tov*. To the contrary, the woman's decision-making process, as well as her decision, is marked by a faithfulness of desire to know the fulfillment of that *tov* most appropriately intended for her. Hers is a *praxis of beauty*: a practice of *tov* or "the good," characterized by a seeing of the good that is followed by a choosing of that goodness which is most appropriate to her fullest thriving and the fulfillment of her highest good. The woman's *praxis of beauty* or choosing of what is *tov* shows us that embracing the good of the Other can be the means through which our own goodness is further realized and fulfilled, making our fullest thriving tied up with the act of embracing the goodness of the Other. In this way, the woman's *praxis of beauty* emerges as an expression of *erotic faithfulness*. *Erotic faithfulness* in turn describes a faithfulness of intent that, when mediated by human desire for our fullest *tov*, is vital to empowering the fulfillment of humanity's highest vocation to be "God-bearers" engaged in the work of co-creating with the Divine. Just as God is described in Genesis 1 as seeing the good and engaging in relationship with it, so the woman is described in Genesis 3 as seeing the good—indeed, she is the first in creation to imitate God in this divine practice—and then engaging in relationship with it.

In all this, it should not be missed that the woman's hospitality towards the good that is Other to her includes a deep desire for the fulfillment of her own *tov*. The woman, like God, is inspired by desire for that goodness which would fulfill her capacity to embrace relationship with the goodness in creation that is Other. The woman acts not only from an appreciation of the good that lies in another, but from an *eros* for what is possible for herself—including the actualization of her fullest wisdom. In this way, she is not unlike God, whom we see in Genesis 1 acting to fulfill God's nature as relational by entering in relationship with that which is not God, but Other. Thus the *erotic faithfulness* exemplified by the woman can be understood as expressing a version of feminist virtue that refuses to indulge in debilitating self-deprivation or self-sacrifice and instead embraces love of one's own fullest goodness as the most powerful way to be oneself in relationship to the goodness of that which is Other. Through *erotic faithfulness,* the woman owns the agency of human freedom to enact a faithfulness towards the good of that which is Other to us—because that faithfulness of desire for the good found in relationship with the Other not only empowers her greatest good but also calls forth the fullest *tov* in others. Indeed, in loving the good that is Other to herself, as God did, the woman actualizes the fullest goodness of herself and others, creates the fullest goodness possible in relationship, and rightly earns the name Eve, *mother of all living.*

Bibliography

Farley, Wendy. *Eros for the Other: Retaining Truth in a Pluralistic World.* University Park, PA: Pennsylvania State University Press, 1996.

———. *Tragic Vision and Divine Compassion: A Contemporary Theodicy.* Louisville, KY: Westminster/John Knox, 1990.

———. *The Wounding and Healing of Desire: Weaving Heaven and Earth.* Louisville, KY: Westminster John Knox, 2005.

Julian of Norwich. *Showings,* trans. Edmund Colledge, O.S.A., and James Walsh, S.J. New York: Paulist, 1978.

Schleiermacher, Friedrich. *The Christian Faith,* eds. H. R. Mackintosh and J. S. Stewart. Edinburgh: T&T Clark, 1989.

SEVEN

Farley's Gathering: A Jewish View

C. A. Levenson

WENDY FARLEY'S CHRISTOLOGY, *Gathering Those Driven Away*, draws its title from the Book of Micah.

> I will assemble the exiles and those I have brought to grief. I will
> make the lame my remnant, those driven away a strong nation
> ... (Micah 4:6–7)[1]

Those driven away are for Micah the Jewish people. They are broken, exiled. *But a day is sure to come when they are gathered back.* And this return, this gathering, will be achieved, Micah says, by a prince to be born in Bethlehem, a prince of ancient lineage. The prince will reach to "the ends of the earth" and will "be their peace" (5:2).

I am a teacher of philosophy whose favorite philosopher is Plato; I am also Jewish and can't quite divorce Micah's lines from the course of Jewish history. The exile Micah refers to does finally come to an end—in 539 BCE—but this first exile turns out to foreshadow a second; and the second exile, with its ghettoes, pogroms, and monstrous holocaust, lasts for two millennia—to my parents' generation. As for peace "to the ends of the earth," we have not yet seen it.

And what of the Prince of Peace? The story emerges centuries after Micah that the Prince had actually come—in Bethlehem, just as foreseen—and that his death had fulfilled his mission. But something in the

---

1. Translations from Hebrew and Christian scripture based on *The Holy Bible,* New International Version, Biblica, 2011.

telling of the story drove the Jewish people away while attracting many outside Judaism; and the narrative in question, as Martin Buber puts it, was *torn out* of Jewish history and consciousness.[2]

The dispersion of the Jewish people and the Jewish–Christian tragedy is not, to be sure, a theme of Farley's book. Her title alludes to it and perhaps serves to keep it in view, but she says very little about it. Still, every exile in history in some way mirrors every other. For Farley, *those driven away* are the dispossessed of our time: the poor, abused women, gays, those who are transgender—all of whom have been hurt by Christianity.

> The wound that moves in this particular piece of writing is the fight over sexual minorities in the Christian churches. It pierces me like a knife to know that some Christians insist that desire obscures the divine image. It renders lovers of Christ unable to minister, unable to parent, unable to share communion, unable to be people of faith.[3]

Farley is a Christian Platonist—that is, a Christian who experiences her faith while sharing in Plato's spirit; and she is a gifted practitioner of the Platonic style of philosophy, which my job over the years has been to teach. The perennial challenge of Platonism is to see with the clarity of reason all that is falling short (in oneself as well as the world), and still take joy in an omnipresent good—*the Good that has no need to be*, as Platonists say so mysteriously. In Farley's case, "the genesis of theology is pain," yet she describes her book as a "love-letter to the Beloved"; and it is suffused on every page with Platonic Eros.[4]

As a Jewish teacher of Plato, I would like to elaborate in my own way five theses I find in her writing.

1. God is beyond being.

2. That which transcends being is best construed as *Eros*.

3. Divine Eros—or Sophia—or Logos—must be seen in its feminine aspect.

2. Buber, *Two Types of Faith*, 11–13. The Christian story was in fact *turned against* Judaism; and yet, Buber writes: "From my youth onward, I have found in Jesus my great brother . . . I am more than ever certain that a great place belongs to him in Israel's history of faith, and that *this place cannot be described by any of the usual categories* [italics added]."

3. Farley, *Gathering Those Driven Away*, 2–3.

4. Farley, *Gathering Those Driven Away*, 2–3.

4. Divine transcendence entails ubiquitous incarnation.

5. The encounter with Christ remains in certain ways unique.

1. God beyond being

Jews are always trying to say what it means to be Jewish and never succeed very well, but I once heard a definition worth repeating in this context. *To be a Jew is to shun idolatry.* The definition is based on the second commandment: "You shall not make for yourself a graven image. . . . You shall not bow down to them or worship them. . . . I, YHVH your God, am a jealous God."

A friend of mine, a Kabbalist from New York, came to our home in Idaho. On the spiritual path, this man was in most ways ahead of me, but in the capacity to respond to the greatness of other religions I found myself—somewhat uncomfortably—ahead of him. Noticing on my desk a rather elegant anthology called *The Trinitarian Controversies*, he asked if I did not agree that an element of idolatry was *intrinsic* to Christianity.

"You would not say that," I replied, "if you read books by Christians, heard their voices. Christians are no more idolatrous than we Jews are despisers of love."

Having challenged my friend in this way, I thought to myself that it was sad, but perhaps fated, that the telling of the story in the Gospel— where to see Christ *is* to see the Father—should have aroused in ancient Israel that long-standing *mistrust of images* which the second commandment had been inculcating so effectively. Odd, too, that the commandment forbidding images had itself evoked an image: God as lover who grows angry when betrayed. The path of transcending idolatry is not a straight one.

Wrestling with idols and images, we Jews may seek help outside Judaism, and certainly from Christian Platonism as Farley represents and challenges it.

> *You shall not make for yourselves a graven image. . . .* The austerity demanded by this commandment seems entirely alien to the human heart. . . . But it is the tenderness and generosity of our Beloved to impose this hard commandment.[5]

---

5. Farley, *Gathering Those Driven Away*, 54.

Like Plato, Farley is a writer who loves images but stays focused on what lies beyond them. She knows quite well that, even when the beloved is a mere human being, it is not that person's image or manifest personality, but something out of reach—like light playing on the sea, as she puts it—that draws us in most deeply. A merely human beloved might be tempted to accept an idolatrous devotion, actually believing that the virtues he or she had disclosed to us were the *reason* for our vehement passion. But "the tenderness and generosity" of the divine beloved is to reject this misunderstanding. Christ, as Tillich explains, might have made himself a symbol of God. On the cross, he renounced that satisfaction.[6]

We can go further. If the second commandment is carried forward to its logical conclusion, we will reach the Platonic paradox that even to assert *God exists* must involve traces of idolatry, since the reality of God is beyond any concept we can form, including the concept of being. *Sefer Yetzirah*, one of the oldest and most mysterious of the Kabbalistic texts, offers the following on its first pages:

> Ten Sefirot of Nothingness,
>   Twenty-two letters . . .
> Ten Sefirot of Nothingness,
>   like the number of ten fingers, five opposite five . . .
> Ten Sefirot of Nothingness,
>   Ten and not nine, ten and not eleven.[7]

The Sefirot are spiritual "flows" or "flows of the sacred" that we encounter within us and around us. This is not the place to explore the numbers in the text—22, 5, 10, 9, 11—but let us underline the crucial word "Nothingness." The flows are divine veils; for God can only appear to us through veils; even these veils are so remote that they remind us *nothing*: they are more like absence than presence.

Kabbalah may be seen as a Jewish type of Neo-Platonism, just as the work of the "Pseudo-Dionysus," to which Farley frequently refers, is Christian Neo-Platonism. But let us turn now to Plato himself. Probably Plato never heard our Shema prayer, the core prayer of Judaism drawn from Deuteronomy:

> Listen Israel, YHVH our God, YHVH is one!

6. Tillich, *Systematic Theology.*
7. Kaplan, *Sefer Yetzirah,* 285–8.

Yet it is really as if Plato were explicating our prayer—as if helping us to remove from it all lingering traces of idolatry—when he works out in the *Parmenides* the conceptualities of "oneness," contending that "Unity itself" must escape the *need to be* on pain of slipping toward duality; for "unity" and "being" are *two, not one,* and "Unity itself" cannot be that.[8]

Simone Weil, a Jewish mystic who lived through the Holocaust and felt closely connected to both Platonism and Catholicism, writes:

> A case of contradictories that are true. God exists: God does not exist. Where is the problem? I am quite sure that there is a God in the sense that I am quite sure my love is not illusory. I am quite sure that there is not a God in the sense that I am quite sure nothing real can be anything like what I am able to conceive when I pronounce this word.
>
> The void is the supreme fullness, but man is not permitted to know it. The proof is that Christ himself was at one moment completely unaware of it.[9]

The moment when Christ was "completely unaware" of truth is the moment when, about to die, he asks why God has forsaken him. The truth, however, is that no one is ever forsaken. The absence of God in the world is God himself Weil says.[10] Staggering words since, when she wrote them, the Holocaust was raging around her.

2. That which transcends being is best construed as Eros

God is certainly unnamable, but the best name for God, Farley suggests, is love. Not that "God is a divine father who loves" but rather that "God *is* love." [11] The phrase "Abyss of Eros" reverberates through Farley's writings.

Some of my Evangelical friends cannot forbear to tell me how sorry they are that I believe in the Jewish God of Judgment rather than the Christian God of Love. I assure them we are friends of love too.

If you ask a Kabbalist whether "God is love," the reply might be that one of the spiritual flows by which Divinity expresses itself is indeed Love or *Hesed*; but this is balanced by another flow, that of *Gevurah* or Severity. Sheer love would flood everything, wash everything away, or make

8. Plato, *The Collected Dialogues of Plato.*
9. Weil, *Gravity and Grace*, 114, 23.
10. Weil, *Gravity and Grace*, 110.
11. Farley, *Gathering Those Driven Away*, 66.

everything merge with everything. Severity keeps things in bounds, keeps the sea from swallowing the land, so to say. Thus it holds things back; it is the *strength* that holds back. It preserves throughout the universe the space of separation—including God's distance from ourselves (since the absence of God is also God). And while the divine Severity is dangerous—for the Devil himself, we are told, takes his rise there—iniquity irrupts only when things get out of hand. What is wanted is perfect balance. One must balance Love and Severity. From the balance, there emerges *Tifferet*: the spiritual flow which is *Beauty*. In a Kabbalistic meditation, Love might be identified (somewhat playfully) with one's right arm, Severity with one's left, and (more seriously) Beauty with one's heart, the "core" of physical presence.[12]

There are times when the world shows a loving face, at other times a severe one, and a person grown proficient in "Jewish meditation" (to use the term of Aryeh Kaplan) might try to find the Beauty-*Tifferet* in the "balance" he or she has experienced. Yet we know that many human beings live under very severe conditions, with the necessities of life withheld in monstrous fashion; but it is said that, if the power of discernment grows strong enough, so we see beyond the flow of "Love-tempered-by-Severity," we may then gain a glimpse of a higher, more encompassing flow—the one called *Keter* or "Crown"—where there is nothing but Mercy and Freedom. For Mercy is God's true name, as we affirm, or actually sing (citing Exodus 34:6), when we take the Torah from its ark.

The affirmation that "God is love" has deep roots in Plato. There is a discourse in the *Symposium* (194e-195e) in which Love—that is, Eros—is declared to be the cause of all good because, when we are in love, we feel inspired, creative, eloquent, and fruitful, as if some higher "Self" had taken shape within us, wielding beneficent power. In love, we feel that beauty flows everywhere, sweetness and gentleness everywhere; yet we know, too, that Love is very strong, since Ares—"Strife himself"—quickly surrenders to Love, Aphrodite having seduced him. To be sure, harsh Necessity (Ananke) once ruled, turning generations against one another and smashing their dreams with reality; but Love can loosen Necessity,

---

12. For Kabbalistic background, I have drawn especially from Matt's annotated translation of the *Zohar*; Kaplan, *Sefer Yetzirah*; and Kaplan, *The Bahir: Illumination*. Also see Scholem, *Mystical Shape of the Godhead*, especially "'Tsaddik: The Righteous One" and "Shekhina: The Feminine Element in Divinity." On the sefirot as "spiritual flows," see Wolf, *Practical Kabbala*.

and we have entered now the Age of Love.[13] In brief: a new dispensation is now displacing the old—but the supersession in question has nothing to do with Laws of Sinai. What is loosened is Ananke-Necessity, the power that decrees, for example, that that the rise of the young *must* mean the fall of the old—a cosmically fatal necessity, as Greek and Hebrew prophets warn us.[14] Now, the loosening of Necessity cannot be achieved through force; for how can Necessity be forced? But Persuasion, driven by Love, can change her decrees (*Symposium*, 197a; *Timaeus*, 47e; *Laws*, 5.741a).[15]

"God is Love" thus emerges, but it emerges, let us note, in a discourse ascribed, not to Socrates but rather to Agathon, a tragedian of very high rank. The setting is a banquet, a celebration of Agathon's achievement. He speaks about Love, as have five previous banqueters; of them all, he praises Love most lavishly. "We are told," he says (referring to Hesiod):

> that, in the beginning, there were many strange and terrible happenings among gods [the strife between young and old] because Necessity [*ananke*] was sovereign, but ever since the birth of the young god Love, the love-of-what-is-lovely has showered every kind of blessing on gods and human beings. And so, I am stirred to speak in numbers, and to tell how it is that Love brings
> > Peace upon earth, the breathless calm
> > That lulls the long-tormented deep,
> > Rest to the winds, and that sweet balm
> > And solace of our nature, sleep.[16]

"Who is this that the wind and sea obey him?" Agathon already knows; in the Gospel, the disciples guess clumsily (Mathew 8:27). Agathon's discourse is perhaps a bit giddy, a bit overwrought, as if a truth too immense to utter were throwing him off balance to some extent. In his bearing, however, he displays a bold androgyny and often leans toward the feminine. "Are you a woman?" a kinsman asks him. "My dress,"

13. Plato, *The Collected Dialogues of Plato.*

14. Hesiod, for example, is surely uneasy; for he shows in the *Theogony* that Cronos had to fight his father Sky, and Zeus his father Cronos, and Zeus, too, must fear his offspring/destroyer. All such battles shake the earth. We read in Plato of Necessity at work here (see below). On the Jewish side, between the time of Hesiod and Plato, the Hebrew prophetic canon closed with a warning from Malachi: If the hearts of parents and children do not—with Elijah's help—"turn toward" each other, God will "smite the land with utter destruction" (Malachi 3:22–23).

15. Plato, *The Collected Dialogues of Plato.*

16. Translation based on Joyce, *Plato's Symposium: Or, the Drinking Party* 197a–c.

he answers, "is in harmony with my thought . . . " (Aristophanes, *Thesmophoriazusae* 142).

Farley's book is dedicated to sexual minorities that have suffered at the hands of Christianity, and it seems proper to point out that, as a matter of historical fact, the concept "God is love" had its first thorough elaboration in a discourse ascribed to Agathon, a figure who would certainly be marginalized today by conservative religious communities that tend to an excess of severity. Socrates replies to Agathon by contending that Love is longing, and longing is made up of *lack*: the gender-fluid poet has discovered a god who is "lack" (Aristophanes, *Thesmophoriazusae* 199c-201c). Thus, the "Void-which-is-Fullness"—the true Abyss of Eros—is glimpsed for a moment, but the dialogue then rushes on. The setting is a banquet in Agathon's honor, and though the guests have decided to drink only water, wine starts to flow unexpectedly, and soon everyone partakes (213e).

3. Feminine Aspect of the Word

The terms "masculine" and "feminine" have a meaning, as we know. They refer to variations of anatomy and also to what we, in the shifting freedom of our taste and with our genetic and cultural inheritance, associate with these variations: tones, auras and atmospheres, modes of comportment and perception; indeed, modes of *being*. Androgynous figures like Agathon hint at the fullness of life which cannot—obviously—be confined to only one gender; the Androgyne, for Jung and Eliade, thus becomes a symbol of *totality*.[17] On the other hand, while it may be true, as the Greeks liked to say, that the crown of beauty in a man is always a touch of the feminine and, in a woman, a touch of the masculine, Agathon gave his femininity such extreme expression that he must, to that extent, have seemed less masculine than other men. That was the burden of his finitude, the blessing and curse of incarnation. To be what you are, Necessity decrees, you must exclude much.

The invisible world is not like that. In a way, things are more fluid there. We see that this is so when we ask—with Farley and others theologians—whether the Logos of which St. John speaks—the Logos that is *with* God and *is* God—is best encountered in the aspect of a gender; for example, as masculine or feminine. Tradition speaks of the Father, Son,

17. See Jung, "The Syzygy," and Eliade, "Mephistopheles and the Androgyne."

and Spirit. The Logos is the Son, therefore masculine. The Jewish Platonist Philo, whose explication of the Logos would help shape Christian experience, evokes this principle in superbly phallic terms: it is a "flaming sword . . . it comes before everything, outstrips everything"; it is "swift, of glowing heat."[18] Yet anyone is free to notice that the Logos is more intimate with us, more nurturing, more "maternal," than the remote, inscrutable "Father" of tradition; and even Philo detects *two* aspects of the Logos, one generous and giving, one severe. Going further: Farley and others note that the Logos may be identified with Wisdom (*Chochma* in Hebrew), and then (turning to Greece) with Goddesses like Metis and Sophia. And since the Logos is a place in the meditator's mind as much as in the world or the heights—or the tradition—it will consent, if asked, to be manifest as "Mother," just as, according to Heraclitus, founder of the Logos-tradition, the "One-Who-Is-Truly-Wise is both ready and not ready to be called by the name of Zeus" (Fragment 118). *Ready and not ready*: that fluidity serves even now.

> Wisdom, the Great Mother, expresses the ordering and creative principle of divinity. She is the Cosmic Christ, whose power draws beauty from chaotic nothingness and breathes life in the tiniest weed. It was for her that the morning stars sang together and the children of the earth shouted for joy (Job 38:7). Christians often forget her as they rush in their devotion to Jesus. But without her, there would be no Christ, for She is the divinity in Christ.[19]

Is there perhaps a trace of consternation in this glistening cosmic mother because her son has unexpectedly surpassed her? If so, we will find ourselves approaching a *dangerous* archetype: "The-Mother-Who-Would-Reabsorb-Her-Offspring." St. Augustine, who gave to Christianity its definitive work on the Trinity, had to fight for independence from his earthly mother Monica—to whom, however, he felt he owed his salvation—and he found in the Logos, as compared to the distant "first person" of the Trinity, a nurturing yet frightening intimacy that indeed reminded him of Monica; for she had once crossed the sea, had like Christ stilled the waves with her prayers, in order to reach him when he strayed.[20]

18. Philo, *On Cherubs*, 27–28. Author's translation.

19. Farley, *Gathering Those Driven Away*, 133.

20. Augustine, *Confessions,* VI.1. See Levenson, "Distance and Presence in Augustine's *Confessions.*"

The archetypal sphere is very varied. Shifting currents call up different figures. "The Divine-Daughter-Who-Must-Escape-Her-Father/Lover's-Grip" has recently reshaped the collective work of meditation, inspiring valor in women and (may we hope?) restraint and generosity in men. On the other hand, in patriarchal epochs vexed by father-son conflict, the image of a Father who is severe and inaccessible—yet *finally* at one with his gentler, kinder offspring—opens for fathers and sons a path of reconciliation, although Christ's submission on the cross might suggest, if you lack eyes to see, a tyrant-father's unjust victory. In Hesiod's *Theogony*, we find jealous divine fathers who want to annihilate son-rivals, but the mother, the Great Goddess, bravely intervenes to stop the carnage. Jung used to say that if a divinized Mary did not join the Trinity as a "fourth" equal to the others, the Devil would make the fourth and we would all pay.[21]

Mythology guides meditation, and a favored mythology, one energized by an epoch or a tradition—or perhaps by one's own psycho-history—may exclude certain meditative paths while promoting others. In this way, too, incarnation means restriction. And I would guess that if I ever encountered Isis the way Apuleius did, or the Ancient of Days the way Daniel did, or Christ the way Saint Paul did, I would meet a divine presence so emphatic in personality—so alive and so fully actual—that I would not dare even to *conceive* of dissolving this figure into the flows of meditative life. That said, anyone who meditates may, if she or he cares to, gain a glimpse of that fluidity that we incarnate ones had to renounce—as the price of ever having been born.

The critic Harold Bloom, who declares himself a Jewish Gnostic, admits that the Kabbalists are "nothing if not sexist"[22] . . . yet they apprehend the fluidity to which I am referring. Meditating on the diverse aspects of the sacred, the "flows" of divine manifestation, they see (or sense the tone, the atmosphere of) one gender or another, and sometimes they see certain "flows" that unite both genders, or transcend gender completely. At the level corresponding to the Word, we find Chochma (Wisdom), who is usually felt to be masculine (though *chochma* is grammatically feminine), and we find Binah (Understanding) who is sheltering, receptive, maternal. So Chochma is like a point, a flash of intuition, whereas Binah is like the sea: one thing deriving from another, wave flowing from

21. Jung, *Answer to Job*.
22. Bloom, *Kabbalah and Criticism*, 29.

wave. But Chochma and Binah have attained a closeness so perfect that whoever detects the masculine presence will almost always find the feminine; and we may wonder if the difference between them is more in our minds than their reality. And since both are like musical notes that can "sound" at higher modalities, we will always sense above Binah a higher mode of Chochma but will equally sense above Chochma a higher mode of Binah. These invisible gender hierarchies are by nature always in flux, although—for better or worse—myth and tradition may stabilize them.

Closer to the human reality, we find the masculine beauty of Tifferet and his exquisite bride Malchut, the face of Divine Immanence. The volatility of this cosmic couple (in contrast to Chochma and Binah) is linked to the absurdity that besets human experience; for the Absurd, Camus says, is "the divorce between Mind and World" (to rename our volatile couple), a divorce intermittently relieved, Camus says, by mysterious "Nuptials Rites"[23]—or Shabbat, as we Jews express it.

In the paths of Kabbalistic meditation, it is sometimes crucial that feminine energies join with feminine, and masculine with masculine. The Zohar teaches, for example, that when Binah and Malchut come together, the world grows lavish and blossoms. They are pictured as mother and daughter, but need not be imagined in that way. There is also a certain androgyny in the spiritual flow of Malchut, in whom meditators sometimes detect the virile presence of David. Indeed, the terms "masculine" and "feminine" seem at times too unsubtle for these descriptions of planes of meditation; and even on the plane of anatomy, the Talmud long ago recognized a continuum of sexual identities—what we now call intersexuality (*m. Bik.* 4:5). That said, controversies concerning homosexuality and androgyny still beset the Jewish community and in spite of progress still cause pain.

4. The Ubiquity of Incarnation

"But what *is* your opinion of Christ?" a Mormon friend once asked me. We had been touring Temple Square in Salt Lake City and now we were gazing up at a towering statue of Christ, a Christ who dwarfed the luminous earth (also portrayed); but this Christ, for all his vastness, was human.

---

23. Camus, "The Myth of Sisyphus" and "Nuptials."

"Should I have an opinion?" I asked. "Really, I do not know. It seems to me that the Word is always ready to be incarnate, always waiting and wanting to manifest. Yet it may be that, under the conditions of existence, incarnation can never be complete. Another 'coming' is always required."

"Are you saying," a worried Evangelical student asked me, "that Christ was a great teacher, a great example, but finally only human like the rest of us? Then you'd best face the 'shocking alternative' that C.S. Lewis described in *Mere Christianity*.[24] If he claimed to absolve us from sin and called himself 'Son of God'—and said that to see him was in some sense to *see God*—and all along was 'human like the rest of us'—then he was certainly a lunatic or worse. He was hardly 'a great teacher.' So either worship him or despise him. That's your 'alternative.' Unless the ones who told his story had gone mad . . ."

"A madness of love and faith," I said. "What Plato in the *Phaedrus* calls the noble (or "right-sided") madness, the wellspring of all philosophy, all purifying rites and all prophesy, and—of course—all romantic passion (244b).[25] These four streams, Plato says, flow from a single source: that True and Noble Madness which is also called the Holy Spirit. In the Gospel that's mostly what I see.

"I'll go further. Apart from removing the elements of anti-Semitism, I'd be afraid to change a word of that text. In its kind, I believe it unsurpassable. I can't imagine a better Christ, any more than I can imagine a tragic protagonist better than Hamlet. My judgment, if you like, is merely literary, but the Gospel, as David Tracy taught us, is in the first place a classic of literature, whatever else it may be.[26]

"Nor do I deny altogether the *factuality* of the story. What gives rise to a discourse of this magnitude must be something tremendous, an event-wave beyond our comprehension. Why should Caesar be a 'fact' and not Christ? It's just that the world is so harsh . . .

"And that's the trouble. Necessity's grip is too tight. When the old and new are at war, the best of both may be annihilated. Certainly peace hasn't come.

"My Orthodox Jewish friends remain true to the Law—the ethical law and the complex religious laws; and the numinous patterns of their lives provide a taste of *olam ha-ba*—the world which is to come

24. See Lewis, "The Shocking Alternative."
25. Plato, *The Collected Dialogues of Plato*.
26. See Tracy, *The Analogical Imagination*.

(or *always* coming). Whether the early Christians damaged this evolving path, blocking its spread too impatiently, is more than I can determine. But my *literary* judgment—if it is not absurd to speak of it—is that the definitive 'personal-messiah narrative' will continue to be the one written by those early Christians. The difficulty, again, is that the story remains incomplete since another 'coming' is called for; but I'm not sure that any-one—not even God—could manage to tell the next part of the story in a manner worthy of the previous installment without overturning the genre . . . and the story-telling medium itself.[27]

"As for me, I remind myself every day that there are small epiphanies everywhere and that, for the rest—even if I'm not conscious of it—the absence of God is also God. Rebbe Zalman, the great Kabbalist, said it. Simone Weil (at heart a Kabbalist) repeated it (the tormented core of her Christology). This secret somehow stays secret even though, across mil-lennia, many have loudly shouted it. Earth swarms with varied life, and only God is there . . . because even God's absence is God. The ubiquity of perfect incarnation."

For Farley and many others, the issue of *gender* as it pertains to *in-carnation* remains especially vexing.

> I am grateful that feminist theologians raise the issue of whether a male savior can save women. An easy answer is yes, if he is God and can walk on water and whatnot, he can save women, too. Problems undoubtedly remain.[28]

If a woman is asked to become Christ-like, will she not feel her gender restricts her? She can tell herself, to be sure, that it's a matter of spirit, not body; yet surely the story in the Gospel is *about* self-expression through body. In that absurd adventure, *her* flesh contrasts with his. No doubt, she can still run the race; but she will be handicapped.

On the other hand, to look at the question from the opposite point of view, let us glance at a young man who feels happy when a pretty girl smiles at him. In her smile, he sees the promise of the sacred. Perhaps he sees the best he has experienced. Can we easily tell him that the Word, when it incarnates, has an eternally masculine face? In his heart he knows it isn't so.

---

27. Of course, the fact that I can't imagine a story doesn't mean it's impossible to tell. Shakespeare in *The Tempest* transcends tragedy and comedy, and I'd have declared *that* impossible . . . except that I've read *The Tempest*.

28. Farley, *Gathering Those Driven Away*, 152.

Beyond being, there are no genders, and the boundaries of culture and tradition also melt away. Farley says she learned something crucial about the incarnation when she met the Dalai Lama. Her story ought to come from her pen, but I should like to tell my own. I wasn't personally introduced to His Holiness—there were about two hundred of us—but we, all two hundred of us, had a wonderful talk, a wonderful conversation. The thing that struck me was that, at the precise moment when he and his companions entered the room, I felt *the silence of meditation* enter the room with them. All meditators know that silence: the silence of snow-covered peaks, of still lakes, a silence encompassing (not negating) sound, a silence in the meditator's mind as much as in the world—a silence that *united* mind and world, the "nuptials" Camus describes so well. The Dalai Lama and his friends brought *that* into the room, and when they left—at that precise moment—the silence went with them.

"Ha!" I said to myself. "That's a trick it would take time to learn!" But in the world there are many wonders. When Fitzgerald's Gatsby smiled at you, you felt that he already saw in you "what at your best you hoped to be"; I've known people who smile like that, too. And they say that when you sat near Socrates—that is, in the aura of his daimon—your mental powers quickened and the most wonderful thoughts came out of you as if some midwife had silently delivered them. I've known teachers who could do that. And some of my students have done that for me.

There may be times, Homer tells us, when we think we're talking to a friend, a lover, a slave or fellow warrior—but really it is the god. Experts spot these gods in disguise from the way they walk, but most of us are not expert (*Iliad*, XIII.80; XXIV.440). In the same way, the patriarch Abraham could never be quite sure when a guest in his tent might be an angel in disguise, or when an angel might be God himself. Everything is fluid and you never know who you are addressing. Jesus tells us to seek him in the poor, the sick, the dispossessed, the lonely prisoner desperate for friends. A man who foresees his cross will want to unite himself in advance with those who, across millennia, will be sharing his pain.

5. The Face of Christ

Drawing on Nicolas of Cusa, Farley suggests that the face of Christ is always in some sense *your* face. It's not that the face of Christ is generically human, displaying features all humans have in common, but that the uniqueness of *his* face is also the uniqueness of *yours*—whether you are a man or a woman, straight or gay, rich or poor, black or white.

> Christ's face shines in the uniqueness of our own face as if this very face alone, in its peculiarities, bore Christ's own face.
>
> Every person bears the face of Christ as if it were hers alone, even lions and oxen and eagles. This requires us to move toward the paradoxical awareness that what we encounter in Christ is both utterly proximate to us, familiar, like us bearing our burdens, beautiful in the way we are beautiful and at the same time proximate to every being in the cosmos *in precisely the same way.* By cherishing the uniqueness of our own Christ-face we are moved to cherish the Christ-face of every being.
>
> The face of all faces, the truth of my own face, is itself not a particular face. It is not an essence in the way philosophy conceives of essences. It is the face of divine emptiness: empty of form and transparent in the form of every face.[29]

Now I wonder if we could say as well that the face of Mary is *your* face; the face of Socrates *your* face; the face of Buddha *your* face. Each face, in its essence, shines with the same divine emptiness. Someone asks me: "Who do you say I am?" The answer is: One who escapes me. But could there not be something in Christ's face, in the image evoked by his story, that uniquely mirrors one's own face in its elusiveness? I am sure that sometimes happens. How often I cannot say.

This much, at least, is sure. There is truth behind Xenophanes' comedy in which lions, drawing pictures of their gods, unfailingly draw other lions. "This is the sad paradox," notes Farley, "which allows us to recognize in every face the face of Christ but also to refuse the presence of Christ's face in those different from our own."[30]

In my last years of teaching in Idaho, students from the Middle East came to study on our campus in large numbers, and many enrolled in my classes. Most were practicing Muslims. I'd have travelled far to meet them. Islam sought from its earliest days to create a "third term" that would reconcile Christians and Jews; and at times it sought to describe a vast mediating world—'alam al-mithal, the "imaginal" world—where essence and instance merge in a single way of being, so that spirit has bodily fullness and all earth shines like the sky.[31] Now, what I want is to

---

29. Farley, *Gathering Those Driven Away*, 182–4.

30. Farley, *Gathering Those Driven Away*, 183.

31. This world, though dreamlike, is real. One can enter it unawares, without

gather everything—all the religions I love—and the great atheisms too—in just such a tangible spiritual landscape. Yet what I take to be the Esoteric Unity of Religion[32] is perhaps more like an opening through which *religions*—in all their diversity—come rushing toward me.

I would like to end with a fable by the Persian poet Attar, whose name means "the Perfumer." It is called *The Parliament of Birds.* Thirty bird-pilgrims approach the throne of the Simurgh, the King who will redeem them from anarchy. They have crossed the seven *wadis* or seas, "the penultimate of which is Vertigo and the last of which is Annihilation." Many comrades have fallen away. Only the thirty now remain. But the name of the Simurgh actually means "30 birds," and this foreshadows a final revelation which the fantastic writer Borges recounts in "The Approach to Al-Mu'tasim."[33] Borges' brief summation ends with Platonic explication, with which this essay, too, had best conclude.

> Purified by suffering, [the pilgrims] reach the great peak of the Simurgh. At last they behold him; they realize that they are the Simurgh and that the Simurgh is each of them and all of them. Plotinus [*Enneads*, V, 8, 4] also posits a divine extension of the principle of identity: "All things in the intelligible heavens are in all places. Any one thing is all other things. The sun is all the stars, and each star is all the others and the sun."[34]

Bibliography

Bloom, Harold. *Kabbalah and Criticism.* New York: Continuum, 1995.

Borges, Jorge Luis. "The Approach to Al-Mu'tasim." In *The Aleph and Other Stories, 1933–1969: Together with Commentaries and an Autobiographical Essay,* translated by Norman Thomas Di Giovanni. New York: Dutton, 1970.

Buber, Martin. *Two Types of Faith.* Translated by Norman P. Goldhawk. New York: Macmillan, 1952.

---

noticing the shift except in retrospect. See the writings of Corbin, especially *Spiritual Body and Celestial Earth.*

32. See Schuon, *Transcendent Unity of Religions*; and Smith, *The Forgotten Truth.*

33. Borges, "The Approach to Al-Mu'tasim," 27–34.

34. Borges, "The Approach to Al-Mu'tasim," 33. Borges' story mirrors Attar's. In it, humans prove capable of great iniquity, but also of great goodness, a goodness always done in imitation of a man called Al-Mu'tasim, whose name means "Seeker after Help." Al-Mu'tasim is the Axis of the World; but every seeker finds his/her own face in him. God, too, may be "in search of Someone, and that Someone of [a higher] Someone"—and so on "endlessly or cyclically."

Camus, Albert. "The Myth of Sisyphus." In *Lyrical and Critical Essays*, edited by Philip Thody. New York: Vintage, 1970.

———. "Nuptials." In *Lyrical and Critical Essays*, edited by Philip Thody. New York: Vintage, 1970.

Corbin, Henry, and Nancy Pearson. *Spiritual Body and Celestial Earth: From Mazdean Iran to Shīʿite Iran*. Princeton, NJ: Princeton University Press, 1977.

Eliade, Mircea. "Mephistopheles and the Androgyne." In *The Two and the One*, translated by John Michael Cohen. London: Harvill, 1965.

Farley, Wendy. *Gathering Those Driven Away: A Theology of Incarnation*. Louisville, KY: Westminster John Knox, 2011.

Jung, Carl Gustav. "The Syzygy: Anima and Animus." In *Aion: Researches into the Phenomenology of the Self*, Vol. 9, Part 2. Princeton. NJ: Princeton University Press, 1969.

———. *Answer to Job*. Translated by Richard Francis Carrington Hull. Vol. 11. Princeton, NJ: Princeton University Press, 2011.

Kaplan, Aryeh, trans. *Sefer Yetzirah: The Book of Creation: Theory and Practice*. York Beach, ME: Weiser, 1997.

Levenson, Carl Avren. "Distance and Presence in Augustine's 'Confessions.'" *The Journal of Religion* 65, no. 4 (1985): 500–512.

Lewis, C. S. "The Shocking Alternative" in Mere Christianity." In *The Complete C.S. Lewis Signature Classics*, edited by Kathleen Edwards. New York: Harper, 1992.

Matt, Daniel Chanan, trans. *The Zohar*. Pritzker Edition. Vol. 1. Stanford: Stanford University Press, 2003.

Neḥunya ben ha-Kanah. *The Bahir: Illumination*. Translated by Aryeh Kaplan. York Beach, ME: S. Weiser, 1979.

Plato. *The Collected Dialogues of Plato*. Edited by Edith Hamilton and Huntington Cairns. Translated by Lane Cooper. Bollingen Series LXXI. Princeton, NJ: Princeton University Press, 1962.

———. *Plato's Symposium: Or, the Drinking Party*. Translated by Michael Joyce. London: Everyman's Library, 1935.

Scholem, Gershom Gerhard. *On the Mystical Shape of the Godhead: Basic Concepts in the Kabbalah*. Translated by Joachim Neugroschel. New York, NY: Schocken, 1991.

Schuon, Frithjof. *The Transcendent Unity of Religions*. Wheaton, IL: Quest, 1984.

Smith, Huston. *Forgotten Truth: The Common Vision of the World's Religions*. New York: Harper One, 1992.

Tillich, Paul. *Systematic Theology, Volume 2: Existence and the Christ*. Chicago: University of Chicago Press, 1975.

Tracy, David. *The Analogical Imagination: Christian Theology and the Culture of Pluralism*. New York: Crossroad, 1981.

Weil, Simone. *Gravity and Grace*. Translated by Emma Craufurd. London: Routledge, 1972.

Wolf, Laibl. *Practical Kabbalah: A Guide to Jewish Wisdom for Everyday Life*. New York: Three Rivers, 1999.

EIGHT

Suffering the Good:
Constructing Solidarity in the Theodicies of
Scripture and Thérèse of Lisieux

Janelle Peters

IN THE JEWISH AND Christian traditions, to know is to suffer. First, the fall of Adam and Eve brings knowledge of good and evil, which entails enculturation into a *habitus* in which clothing the body and tilling the soil seem vital.[1] Then, the fall of the Watchers endows humanity with other divine epistemologies—not the least of which are cosmetics—and leads to a catastrophic flood of that soil.[2] That these divine incursions into the world are the cause of suffering gives rise to the problem of theodicy, that is, the disquieting suspicion that a good God allows us to feel pain we have not brought upon ourselves.[3] Each of us *will* suffer, whether by natural or by manmade disaster. This, not sin, according to Wendy Farley, is "at the center of the problem of evil."[4]

Suffering being a given, the individual has two options: to turn inward toward the self and sacrifice the world or to turn outward toward

---

1. Bourdieu, "Habitus," 43–52.

2. Gen 6:1–4; *1 En.* 15:2–3.

3. The enigmatic nature of theodicy is framed nicely by Martha Nussbaum: "We should not confuse Greek religion with Judaeo-Christian religion, where it is generally true that the actions of God are to be received as the mysterious doings of a basically moral order." See Nussbaum, *The Fragility of Goodness*, xxxii.

4. Farley, *Tragic Vision and Divine Compassion*, 12.

the world and sacrifice the self. Farley sees erotic faith as the proper response to suffering. Love, to be properly accomplished, desires justice for the other. As the other is of necessity bound to and defined by finitude and mortality, so too does justice locate itself in the present rather than in a distant moment in the eschatological future. In this essay, I will explore the ways in which Farley attaches the pursuit of justice to suffering and martyrdom, focusing particularly on the example of her later work on St. Thérèse of Lisieux. The transformation of the individual comes in the individual's capacity to transcend the grief of suffering and to continue to direct compassion and love toward others in the world. As illustrated by St. Thérèse's interpretation of her tuberculosis as an act of divine charity, to wrestle with the doubts in her faith that emerged from being barred from male ecclesiastical roles (e.g., priest, Doctor of the Church, soldier), the suffering individual uses the logic of the incarnation to direct spiritual efforts not to envisioning heavenly crowns and thrones, but to using her life and very body as the clay that participates in transforming the incarnation. The civic martyr thus sharpens Adorno's maxim: "the need to lend a voice to suffering is a condition of all truth."[5] The tragedy of her demise throws into relief the values that we should hold fast in the world.

Suffering

That suffering is on par with actual martyrdom has been a Christian theological principle since at least the late first century CE letter of 1 Clement. Clement of Rome instructs the Corinthians who have recently ousted their presbyters to sacrifice their own positions in the community for the sake of unity. He equates: 1) the sacrifices made by kings who exiled themselves during plagues, 2) individuals who sold themselves into slavery and death for the sake of another, 3) women who died as martyrs in the arena, and 4) the biblical heroines of Esther and Judith. What did Esther and Judith, who end their narratives triumphantly in their own homes, do to warrant inclusion in a list of sacrifice and martyrdom?[6] Presumably the answer is that Esther and Judith both willingly flirted with sexual violence as a last resort to save their nation. Ancient and modern commentators on Esther have speculated that Esther might well have preferred death to the wretched isolation of being a hidden Jew in

5. Adorno, *Negative Dialectics*, 17–18.
6. *1 Clement* 55. Peters, "Rahab, Esther, and Judith," 94–110.

the Persian court, susceptible at any time to suffer the same relegation to the harem as Vashti and the virgins who preceded Esther in Ahasuerus' bedroom.[7]

In *Tragic Vision and Divine Compassion,* Farley is perhaps more precise than the Apostolic Fathers—who did not yet have access even to Augustine's concept of interiority—in locating the equivalency of suffering and martyrdom in the effect of the external situation rather than the external situation itself. We may strain to see the "death camps, torture chambers, or famine-stricken countries" as merely "more dramatic examples" of the destructive force of suffering.[8] However, the internal state that these grim physical conditions stimulate is the same as that occasioned by more banal conditions such as the desperate housewife and the "Willy Lomans of the world." The human spirit has a myriad of evils, unleashed since Hesiod inscribed them into Pandora's jar, that can cause the soul to lose hope and despair.[9] For the Greeks, such a condition meant to believe in the Olympic deities, who were not always benevolently inclined toward humanity. For Kristeva, such despair entails atheism, a giving up of a hope that is, in a Christian spiritual economy, God.[10] However, in all cases, it is clear that the snakes that bite away human happiness are not restricted to a theological-historical moment in the Garden of Eden but follow us through life, springing up incessantly as though from the head of the Hydra.

When experiencing the suffering that inexorably confronts humans as they plod through the divine plan, the challenge for the individual thus becomes how to continue to live without allowing suffering to triumph over one's existence. Farley cites Simone Weil's axiom that at "the very best, he who is branded by affliction will keep only half his soul."[11] Radical suffering so scars the individual that he or she can neither savor life nor even momentarily escape from the experience of trauma. Tolkien's Frodo exemplifies the irreversibly traumatized soul: "I am naked in the dark, Sam, and there is no veil between me and the wheel of fire."[12] Such permanent occlusion of sense-perception by the suffering soul was

7. *Aggadat Esther* 11.9; Bronner, "Esther Revisited: An Aggadic Approach," 183.

8. Farley, *Tragic Vision and Divine Compassion,* 118.

9. Hesiod, *Works and Days,* 83–104. See Zeitlin, *Playing the Other,* 64.

10. Kristeva, *Black Sun Depression and Melancholia,* 4.

11. Farley, *Tragic Vision,* 59; Weil, *Waiting for God,* 122–23.

12. Farley, *Tragic Vision,* 58; Tolkien, *The Return of the King,* 215.

conjectured by Augustine to be the "unforgivable sin."[13] Likewise, Farley observes that radical suffering is an incurable wound that prevents an individual from fully participating in his or her future. This is not the gaping wound of the Auschwitz gallows that Wiesel found redemptive; it is the refusal to allow the moments of life after the trauma to count as admissible evidence.[14]

Humans sometimes must endure existence—for not simply a day or a year, but the course of their entire lifespans—in a network of relations designed to dehumanize and demoralize them. Examples range from the South African apartheid system to the Nazi death camps. Farley contends that the goal of the designers of these vices of human souls is to "produce in the victim a 'self-disgust' to the point of wanting death or even committing suicide."[15] This can, I think, particularly be seen in the case of the Nazis, who had the benefit of scholarly work done on sacrifice. The Nazi desire that the victim accede to self-destruction resonates with the "myth of innocence" connected to ancient Greek animal sacrifice, a myth that was beginning to be identified by structuralists as underpinning sacrifice.[16] In ancient Greece, sacrificial animals were made to nod their assent by water thrown on their heads and to reveal the sacrificial weapon in the dust with their own hooves by a carefully guided rope. This was the logic deployed by the Nazis, who also transported their victims to the death camps in train cars meant for freight or livestock while retaining their victims' humanity in name only by booking them as passengers.[17] Hannah Arendt, as Farley reminds us, employed language games that transmogrified genocide into the "final solution" and murder into "evacuation" (*Aussiedlung*) or "special treatment" (*Sonderbehandlung*).[18] Thus, though everyone in Nazi Germany knew what was happening, they lost the epistemology that would have told them what was happening was "murder and lies." It was not simply that the Jews were losing their lives; they were also losing the language that would have validated the

13. Fredriksen, *Augustine and the Jews*.

14. Wiesel, *Night*, 78.

15. Farley, *Tragic Vision*, 54; Fackenheim, *To Mend the World*, 12.

16. Hubert and Mauss, *Sacrifice: Its Nature and Function*; Meuli, "Griechische Opferbräuche," 185–288; Bruce Lincoln, "Rewriting the German War God," 193; Lincoln, "Chapter One: From Bergaigne to Meuli," 13–31.

17. Berger, "The 'Banality of Evil' Reframed," 610.

18. Farley, *Tragic Vision*, 44.

horror of this experience as such. The physical suffering of the Shoah was compounded by the psychological and linguistic suffering of the Shoah.

Farley names this psychological and linguistic suffering as the most extreme violence that occurs to a human being. Barred from access to language, the individual loses even the capacity to describe humiliation and pain. The victim has been deprived of the basic right to self-defense. This is the same conclusion, we will remember, of George Orwell's *1984*, where the protagonist has been broken by his worst fear, rats, and proceeds to so meld his mind with that of his oppressors that they allow him to wander the metropolitan bars before exterminating him like a rat on the street. Farley, though, goes further. For Farley, the soul displaced by radical suffering has been forcibly evicted from the quotidian reenactment of God's creative work in which every human being is intended to participate. "To have a servile soul," as Farley echoes Levinas, "is to be incapable of being jarred, incapable of being ordered."[19] Creation did not come into being *ex nihilo*.[20] Rather, God ordered the chaos that He found at the beginning. Likewise, the chaotic soul is continually ordered and veering back into an oozing state ready to be jarred again. When humans ate from the Tree in the Garden, they became godlike and thus simultaneously restarted and joined in the process of ordering the chaotic. The soul crushed by radical suffering has been so obliterated that it can no longer participate in the ongoing transformation that is Creation. The suffering soul is static—without motion, without language, without emotion, without motions of defense.

In contrast to the annihilated soul, Farley praises the martyrs and tragic heroes who testify in two directions: negatively and positively. First, martyrs and tragic heroes point out the injustice being committed against them in "a world order in which the good are defeated by the wicked or the strong." Second, they demand vindication by articulating a powerful vision of a world order beyond the one oppressing them. This world order legitimates the martyr's or hero's claims to honor and status. For Farley, Levinas provides the example *par excellence* of the civic martyr who never relinquishes self-respect.[21] This civic martyr is Socrates.

19. Farley, *Tragic Vision*, 44; Levinas, *Collected Philosophical Papers*, 16.

20. Here, Farley's thought takes a different approach to creation than does that of Edward Farley, who juxtaposes Christian creation *ex nihilo* with Greek repetition and renewal. See Farley, *Divine Empathy*, 138.

21. Such a choice of emphasis extricates Farley's theology from the problems encountered by the post-Shoah theologies of Jürgen Moltmann and Dorothee Sölle. In

As presented in Plato's *Apology*, Socrates did not simply disavow the charges leveled against him. He argued that the *polis* should honor him as a successful athlete and provide him with free meals for the rest of his days.[22] In the face of imminent death, Socrates refused to plead for his life, preferring to negotiate for honors according to the logic of the civic apparatus in which he was enculturated.[23] The immediate context of civic tragedy and transgression is peeled back by Socrates' invocation to remind the audience of the basic moral order to which they all adhere. The ingenuity of his self-defense against the charges of corrupting the young citizens of the *polis* is to recall that he has not corrupted anyone so much as to receive the honor of free meals at the Prytaneum. The civic martyr conjures up the values of the *polis* when its citizens have forgotten them. In so doing, the civic martyr is the *polis'* foremost citizen.

Where is God? Theodicy and the Tragic Structure of the Creation

But why must the civic martyr suffer and die? In the world of drama, the playwright has the option of saving her characters with a *deus ex machina*. The spiritual equivalent of saving particular individuals from the logic of the divine plot need not be a miracle in terms of an extraordinary supernatural sign, as the biblical literature involving the figure of Daniel makes

---

necessitating a God who suffers with us, they leave little room in their theology for Jews, who do not believe in Jesus' redemptive death and resurrection. For Wiesel, for instance, God dies on the gallows at Auschwitz. His suffering is not a sign of solidarity. The image suspends Wiesel's audience within a catastrophic moment. Farley's theology honors this moment while attempting to reintegrate the traumatized into society and to restore a sense of life.

22. *Apology* 36d. On the elite connotations of these meals as commensality at the royal hearth, see Bowra, "Xenophanes and the Olympic Games," 274.

23. As Vasilou reminds us, this aspect of Socrates' remembered character is a deliberate function of the genre of the *Apology*, which is constructed by Plato to present Socrates narrating himself as a civic martyr: "One unique aspect of the Apology as compared with the other early dialogues is that Socrates has been called upon to speak in a positive way about himself and his life. As we have seen, he is required, for example, to say what he believes would be a just punishment for him, not merely to question others about their views. In addition, Socrates is speaking to a large audience. While conditional irony indulges an interlocutor's belief that he has knowledge, in this context he cannot be sure that his audience holds any given opinion; he must address them *en masse*." Vasilou, "Socrates' Reverse Irony," 226.

clear.[24] The Danielic literature includes salvation by both human and supernatural means. In Daniel, God literally inscribes the king's walls with writing that Daniel, who possesses the more acute interpretative skills of the colonized, can read better than the king's own interpreters. The semiotics of divine will could not be less numinous.[25] However, in an addition to the Book of Daniel, Susanna is saved from execution by secular juridical procedures. Although she must endure the humiliation of being put to trial and condemned to death, God inspires Daniel to convince her community to authorize him to question the only two witnesses to the crime, the elders who accused her of adultery after she refused to submit to their licentious desires. Daniel proves their conspiracy, and the elders receive the punishment they sought to inflict on Susanna. The Danielic literature abounds in miracles. Why does not God consistently intervene in this manner? Why does Socrates die of hemlock when his community wrongfully convicts him? Why can God keep a menorah lit for an extraordinary duration but allow a mother to watch her sons die for their faith? Of all the valiant men at Masada, why does only Josephus live in order to serve the Roman emperor Vespasian as a prophet of the Jewish God? At the personal, communal, and political levels, we must conclude that there are times when God allows the innocent to suffer and die.

The "hidden face" of God, particularly in the face of suffering, is a recurring motif in the later books of the Hebrew Bible and the ecclesiastical leaders in the age of composition of the New Testament. Both Job and Jesus question the wisdom of God's mandate that they sacrifice comfort and risk both their lives and the lives of the ones they love.[26] The original ending of Mark leaves its audience in the cathartic moment of mourning the loss of Jesus. Suffering becomes an integral component of creation for Christians, as seen in the statement of second-century martyr Ignatius:

24. The ambivalence of the Danielic literature in the interplay of the threat of martyrdom and salvation was picked up by female interpreters in the nineteenth century. See Grammer, *Some Wild Visions*, 107.

25. Bal, "Lots of Writing," 89–114.

26. In Job 19:9–10, Job is stripped of honor and his crown, and then "broken down on every side." The imagery recalls the brokenness of the temple of Jesus' body predicted in the Gospels. This similarity is partially behind the depictions of Job as an athlete in late Antiquity and the Middle Ages. See Baskin, "Job as Moral Exemplar in Ambrose," 222–31; Poliakoff, "Jacob, Job, and Other Wrestlers," 48–65.

"And the virginity of Mary and her giving birth was concealed
from the ruler of this age, likewise too the death of the Lord,
three mysteries of a cry accomplished in the silence of God."[27]

This divine silence is a function of the sovereign rule imputed to God.
Once God became omnipotent, suffering had to be interpreted as a divinely preordained component of a divinely preordained creation.[28]

Since, as Genesis tells us, God deemed each act of his creation good,
the entire creation must be good. As a punishment for disobeying divine
orders, certain hardships have been placed upon humanity, such as the
necessity of toil and painful childbirth, but those conditions most people
would agree cause the most suffering—e.g., genocide, leprosy, social isolation—are not said to originate from the Fall. Thus, creation is good, and
suffering is actually a part of the divine order. It is merely that creation
has a tragic structure. For Farley, this is theodicy.

Scripture encodes within it the causes of theodicy. Because theodicy
is not the result of the personal interventions of God, as Farley has argued, we find in Scripture a theology of vulnerability. I will trace the *topos*
of vulnerability as it unfolded in Scripture historically and then connect
the theme with Farley's thought on the vulnerable avoiding table fellowship with idols. This will take us from Farley's identification of theodicy
as the tragic structure of creation in *Tragic Vision* to her constructions of
ways for human beings to experience the divine incarnation of creation
as they suffer through its tragic structure.

The Vulnerability of Faith

Scripture demonstrates suffering's hold on humanity and the need for
mutual compassion. In the Torah, perhaps in anticipation of Israel's im-
pending loss of statehood, we find authors who present their state's divine
mandate for the destruction of the memory of Amalek without remorse
(Exod 17:14–6; Deut 25:19).[29] Amalek had assailed the Israelites as a nation as they fled Egypt to found a state.[30] The Israelites were still only a
nation, a weary band of ex-slaves marauding about the countryside.
For Amalek to attack a group without substantial property was sheer

27. *Letter to the Ephesians* 19.1.

28. Farley, *Divine Empathy*, xv.

29. Wright, "The Commemoration of Defeat," 433–73.

30. Sagi, "The Punishment of Amalek," 325.

bellicosity. In retribution for the Amalekite disregard for ancient theories on what constituted a "just war," the Israelites were to blot out their memory under heaven when they came to the land on which they would establish their state. Later, in 1 Sam 15:3, we learn that this is not simply a *damnatio memoriae* of the Amalekite nation but a wholesale purge of even the animals of the Amalekites. Since the Amalekites were no longer a threat at the time they were written into the Torah, we can only presume that recounting this genocide is meant to throw into relief the amazing character of the Jewish survival as a nation during the period of captivity in Egypt and the exodus from Egypt. Theodicy is averted as the Amalekites are defeated and cultural protections for the vulnerable are established.

After the exile in Babylon, ruminations on theodicy become more trenchant and less sanguine. Books such as Job, Lamentations, Isaiah, Esther, and Ezekiel all pose the question of why God fails to respond to the suffering of His people. Esther, of course, best exemplifies the sensitivities and anxieties of this new postexilic theology. Haman, the adversary of Jewish courtier Mordecai, is descended from Agag, king of Amalek. Mordecai, Esther's uncle, is a descendant of Saul, king of Israel. Thus, the author quite consciously recasts the pre-exilic history of 1 Sam 15 in an imagined exilic past to orient postexilic theology.[31] Esther's scroll exhibits a new awareness of the tenuousness of political power—there is a sense that any political structures created will not discriminate between the Jews and the *goyim*.[32] When Haman describes to Ahasuerus the perfect honor, envisioning himself in the palmary role, he finds himself leading Mordecai through what he imagined to have been his triumph. Haman hangs on the gallows he has erected for Mordecai. And, despite Esther's

31. The identification of Haman as an Amalek appears to have been accidental in the earliest versions of Esther. Esther 3:1 merely calls Haman an "Agagite." The Septuagint knows nothing of Haman's Amalekite ancestry and instead places his familial provenance in Macedonia, an enemy of both Jewish and Persian nations. Later theological interpretation strengthened the connection between Haman and Amalek (*Ant.* 11.209, *Megillah* 13a, *Pesiqta Rabbati* 12, *Midrash Esther Rabbah* 3.1 and 7.4). See Feldman, *Studies in Josephus' Rewritten Bible*, 525. In contemporary Jewish thought, Amalek has become a metaphysical descriptor for anti-Semitism. See Piekarz, *Hasidut Polin bein Shtei Milhamot ha-Olam*, 327.

32. The mechanistic nature of the theodicy in Esther anticipates the theodicies constructed by Enlightenment and post-Enlightenment thinkers such as Newton, Descartes, Leibniz, Spinoza, Hume, Kant, and Hegel. As in Esther, the absence of the name or figure of God for these thinkers mandated the need for a theodicy that worked by de-personal systems rather than by a personal deity.

successful commensal negotiations at court, it is impossible to reverse the original edict permitting a *pogrom*; the king can only issue an edict permitting a *pogrom* for those who would start a *pogrom*. The Jews are allowed to fight in self-defense, just as they were to be attacked because their presence had been construed as a threat. Mordecai, of course, has known about the interchangeability of fates all along—this is exactly why he has allowed Esther to undertake the dubious mission of entering the king's harem. Whereas in the Torah Israel's victory over Amalek is clear and reassuring, Esther presents a vision of theodicy where suffering is averted only by having drawn a lucky lot (*pur*).

As the Amalekite traditions develop from Exodus to Esther, we learn that life is fragile in *all* contexts—in exile, in the diaspora, and in one's own state. Our enemies are not those in power; they are those who would go after the weak instead of the powerful. Theodicy is not the intentional design by the sovereign to refuse to intervene in suffering; it is characterized, with the possible exception of the divine litigator Job, as divine amnesia and absence. While Farley emphasizes the question of why a good God allows the strong to attack the weak, I think her related concern of how a good God permits his beloved children to have table fellowship with idols is even more salient. Just as one can sacrifice oneself for idols rather than the beloved, one can deny one's associates solidarity in the hopes of rising above them in the hierarchy. In the Amalekite passages and the Book of Esther, the problem of theodicy arises from the weak attacking each other. The hiddenness of God's face illumines the injustices and unrealized moments of solidarity perpetrated by humans on each other.[33]

We can find this motif elsewhere in Scripture. Abuse from one's associates, of course, is precisely the cause of Job's psychological miseries. When God takes away his opulent lifestyle, his own friends assume that his misfortune is due to sin. Similarly, Jesus must teach people that disability is related neither to the sins of an individual nor to the sins of an individual's parents. Part of the work of Job and Jesus is to convince their audiences that no one's sin is responsible for the broken nature of the world. It is merely the work of the good to respond compassionately to heal the parts of creation under duress. Theodicy is the crucible in which the self-sacrificing good are smelted.

33. Thus, in one Talmudic source, we discover the descendants of Amalek and Haman converted to Judaism and produced some of its most respected teachers (*b. Sanhedrin* 96b).

A potential danger is that the principle of sacrifice as a good will be misapplied, leading individuals to suffer for the good without achieving transformation of themselves or the world. Desiring to sacrifice oneself for the good, one instead only achieves self-abnegation by listening to false scripts. The *auteurs* of these false scripts are not voices within the individual. Rather, humans sacrifice themselves for their societies and thus follow social scripts. This is why Levinas eschews theodicy as a totalitarian project that subordinates the cost of human sacrifice to ultimate designs, resulting in "a teleological drama."[34] Theodicy can be and has been too easily exploited by totalitarian states like the Nazi, Stasi, and Soviet regimes. Indeed, Farley connects the demons at table-fellowship in 1 Corinthians and the command to cut off body parts causing one to sin in the Gospels with the onus placed on certain groups of individuals within a society. Like Origen and other early Christian men who may have literally emasculated themselves in order to serve as faithful "eunuchs of the kingdom," self-sacrificing individuals sometimes yield their very bodies to false goods, such as preserving an abusive marriage or serving in the military of an illegitimate state.[35]

David Blumenthal, I think, provides a helpful example from the Shoah that illustrates the relational dynamics of positive sacrifice Farley advocates. Positive sacrifice demands self-respect on the part of the would-be sacrificant in the incarnational theology of Farley, because the tragic hero must remind society of the values it in fact upholds.[36] In the Shoah, two-thirds of the rescuers interviewed by one research team, the Oliners, risked their lives to help Holocaust victims in response to a request by the victim or a mutually respected acquaintance.[37] Had these individuals not taken the initiative to secure their own safety, the death toll surely would have been higher. Here, a death is not necessary to create a tragic hero; it is the request for help that summons forth in the rescuer the recognition of the tragic structure of the cosmos, the heroic nature of the victim, and the need for the rescuer to respond in kind.[38] One thinks of the saying of Jesus preserved in Matthew and Luke that the Father will not give snakes to His children asking for bread (Matt 7:10; Luke 11:11).

34. Ajzenstat, "Beyond Totality," 116.
35. Caner, "The Practice and Prohibition," 402.
36. Farley, *Tragic Vision*, 27–28.
37. Oliner, *The Altruistic Personality*, 312–17.
38. Blumenthal, *The Banality of Good and Evil*, 45.

In order for humans to hold fast to the self-assurance they need to perform extraordinary feats like seeking shelter in Nazi-occupied territory, they need such sacred promises that God and creation are intrinsically good. We need to hear that "this too shall pass." Given the frailty of human beings and their societies, Farley finds that the natural order provides the surest sign that God's creation abounds in His love. She cites Jesus' teaching that the lilies of the field persist in order to inspire hope in creation's saturation with God's love even through tragedy:

> Jesus walks past some wildflowers and insists they are more beautiful than Solomon in his glory. This is how God clothes grass in the field, weeds that live today and tomorrow are thrown in the oven (Matthew 6:28–30): random, irrelevant, useless beauty. They serve no purpose. People pass by every day without noticing or caring. This beauty does not feed them when they are starving or save them when the soldiers come pillaging. But because they are naked to the inflowing energy of the Divine Eros, the flowers are radiant with an intensity of beauty that no human wealth can manufacture. When Jesus says the divine empire is within and all around us, perhaps he is saying that this influx of beauty is constantly available to us, is always raining down on us, purposeless and perfect.[39]

Within the tragic structure of creation, then, we discover the radiance of divine love. When we find ourselves outside the camp as social or literal lepers and our worldview turns to anomie, we still have the natural order to remind us of the beauty and hope inherent in creation. The chaos of the beginning remains ordered by God, even if it is only apparent in the beauty of the wildflowers. Even amid the nettles and poison ivy, beauty springs up to nourish our senses and offer us hope.

Thérèse of Lisieux

The tragic structure of the universe remains invisible until it takes form in particular instances of human suffering.[40] In *The Wounding and Healing of Desire: Weaving Heaven and Earth* (2005), Farley introduces Thérèse of Lisieux as a model of the ways in which a martyr or tragic hero can pull back the fabric of the illusion of suffering to reveal the essential good of

---

39. Farley, *Gathering Those Driven Away: A Theology of Incarnation*, 222.

40. Surin, "Theodicy?," 232.

creation underneath. Thérèse views her death from tuberculosis in her early twenties not as a hardship but as a blessing. The value of divine benefaction, to Thérèse, lies in salvation from earthly disappointments rather than in imagination of heavenly delights.[41] The historical work of Steffen Lösel provides further evidence to support Farley's theological claims.[42] According to Thérèse's sister Céline during the first ecclesiastical process concerning her benediction, Thérèse had expressed gratitude at being permitted to die at age 24, the age when men could be ordained as priests: "The good God allows me to be sick, so that I could not have gone there and I would have died before I had exercised my ministry." Thérèse proves Farley's point when she confides her vision of heaven to Céline. Heaven, it seems, will admit the priests and the female virgins so that "those who have desired it on earth will partake in heaven of the honors of the priesthood." Thérèse's desire is no idle fancy—she has her sisters cut her a tonsure. Yet, Thérèse is clear that she is going to heaven not as an angel or priest but a virgin. This is no mystic vision of the ways in which heaven differs from earth, such as the insistence of Matthew's Jesus that in heaven men and women will not be given in marriage but will be like the angels or the assertion by Paul that we see heaven only as through a glass darkly. For Thérèse, her vision of heaven, afforded by her tragic case of one of the common diseases of the nineteenth century, permits her to throw into relief the way life should function on earth. Indeed, her cult in the 1920s became one of the cults associated with the traditional sites of Germanic healing deities.[43] It was not, as Vita Sackville-West has suggested, that Thérèse presided over the "treacly dulcification" of a feminized French Church by doing ordinary things extraordinarily well, excelling at the Victorian-era Cult of True Womanhood.[44] Rather, as Farley has urged us to see, pilgrims to these shrines left votives and tablets as thank-offerings indicating she was restoring a sense of life as it should be, that is, joyous in a way that she had not been able to experience. Thérèse gave these more secular believers hope because she had persisted in the face

41. Farley, *The Wounding and Healing of Desire*, 84.

42. Lösel, "Prayer, Pain, and Priestly Privilege," 273–306.

43. According to a 1935 report in the *Tyrolean Informer*, interest in a chapel outside Innsbruck "grew from day to day, as the ever increasing votive and thank you tablets on the walls [and] the great stream of visitors attested." See Waddy, "St. Anthony's Bread," 352.

44. Sackville-West, *The Eagle and the Dove*, 146. Cf. Pope, "A Heroine without Heroics," 46–60.

of adversity, knew her body would be corrupted, and yet still believed in the possibility of the restoration of bodily integrity. Though her body was being cut off, her soul remained intact.

Joseph Ratzinger, Roman Catholic theologian and retired pope, anticipates both historian Lösel and theologian Farley in his choice of Thérèse as a paradigm of faith. Like both of them, he redeems Thérèse from the realm of quotidian kitsch to which the historiography of Sackville-West would relegate her. And, like Farley, he centers his scrutiny on her moments of doubt and atheism arising from her perception of theodicy. In his *Introduction to Christianity* (1969), he underscores that Thérèse has been enculturated into the worldview of her religious community, being "so completely molded by the faith of the Church that the invisible world became, not just a part of her everyday life, but that life itself."[45] Despite this, she began to put herself in "sinners' shoes" and contemplate a chasm that lay beneath those shoes and her neatly ordered religious life. Even within the physical and metaphysical cloisters of her religious order, her illness, and her life of sanctity, she was able to have compassion for the more secular doubters by doubting herself. For Ratzinger, this intellectual progress beyond her self-assured and continually reinforced faith exhibited a great spiritual gift to the *perhaps* advocated by Buber. In a post-Enlightenment age, we are no longer able to imitate Mary's divine "yes"; the transformational individual sees the Enlightenment critique of belief in God and nonetheless says *perhaps*.

Reading Farley and Ratzinger in tandem, we behold Thérèse as a civic martyr who at once bears the burden of witnessing to an ideal civic order (Farley) and yet is allowed to doubt all order (Ratzinger). For Farley, Thérèse uses her illness as a catalyst to push for her vision of female leadership in roles traditionally reserved for men, such as priest, Doctor of the Church, and soldier. For Ratzinger, Thérèse is a perspicacious theological intellect who has compassion for those in a post-Enlightenment world by envisioning herself in "sinners' shoes" and identifying her fate with those outside her cloister. At no point in time for these two theologians does Thérèse spend her time rhapsodizing about the martyr's crown she would receive in heaven. When Thérèse theorizes justice in heaven, she is actually promulgating justice on earth. This meditation appears to have had transformative power for Thérèse since, as Lösel notes, she stopped competing with priests and started viewing herself as their

---

45. Ratzinger, *Introduction to Christianity*, 42.

co-worker. In other words, in the mind of Thérèse, she no longer needed to become a priest; *she already was one.*

Conclusion

Affliction—whether from biological or social oppression—is an inexorable component of the life of every human being. Suffering is a part of creation. This means that our participation in creation will entail the experience of theodicy, suffering beyond our control but within our capacity to transform. Farley frames this human condition within the realm of drama. The human drama is not the teleological drama feared by Levinas but a redemptive tragedy. The parameters of this tragedy summon the good within individual humans just as the tragic hero or martyr inspires within another a call to action. What is essential in this martyrology is not the construction of heaven but the construction of lived experience "under heaven," to borrow the scriptural phrase. Farley's example of St. Thérèse of Lisieux emerges from the contemporary theological project to save the nineteenth-century saint from her kitschy historiographers and to prove that St. Thérèse was indeed a theological intellect worthy of veneration as a Doctor of the Church. Farley focuses on Thérèse's desire to inhabit such male roles, as Doctor of the Church had been an exclusively male prerogative in the lifetime of Thérèse, as part of the heroic vision for the transformation of this world as a foretaste of the one to come. While dying a horrific death of tuberculosis, Thérèse resisted the temptation to fixate on the somatic and instead both elevated herself to the role of priest and humbled herself in seeing herself as a secular sinner. Rather than withdrawing inward from the pain, she kept her soul in communion with her society. And it is Thérèse's call to communion that is Farley's contribution to theology on the incarnation of the divine in creation.

Bibliography

Adorno, Theodor. *Negative Dialectics*. Translated by E.B. Ashton. London: Routledge & Kegan Paul, 1973.

Ajzenstat, O.E. "Beyond Totality: The Shoah and the Biblical Ethics of Emmanuel Levinas." In *Strange Fire: Reading the Bible after the Holocaust,* edited by T. Linafelt, 106–20. New York: New York University Press, 2000.

Bal, Mieke. "Lots of Writing." *Poetics Today* 15.1 (1994) 89–114.

Baskin, J.R. "Job as Moral Exemplar in Ambrose." *Vigiliae Christianae* 35.3 (1981) 222–31.

Berger, Ronald J. "The 'Banality of Evil' Reframed: The Social Construction of the 'Final Solution' to the 'Jewish Problem.'" *Sociological Quarterly* 34.4 (1993) 597–618.

Blumenthal, David R. *The Banality of Good and Evil: Moral Lessons from the Shoah and Jewish Tradition.* Washington: Georgetown University Press, 1999.

Bourdieu, Pierre. "Habitus." In *Habitus: A Sense of Place,* edited by Jean Hillier and Emma Rooksby, 43–52. Burlington: Ashgate, 2005.

Bowra, C.M. "Xenophanes and the Olympic Games." *American Journal of Philology* 59.3 (1938) 257–79.

Bronner, Leila Leah. "Esther Revisited: An Aggadic Approach." In *A Feminist Companion to Esther, Judith, and Susanna,* ed. Athalya Brenner, 176–187. Sheffield: Sheffield University Press, 1995.

Caner, Daniel F. "The Practice and Prohibition of Self-Castration in Early Christianity." *Vigiliae Christianae* 51.4 (1997) 396–415.

Fackenheim, Emil. *To Mend the World: Foundations of Future Jewish Thought.* New York: Schocken, 1982.

Farley, Edward. *Divine Empathy: A Tragedy of God.* Minneapolis: Fortress, 1996.

Farley, Wendy. *Gathering Those Driven Away: A Theology of Incarnation.* Louisville: Wesminster John Knox, 2011.

———. *Tragic Vision and Divine Compassion.* Louisville: Wesminster John Knox, 1990.

———. *The Wounding and Healing of Desire: Weaving Heaven and Earth.* Louisville: Wesminster John Knox, 2011.

Fredriksen, Paula. *Augustine and the Jews: A Christian Defense of Jews and Judaism.* New Haven: Yale University Press, 2010.

Grammer, Elizabeth Elkin. *Some Wild Visions: Autobiographies by Itinerant Female Preachers in Nineteenth-Century America.* Oxford: Oxford University Press, 2003.

Hubert, Henri, and Marcel Mauss. *Sacrifice: Its Nature and Function.* Chicago: University of Chicago Press, 1964.

Kristeva, Julia. *Black Sun Depression and Melancholia.* Translated by Leon S. Roudiez. New York: Columbia University Press, 1992.

Levinas, Emmanuel. *Collected Philosophical Papers.* Translated by Alphonso Lingis. Dordrecht: Martinus Nijhoff, 1987.

Lincoln, Bruce. "Rewriting the German War God: Georges Dumézil, Politics and Scholarship in the Late 1930s." *History of Religions* 37.3 (1998) 187–208.

Lincoln, Bruce. "Chapter One: From Bergaigne to Meuli." In *Greek and Roman Animal Sacrifice,* edited by Christopher A. Faraone and F.S. Naiden, 13–31. Cambridge: Cambridge University Press, 2012.

Lösel, Steffen. "Prayer, Pain, and Priestly Privilege: Claude Langlois's New Perspective on Thérèse of Lisieux." *Journal of Religion* 88.3 (2008) 273–306.

Meuli, Karl. "Griechische Opferbräuche." In *Phyllobolia: Festschrift für Peter von der Mühll zum 60. Geburtstag am 1. August 1945*, edited by O. Gigon, 185–288. Basel: B. Schwabe, 1946.

Nussbaum, Martha C. *The Fragility of Goodness: Luck and Ethics in Greek Tragedy and Philosophy, Part 2*. Cambridge: Cambridge University Press, 2001.

Oliner, S. and P. *The Altruistic Personality: Rescuers of Jews in Nazi Europe*. New York: Free, 1988.

Peters, Janelle. "Rahab, Esther, and Judith as Models for Church Leadership in 1 Clement." *Journal of Early Christian History* 5.2 (2015) 94–110.

Pope, Barbara Corrado. "A Heroine without Heroics: The Little Flower of Jesus and Her Times." *Church History* 57.1 (1988) 46–60.

Ratzinger, Joseph Cardinal. *Introduction to Christianity*, second edition. San Francisco: Ignatius, 2004.

Tolkien, J.R.R. *The Return of the King*. London: George Allen & Unwin, 1966.

Vasilou, Iakonos. "Socrates' Reverse Irony." *Classical Quarterly* 52.1 (2002) 220–30.

Waddy, Helena. "St. Anthony's Bread: The Modernized Religious Culture of German Catholics in the Early Twentieth Century." *Journal of Social History* 31.2 (1997) 347–70.

Weil, Simone. *Waiting for God*. Translated by Emma Crawford. New York: Harper & Row, 1973.

Wiesel, Elie. *Night*. Translated by S. Rodway. London: Penguin, 1981.

Wright, Jacob L. "The Commemoration of Defeat and the Formation of a Nation in the Hebrew Bible." *Prooftexts* 29.3 (2009) 433–73.

Zeitlin, Froma I. *Playing the Other: Gender and Society in Classical Greek Literature*. Chicago: University of Chicago Press, 1996.

NINE

Eros for the Natural World: Reading Wendy Farley's *Eros for the Other* as a Resource for Environmental Theology

Leigh Pittenger

IN *EROS FOR THE OTHER: Retaining Truth in a Pluralistic World*, Wendy Farley addresses the difficulty of maintaining conceptions of "truth" or "reality" in a postmodern context. While crediting postmodern theories such as deconstruction with exposing the constructed character of certain predominant assumptions about reality, Farley argues against a sensibility that would see *everything* as constructed and consequently deem it impossible to make any truth claims or moral judgments. To accept the position that social construction "goes all the way down" and that no truth exists would eliminate any foundation for the pursuit of justice. Farley recognizes human beings have a "vocation to truth" that depends on maintaining "truth" and "reality" as pertinent categories.[1] Drawing on Hannah Arendt and Emmanuel Levinas to illuminate the connections between eros, ethics, and truth, Farley employs the phrases "eros for the other" and "passion for reality" to describe the ethical relationship of human beings to the real. She states that a "passion for reality, that is, the reality of other beings, is the beginning of ethical practice."[2]

---

1. Farley, *Eros for the Other*, 199.
2. Farley, *Eros for the Other*, 12.

Farley's conception of a "vocation to truth," characterized above all by a "passion for reality," offers a resource for environmental theology, as Farley extends the conception of the "other" or the "real" to include not only human beings but also *all* living beings. Against those who might suggest that terms such as "nature" or "natural world" refer to mere constructions, Farley makes a compelling case that multitudinous beings (animals, insects, flowers, forests, landscapes, watersheds, ecosystems) are indeed realities that should evoke a passionate and committed response from human beings. Utilizing Levinas and Arendt as philosophical sources, offering a provocative description of eros, and advocating the necessary practice of an erotic/ethical imagination (as distinct from fantasy or illusion), Farley's work reveals the cultivation of an eros for the natural world.

Farley's Critique of Totality and Conception of Reality

In *Eros for the Other*, Farley describes ethics in terms of an attentive, responsible, joyful, and compassionate orientation toward the real. One obstacle to living ethically is that the individual mind tends to drift into solipsism or fantasy, which results in viewing other beings either as mere extensions of the self or as objects designated to fulfill the self's needs and desires. The second obstacle, on a grander scale, is that totalizing ideologies lead to the construction of systems that serve only to reproduce the ideology (totalitarianism being the prime example). Such systems ensure that all facts that do not promote the ideological view are ignored or suppressed, and they reduce all beings to mere functions within the system. If a being does not conform to the system, or should fail to fulfill its assigned role, that being will be discounted as a "being" at all—demonized, degraded, outcast, or destroyed. These two obstacles are both characterized by a narrow, limited worldview based on illusion; for the sake of preserving the One, either a narrowly conceived Self or System, the goodness and value of multiple beings is obscured. In Levinas's terms, the other is reduced to the same. This is what is meant by "totality." Totality circumscribes one's vision in such a way that it is almost impossible to break out of it. How can totality be resisted, then? How can human beings learn to *see* reality and live in proper relation to it?

Part of the effort to resist totality involves understanding how it works. Developing her critique of totality, Farley draws on the writings of Levinas and Arendt, Jewish thinkers who personally experienced the rise of the Nazi regime in Germany and who subsequently developed profound critiques of totality—Arendt by offering a historical and political analysis of the rise of totalitarianism in Nazi Germany and Stalinist Russia, and Levinas by offering a stringent critique of the Western philosophical tradition as "an ontology: a reduction of the other to the same by interposition of a middle and neutral term that ensures the comprehension of being."[3] As Farley writes, "Arendt and Levinas both recognize with unusual clarity and radicality the depth of violence accomplished by totality. From two quite different perspectives, they identify and hold open the gap between the violences of history and the claims of persons. Arendt and Levinas engage in a critique of totality in defense of reality, in defense of the individual lives dismembered by totalizing power."[4] Farley's observation that Arendt and Levinas critique totality *in defense of reality* is key. While Levinas and Arendt employ different terminology (with Levinas speaking of "the other" and Arendt speaking of "reality" and "plurality"), they both emphasize that something real exists outside the self and outside of ideology, something that properly evokes a response of respect, obligation, and passion.

Farley draws primarily from Levinas's *Totality and Infinity* for his critique of totality and emphasis on obligation to the other. She embraces his distinction between ethical metaphysics on the one hand (an orientation of infinite obligation to the other) and ontology on the other. Philosophy, understood as ethical metaphysics, is properly understood as the search for truth. Here truth is not defined in terms of ideas or content to be grasped. Instead, following Levinas, Farley describes the desire for truth in terms of relationship or an *orientation toward others*: "The desire for truth would orient one toward other persons and therefore toward ethics because persons exemplify a kind of reality that is stubbornly irreducible to one's own consciousness. On this trajectory, the desire for truth takes one away from self-consciousness and toward others and is therefore an ethical metaphysics."[5] In Farley's view, eros is ethically

---

3. Farley, *Eros for the Other*, 49. The quoted phrase is from Levinas, *Totality and Infinity*, 43. Farley includes a footnote remarking on Levinas's particular usage of the term "ontology," likening it to Derrida's "metaphysics of presence" or Adorno's "logic of identity" (fn. 19).

4. Farley, *Eros for the Other*, 48.

5. Farley, *Eros for the Other*, 49.

significant because it propels the movement outward from the self and toward the real.

While highlighting Levinas's respect for truth and emphasis on obligation to the other, Farley expresses some discomfort with his language of "the other," which possesses an abstract and distancing quality. Moreover, in Levinas's usage, it refers only to the *human* other—the widow, the orphan, the stranger. For Farley, the outward orientation of eros leads human beings not only toward other persons in *their* reality but also toward the natural world in *its* reality. Explaining that she prefers the word "beings" to "others" because of its greater inclusivity, she writes:

> It is necessary to articulate the claims imposed by ethical existence in such a way that all reality is understood to be included. It is not only other persons that are real, beautiful, and vulnerable to wrongful destruction or exploitation. It is the mark of all reality to be beautiful and vulnerable. This is true of persons, of other creatures, of ecosystems, of streams, oceans, deserts—realities that are not particular creatures and yet are real and can be wrongfully harmed.[6]

Farley also uses the word "beings," as she explains, "to contest the construal of reality—of all existence—as thinglike.[7] Despite growing environmental awareness in North America, the construal of the natural world as "thinglike," as a limitless reservoir of "resources" to be exploited for our own use, remains one of the dominant illusions of our society in our time, as evidenced by the continued use of irreparably damaging practices like mountaintop removal, for example, or by the routine treatment of animals as machines for dairy and meat production in factory farms. Farley exposes the totalizing and illusory nature of this worldview by emphasizing the *beauty* and *vulnerability* of living beings. An increased recognition of such beauty and vulnerability should enhance human beings' sense of obligation to cherish and protect the natural world.

While drawing on Levinas to emphasize obligation to the other, extending the meaning of "the other" to recognize all beings as characterized by beauty and vulnerability, Farley turns to Arendt to emphasize *plurality* as another defining characteristic of the real. Farley's analysis focuses primarily on *The Origins of Totalitarianism*, in which Arendt identifies the manifestation of concentration camps as the essence of

6. Farley, *Eros for the Other*, 11.

7. Farley, *Eros for the Other*, 11.

totalitarian evil. Farley notes, while Arendt does not blame Western philosophy for *directly* leading to the construction of concentration camps, she suggests that philosophy was "not altogether innocent."[8] In Arendt's view, philosophy is at fault because it "spoke of man the individual and dealt with the fact of plurality tangentially."[9] Arendt employs the term *plurality* to refer to the distinctive individuality, uniqueness, and agency of human beings in the world. According to her analysis, totalitarianism, with its goal of creating and perpetuating a monolithic system, is designed to eliminate plurality altogether—to destroy the very capacity of human beings to appear in the world as unique individuals capable of spontaneous speech and action. Because the philosophical tradition fails to recognize the importance of plurality as the condition of human speech and action, it fails to help people understand and resist the horrors of totalitarianism.

Farley shares Arendt's appreciation of plurality and affirms it as a defining characteristic of reality. Moreover, just as she extends Levinas's meaning of "the other" to include other-than-human beings, she also extends the meaning of "plurality" to refer to multiple expressions of being, each possessing a unique, irreplaceable value. As Farley observes, "multiplicity is manifest . . . in the almost absurd extravagance of nature."[10] Like Arendt, she advocates more than a simple "tolerance" of multiplicity or plurality. Instead, she calls for a *passion for reality*, characterized by delight: "A passion for reality and acknowledgement of the obligations other beings impose on us require a *delight* in plurality. A capacity to recognize and love plurality is one criterion by which a conception of truth must be judged. It is a criterion imposed by reality itself in accord with its pluralistic and infinitely diverse embodiments."[11] Farley deems it is this passion for reality, delighting in the unique beauty of particular beings and places, that guides the human vocation to truth.

---

8. Farley, *Eros for the Other*, 45. "I suspect that philosophy is not altogether innocent in this fine how-do-you-do. Not, of course, that Hitler had anything to do with Plato . . . Instead, perhaps in the sense that Western philosophy has never had a clear concept of what constitutes the political and couldn't have one, because, by necessity, it spoke of man the individual and dealt with the fact of plurality tangentially." (In *Hannah Arendt/Karl Jaspers Correspondence, 1926-1969*, 166.)

9. Farley, *Eros for the Other*, 45.

10. Farley, *Eros for the Other*, 21.

11. Farley, *Eros for the Other*, 17. Emphasis mine.

Three Dimensions of Eros:
Delight, Detachment, and Compassion

Farley describes the human "vocation to truth" as an orientation toward other beings, involving the recognition of beings as beautiful, vulnerable, multiple, and diverse. Eros is her chosen metaphor to describe the impulse to move away from totality and toward the transcendent other. But how is eros to be understood? How does it enable human beings to break out of totality and to reorient ourselves toward other beings? Farley launches her examination of eros, which draws on thinkers as various as Plato, Audre Lorde, and Ann Carson, with an emphasis on joy. Eros is "first of all a capacity for joy, which connects us to others and which transforms all experiences into forms of excellence and delight."[12] For Farley, this joy *itself* possesses an ethical quality: "The joy of eros is deeply ethical in quality and effect. It is through eros, which is drawn out of itself by the wonder of concrete existence, that orientation toward reality becomes possible."[13]

Farley's emphasis on joy connects closely with her discussion of the first dimension of eros, which she presents as *delight* in response to beauty. Here "beauty" refers not to an aesthetic quality but to the other's exteriority or "absence" (that is, the other's irreducibility to totality, its inability to be grasped or possessed), infinity, and value or "importance" in Alfred North Whitehead's usage.[14] In an encounter with beauty, Farley writes, "a fire licks at the fortress of the self; beauty is a cleansing fire that burns out the fixation upon oneself."[15] This experience of delight in an encounter with the beauty of the natural world quickens our senses, our imaginations, and our impulse to praise. Over the centuries, it has led countless prophets, poets, mystics, naturalists, philosophers, and theologians to bear witness to such encounter in inspired writings, such as Gerard Manley Hopkins's often-quoted poem "God's Grandeur" ("The world is charged with the grandeur of God!") or a lesser-known passage from the thirteenth-century mystic Angela of Foligno:

12. Farley, *Eros for the Other*, 68.

13. Farley, *Eros for the Other*, 69.

14. Farley, *Eros for the Other*, 80. In her discussion of "importance," Farley is calling attention to what she calls the "value-ladenness" of reality (81). See Whitehead, *Modes of Thought* (New York: Free Press, 1938), 11.

15. Farley, *Eros for the Other*, 83.

And immediately the eyes of my soul were opened, and in a vision I beheld the fullness of God in which I beheld and comprehended the whole of creation, that is, what is on this side and what is beyond the sea, the abyss, the sea itself, and everything else. And in everything that I saw, I could perceive nothing except the presence of the power of God, and in a manner totally indescribable. And my soul in an excess of wonder cried out, "This world is pregnant with God!"[16]

As even the most passionate writers have attested, such an encounter with "totally indescribable" beauty transcends even our most inspired attempts to express it in words.

The second dimension of eros that Farley describes is a kind of detachment; she writes that the "cleansing fire" of beauty purifies "through a passionate, *detached* delight."[17] Detachment here does not undermine the emphasis on delight, joy, or passion; it does not imply absence of *feeling* but rather the absence of *self-concern*. In this way, the sensation of delight and wonder evoked by beautiful and vulnerable beings differs from lust or greed.[18] Eros does not seek to possess others as though they were things, making them subservient to the ego's illusory needs; instead, eros is quickened by the *absence* of others, their mystery and irreducibility. Those who view the natural world with a passionate detachment recognize its various life-forms are valuable for their own sakes, not merely for their potential for commercial exploitation or other perceived human benefits. Although we are immersed in the world and dependent on it for nourishment and indeed for our very breath (and in that sense the world is always *present*), the world is also *absent* in that its great variety of life-forms and its various complex processes transcend what we can ever fully see, know, and understand. And, despite whatever illusions we have entertained to the contrary, the natural world ultimately remains beyond human control.

In emphasizing detachment, Farley makes a point of contrasting eros not only with lust or greed but also with shame, guilt, and self-abnegation, conditions that she identifies as an actual *betrayal* of eros, as mere forms of self-preoccupation.[19] She critiques Levinas sharply on this point: he describes the ethical encounter with the "face" of the other

16. Foligno, "The Book of Blessed Angela (Memorial)," 169–70.

17. Farley, *Eros for the Other*, 83. Emphasis mine.

18. Farley, *Eros for the Other*, 83 and 90.

19. Farley, *Eros for the Other*, 90–99.

in rather violent terms, advocating complete self-abnegation. The face "calls the self into question" so radically as to deprive the subject of any remaining autonomy. Farley, by contrast, rejects self-centeredness without rejecting personhood. In fact, she advocates an appreciation of the integrity of *personhood*, arguing that personhood is actually an essential component of responsibility: "Being present in person, with all the complexity of personhood intact—humor, desires, enjoyments, abilities, preferences, needs—is a good deal of the actual content of responsibility."[20] In responding to the natural world, then, human beings are not encouraged to surrender our selfhood completely. While we might recognize the necessity of accepting certain limits (i.e., learning to consume fewer resources), we need not do violence to ourselves. Instead, we embrace health, bringing our whole selves into relationship with other beings.

The third significant dimension of Farley's description of eros is *compassion*. Though she emphasizes joy and delight, Farley does not deny that love of the natural world will involve suffering. She writes, "The simultaneous presence of beauty and its destruction releases two arrows piercing one's heart: wonder and pain. Out of this coupling of delight and suffering, compassion is born."[21] Suffering has always been a human response to the difficult truth of impermanence (the awareness that everything changes and eventually passes away), but it is perhaps intensified in our time, when we must witness—and are implicated in—a great deal of widespread, irreparable destruction of the natural world. If we are paying attention, we are well aware that the beauty of the natural world is being disregarded and degraded on a daily basis. Grief and even heartbreak are appropriate responses to the suffering, degradation, and demise of other beings, especially when human beings have contributed to an excess of suffering. If we permit ourselves to experience both wonder and pain, resisting the temptation to slide into despair or apathy on witnessing the continuing destruction of beings that we cherish, we can also allow a necessary compassion to arise.

Farley's metaphors of eros and "passion for reality" thus contribute to environmental theology by not only emphasizing obligation to the natural world but also by encouraging a fully human response, including the real and valuable emotions of delight, joy, grief, and compassion. To be sure, Farley insists repeatedly on the human *responsibility* to behave

20. Farley, *Eros for the Other*, 97.
21. Farley, *Eros for the Other*, 85.

ethically toward all beings. But the language of responsibility, unaccompanied by the language of passion and joy, might suggest that the human responsibility to protect the natural world is nothing more than a dreary, self-denying burden. Nothing could be further from the truth, for the more we allow ourselves to experience the erotic dimension of our relationship with the natural world, the more we are enlivened ourselves, and the more we come to feel at home in the world.

The Ethical "Leap of Imagination": Cultivating an Eros for the Natural World through the Practice of Imagination

Farley describes the human "vocation to truth" as an ongoing practice, or perhaps a set of practices, characterized especially by *attention*: "Attention rightly implies a kind of effort; it is a practice, a moral discipline. It is a disposition toward the world, one in which eros for others displaces the fascination with the self and with the securities of total knowledge."[22] Similarly, an eros for the natural world is a practice, a mode of attending that can be cultivated. To some readers, the language of practice or cultivation may seem out of place in a discussion of eros. In a sense, eros is wild and untamable; like reality itself (mysterious, unpredictable), it thwarts any attempt to domesticate it. Reality can take us by surprise when we least expect or desire it; it can wrench the focus of one's awareness from one's self to the other with a "dislocating jerk," as Farley puts it.[23] We might experience its disorienting effect sometimes as an unwelcome condition, even an affliction, and at other times as a liberating gift of grace. At any rate, the shift of reorientation associated with the erotic response to the other is not a sensation that we always associate with the steady discipline of a *practice*.

However, following Farley, I argue that eros for the natural world can be consciously cultivated. It is partly a matter of deliberately *seeking* an encounter with other beings, quieting the noise in one's mind, waiting silently and patiently for other beings to reveal themselves, "stalking" them in an Annie Dillard–like way: "I walk out; I see something, some event that would otherwise have been utterly missed and lost; or

22. Farley, *Eros for the Other*, 191. Farley cites Simone Weil and Iris Murdoch in her discussion of attention as a moral discipline.

23. Farley, *Eros for the Other*, 81.

something sees me, some enormous power brushes me with its clean wing, and I resound like a beaten bell. I am an explorer, then, and I am also a stalker, or the instrument of the hunt itself."[24] It is also partly a matter of training the imagination in a particular way. Farley acknowledges the importance of imagination when she speaks of needing to take a "leap of imagination" to see through the illusions that separate us from reality. The problem is that totalizing ideologies severely undermine the individual's capacity even to *imagine* a reality outside of its promoted norms. For example, Farley describes the difficulty of seeing the full personhood of a nursing mother through a patriarchal lens:

> The body of a nursing mother has, for her, an infinitely complex set of meanings. Through it she caresses and feeds her baby; she feels pleasure, strength, exhaustion. It is the site of her varied actions, desires, experiences, memories—many of which have nothing to do with nursing or babies. But within the illusion of patriarchy, none of this really exists. What exists are breasts, which are there to excite desire or repel genteel sensibilities. It would take a leap of imagination to apprehend a person whose meaning is irreducible to this desire and revulsion. . . . This leap of imagination is all but impossible within the confines of illusion.[25]

Farley identifies both totalitarianism and capitalism as totalizing ideologies that, like the patriarchal worldview described above, reduce the full reality of beings to a one-dimensional image. In present-day North America, capitalist ideology in particular strives to create a hegemonic world and undermines our sense of ethical obligation toward the natural world.[26] Industry and advertising collude to promote an image of the "good life" characterized by hyperindividualism, excessive consumption, and economic growth. Just as a "leap of imagination" is needed within a patriarchal system to allow us to see nursing mothers as full persons, it

24. Dillard, *Pilgrim at Tinker Creek*, 14.

25. Farley, *Eros for the Other*, 19–20.

26. Farley, *Eros for the Other*: "For Americans, capitalism produces an entirely different form of unity. Free from the terror of totalitarianism, it nonetheless imposes itself upon the world in ever more complete hegemony, homogenizing cultural diversity into a banal, anesthetizing sameness and reducing all persons to interchangeable parts. . . . In our material situation there is less and less room for diversity of any kind. Capitalism, and in an infinitely more overt sense, totalitarianism undermine the moral obligation to respect and nourish the pluralism through which life is manifest" (42–43).

is also needed to allow us to see and comprehend the enormously high costs of our current lifestyles, including the loss of habitat, the extinction of species, increasing air and water pollution, and the victimization of minority communities and indigenous peoples who bear the brunt of current waste disposal procedures, just to name a few. Imagination is needed to seek other representations of "the good life" to replace our own as meaningful and desirable.

Imagination is also needed to enable those of us who live comfortable North American lives to *change* our lifestyles to live more ethically. Even we who care about the natural world and who strive to make small personal changes, such as recycling, find it difficult to break our numerous destructive habits (driving cars, flying to conferences, and so on). We need imagination to shift our understanding of our own behaviors. For example, Sallie McFague writes of the difficulty involved in imagining the reality of global warming and our own contribution to the problem: "Climate change is slow, insidious, partly invisible—and we are the enemy. Moreover, we are a (largely) innocent enemy: we high-level consumers of energy are merely living ordinary Western lives, doing what everyone else in our society is doing. Even as we gradually learn how deeply our actions are affecting the planet's health, the problem still seems amorphous, abstract, remote."[27] Imagination is required not only to help us identify our ordinary, "innocent" behaviors as destructive and even sinful but also to help us envision effective, life-affirming responses. As a society, can we imagine the effects of our collective behaviors on climate change and create beneficial policies to address the situation? Can we imagine re-creating American cities so that public transportation is improved and fewer people need to rely on personal vehicles? Can we envision communities working together to support local farmers whose treatment of their land and animals is ethical and sustainable? Exercising an outward-oriented imagination characterized by eros will help us ask the necessary questions and find new approaches to our daily routines.

27. McFague, *A New Climate for Theology: God, the World, and Global Warming*, 28.

The Imaginative Dimension of Eros
in Environmental Theology

The essential task of environmental theology is helping human beings cultivate an erotic/ethical imagination that assists us in practicing our vocation to truth. Theology can participate in the deconstruction of a totalizing worldview that binds entire societies in a consumerist illusion and reduces the natural world to a mere set of "resources" for consumption. Theology can help us cultivate and sustain a sense of eros for the natural world. It can help redirect people's attention and desires away from narcissistic self-concern or illusory images of "the good life" and toward regard for the goodness and wonder of creation. As Farley observes, such theology is shaped not by scholarship alone but by a willingness to interact as fully and consciously as possible with the natural world. While the imaginative dimension of eros can be enhanced by inspirational words and images (poetry, photographs, liturgy, etc.), the fullest power of eros arises through direct encounters with the natural world.

Cultivating an eros for the natural world requires us to become more aware of how dominant ideologies attempt to deform the imagination. For example, in her conclusion to *Eros for the Other*, Farley cautions readers against allowing the dominant ideologies to determine how we frame our discussions of the natural world. She warns against framing our questions in a way that "cedes most of the questions in advance to powers bent on the most efficient exploitation of the environment possible."[28] Drawing an analogy with Nazi Germany, she writes:

> It is as if one agreed to accept, "for the sake of argument," the Nazis' characterization of some persons as subhuman and then, on that basis, decided what range of treatment was appropriate: legal distinctions on the basis of true and ersatz humanity, different rations permitted the two groups, then concentration of some into limited areas, deportation, and ultimately liquidation. Resisting this slide from distasteful, perhaps, but still "relatively innocuous" ontological distinctions to increasingly violent relationships should not begin in the midst of destruction, when it is already too late.[29]

28. Farley, *Eros for the Other*, 189.

29. Farley, *Eros for the Other*, 198. Roger Gottlieb, Holocaust scholar and environmentalist, has similarly used the Holocaust as a basis of analogy to illuminate our understanding of the environmental crisis. See *A Spirituality of Resistance*, 28–29 and 68–72, for several parallels between the Holocaust and environmental crisis.

As Farley suggests here, instead of calling for a true "leap of imagination" that changes the way we see the world and ourselves in relation to the world, many discussions of contemporary environmental issues have focused merely on mitigating the effects of the problems that we are determined to continue creating, or delaying the worst consequences for a few more years. Environmentalists like Bill McKibben have similarly observed how our responses have avoided offering any real solutions: "We have tended to focus on the efficiency issues—new technologies, better cars, recycling, and so on—because they are politically and emotionally the most palatable: they allow us to avoid the question of our place on the planet, they offer us the possibility of extending our current patterns of use for at least another generation or two."[30] North Americans may feel better about ourselves if we recycle some of our consumables, for example, but if we continue to define ourselves primarily as consumers and fail to reconsider "our place on the planet," the numerous manifestations of environmental crisis will continue to escalate.

Theology's contribution to addressing these environmental crises involves starting at the beginning—asking and answering basic questions about humanity's place in the world. As Farley writes,

> The struggle for truth against illusion and domination must include a struggle to define the underlying presuppositions about the sorts of beings that inhabit the world. What reality is like, whether beauty is "mere prettiness" or has ethical significance, whether the natural world is really nothing other than a utility, and whether human persons are really most like (admittedly complicated) computers—these are questions that determine the outcome of struggles for justice and even survival. If the struggle for justice is limited to ad hoc, local contests, it becomes little more than negotiation for slightly better conditions, parallel to suggesting that subhumans be given a few more grams or calories in their diet.[31]

A leap of imagination enables us to revisit basic questions of worldview and identity. Who are we as human beings if we are *not* primarily individual consumers? What is our proper relationship with the natural world if it is *not* one of "dominion" or exploitation? What are the unique

---

30. McKibben, *The Comforting Whirlwind: God, Job, and the Scale of Creation*, 43. McKibben draws from the book of Job to advocate a human attitude of humility in the vast and mysterious scheme of creation, as opposed to an anthropocentric sensibility.

31. Farley, *Eros for the Other*, 198–99.

features and the needs of the particular neighborhood and the bioregion where I live? Who is God and how does God relate to the world? Farley's theology of "passion for the real" exposes the inadequacy of using criteria like "efficiency" to guide our relationship with the world. Such theology assists with the reframing of questions in imaginative ways that can lead to significant shifts in how our society sees the world and supports the many valuable beings who share it.

Conclusion: Putting Eros into Practice

Wendy Farley's contribution to environmental theology lies in her description of the human vocation to truth, characterized by a "passion for the real," and her description of the natural world as a "reality" calling forth an erotic response of wonder and responsibility. Reading and writing about the natural world can contribute to ecological literacy and invigorate our sense of eros, but mere scholarship remains an inadequate expression of an eros for the natural world. To live as people inflamed by eros necessitates venturing from our rooms and interacting consciously with the world in a new, humbled, receptive, and imaginative way. It necessitates identifying and rejecting practices that contribute to the "unmaking of the world"[32] and embracing lifestyles that allow multiple forms of beings to flourish. It necessitates using our imaginations to discover and implement sustainable practices. Motivated by eros, we can reimagine the "good life" as joyful participation in the work of cherishing and sustaining a world that is vitally alive.

32. Farley uses the phrase "unmaking of the world" throughout *Eros for the Other* to describe the effects of totalizing ideologies and practices (see pages 17, 34, 61). For example: "The unmaking of the world is not limited to the extremes of the killing fields and death camps. Whenever human beings, the natural world, and societies are transformed into things, when capacities for beauty or compassion are trivialized, when thinking becomes indistinguishable from ideology and religion indistinguishable from consoling fictions, then reality and humanity are under assault" (61).

Bibliography

Angela of Foligno. "The Book of Blessed Angela (Memorial)." *Angela of Foligno Complete Works.* Trans. Paul Lachance, O.F.M. Preface by Romana Guarnieri. New York: Paulist Press, 1993. 169-70.

Dillard, Annie. *Pilgrim at Tinker Creek.* New York: Harper Perennial Modern Classics, 2007.

Farley, Wendy. *Eros for the Other: Retaining Truth in a Pluralistic World.* University Park: Pennsylvania State University Press, 1996.

Gottlieb, Roger S. *A Spirituality of Resistance: Finding a Peaceful Heart and Protecting the Earth.* New York: Crossroad Publishing Company, 1999.

Levinas, Emmanuel. *Totality and Infinity: An Essay on Exteriority.* Translated by Alphonso Lingis. Pittsburgh: Duquesne University Press, 1969.

McFague, Sallie. *A New Climate for Theology: God, the World, and Global Warming.* Minneapolis: Fortress Press, 2008.

McKibben, Bill. *The Comforting Whirlwind: God, Job, and the Scale of Creation.* Grand Rapids: Eerdmans, 1994.

TEN

Lived Faith Seeking Understanding: Learning from Wendy Farley

Catherine Punsalan-Manlimos

WENDY FARLEY'S WORK, *Gathering Those Driven Away*, is a liberating Christology with a surprising invitation to reflect on vocation. As a theologian, I walked with the author as she undertook a "meditation on incarnation"[1] from an optic of those marginalized by the church and guided by the writings of those in the tradition that have been placed on the margins. She writes as one driven away from the perspective of those driven away. She does theology in a manner that enables her to speak about a God that I, as one who has always been on the margins, can recognize. She writes of truths discovered through a personal encounter with Divine Eros; she theologizes as one who has been authorized to speak by a loving knowledge of Divine Wisdom. When the courage to articulate a theology comes with such authority, what is communicated is an understanding of God that is more expansive than what can be captured by any positive theology that fails to account for the mystery discovered only in encounter. Yet, what is produced is a work that demonstrates a "faith seeking understanding," that is, a theology that sees and penetrates the depth of reality and finds there the God who is love. She brings this discovery to expression even in the midst of experiences that seem to deny the God of love.

---

1. Farley, *Gathering Those Driven Away*, 11.

145

The introduction of Farley's work helped me to understand for whom and from whose perspective this work is being written: precisely those who are continually excluded and diminished by the church. And as I read through descriptions of the consequences of exclusion, I began to recognize myself as someone—with my particular social location as a Filipina in the United States within my specific religious tradition of Catholicism—kept at the margins. I came to recognize my inclusion at the Catholic table is not due to an expansion of the table to include contending voices different from those that have dominated the church and its theology. I was allowed to sit at the table because I knew how to partake of the meal that they offered rather than because I had a distinctive dish to bring. To push the table fellowship metaphor, I was allowed to bring lumpia (Filipino eggrolls) but made in a way that I have come to realize does not exist in the Philippines. What I brought to the table looked different on the outside. When you opened the wrapping you don't find pork, bean sprouts, and yams, which are the main ingredients in the eggrolls my mother cooked. Instead, you find hamburger meat and the ingredients of coleslaw.

The metaphor could suggest that there was space created for me to bring something new to the table. Instead, what I felt permitted to bring was something that only had the appearance of being new but did not have the substance of what I actually have to offer. And so, from the beginning, I became keenly aware of my anxieties about sitting at the table: not being quite good enough and feeling less than authentic. I was able to surface my fears and sense of uncertainty and feel both at home with them and confident that it is from such experiences of dislocation and in solidarity with others who are even more marginalized that I can learn to speak most authentically about God. What better initiation to humility about any God-talk than sitting at a table that always reminds you that you may not have it quite right. Yet, the danger of diminishment and self-doubt cannot be ignored.

Farley has my gratitude for the guidance that her work gives me as a theologian in search of my theological voice. She shows the liberating message contained within theologies that have their authority rooted in an encounter with Divine Eros rather than in simple conformity with external authorities, whether that be church or the theological academy. Her work is a reminder that good theology should be able to communicate good news. Faith should lead to God-talk that reflects an encounter with the God of love and justice, the God of silence and presence, the God of Jesus of Nazareth and the Christ of faith.

Farley and Gutierrez: Authorized to Speak About God

The example of God-talk that is presented by Farley is one that echoes wisdom found throughout the history of religions and clearly rendered in the book of Job. I have come to a deep appreciation of Job through the reflection of Peruvian liberation theologian Gustavo Gutierrez. Here I want to reflect on what I have learned from both Farley and Gutierrez regarding the authority to speak about God from an encounter with God, especially in the context of marginalization, exclusion, and oppression.

When confronted with a contradiction between a dominant theology and lived experience, the pressure of the reality of life leads one to question classical theologies. In the face of suffering and anguish, one can face a choice between talk and faith in a God of justice and love. It can feel like a choice between creedal God-talk and talk about a God of history who is concerned about the life of God's people.[2] In reading the book of Job from the perspective of those who suffer from poverty and oppression in Latin America, Gustavo Gutierrez beautifully unpacks this predicament when he examines the tension between the doctrine of temporal retribution embraced by Job and Job's experience of the severity of the suffering that befell him.[3] The incongruence between the "just and upright" Job and the tragic losses that he experienced did not fit into the expectation of God's justice contained in the doctrine. The God suggested by Job's theology could not be made to fit into the circumstances of his life. Job found himself critically questioning his inherited theological worldview when faced with his unshakable faith in a God of justice and

---

2. It is fascinating to consider the fact that when Christian make a profession of faith, the life of Jesus is reduced to the conception by the Holy Spirit, the virgin birth, and the Paschal Mystery and excludes much of his life and ministry. There exists the danger of a living a life of faith that assumes right belief, without consideration for the reality of everyday life, is all one needs. Pope Francis calls this a new form of Gnosticism. On the other hand, a new form of Pelagianism that demands right action and assume the capacity of human beings to accomplish this poses a danger. In both cases, there is the assumption that we have all we need in doctrines and moral teachings to enable the human intellect or the human will to bring about salvation. Such persons are closed off to the possibility of an encounter with God shaping knowledge of God and the discernment of God's call. Pope Francis, *Gaudete et Exsultate*, par. 36–62.

3. Gutierrez, *On Job*, 27–30.

the reality of his unjust situation. Will he surrender his belief in a just
God or his long-held belief in how God exacts God's justice in the world?

The contradiction between lived experience and his theological
worldview led him to question the doctrine of temporal retribution. But
interestingly, it wasn't the experience of suffering as such that led him
to demand an explanation that would enable him to make sense of his
circumstances. It was the oppression he felt by the implicit accusations
of his friends that he somehow deserved his suffering, that he must be
guilty. It was this judgment, spoken and unspoken, that led to him defend
himself and ultimately his God. He ultimately turned to God for answers
when confronted by what his friends said of God and God's justice. Their
account failed to explain the suffering of the innocent and the injustice
in the world that his own suffering made more apparent to him. And it
was ultimately when he fell silent and allowed God to be present to him
that he heard God's voice. And ultimately, God let it be known that God
is bigger than Job's comprehension and expectations.[4]

Job, whom we are told spoke eloquently about God to others prior
to his suffering, would once again speak about God, as one who has suffered and come to understand the suffering of others. But now, his words
would be born of his encounter with God, of being silent and allowing
God to speak rather than simply repeating the theology that he learned
and the worldview against which he judged his life and that of others.

It is a tragedy to be shackled by a theology that mercilessly indicts
the human experience of an expansive loving God. Talk of a loving God
grounded in borrowed concepts and theories can become a source of
oppression rather than liberation, condemning and wounding those
already wounded by the reality of life. God-talk that flows from an encounter with God in the midst of the tragedies of life points to the God
of Jesus Christ. It renders the salvation of God through Jesus Christ more
comprehensible than theology that demands an understanding of God
that fits within the limits of traditional formulas that no longer have the
power to communicate the good news to those cast out.

While acknowledging it as an academic discipline, Farley describes
theology as a "longing for wisdom." More powerfully, she defines it as
"pain seeking understanding."[5] There is something about this perspective, the perspective from the margins, from the wounded, that opens

---

4. Gutierrez, *On Job*, 85–87.

5. Farley, *Gathering Those Driven Away*, 1.

a vista to a God beyond words and beyond human telling. And so, it should be no surprise that apophasis becomes an important part of this theology.[6] When God finally responds to Job's demand for an explanation, God's words ultimately render Job silent because the words he chooses to speak are so self-focused and almost odd in the face of God's self-manifestation (Job 40:4-5). He finds himself in the presence of God, and no words, except words of negation, suffice (Job 42:5-6).[7] The smallness of his expectations is revealed in the presence of a God whose ways are beyond his capacity to intellectually grasp.[8] He comes to know a God who is bigger than the theology that he carries with him and big enough to enable him to paradoxically embrace the gratuitousness of this God's love and justice and the reality of the suffering, pain, and rejection that had become his lot.

As Farley makes clear, the greater pain is not the rejection by strangers or society at large—even as these remain devastating and destructive—but the pain caused by being told by those one holds most dear that one is also rejected by God.[9] What cuts most deeply is to be told by the community to repent of your sin. This is compounded by the knowledge that you are innocent. You are judged and condemned by the very ones you count on to be with you in your suffering. And in the end of Job's tale, it is they who are judged by God as speaking wrongly about God. Their defense of their theology leads them to distort God and God's love and justice.[10]

Job does not begin to question God or his received theology in the face of his suffering until his friends begin to invite him to repent of his sins, sins for which he must be guilty in a world where God rewards the good and punishes evil. Job's well-intentioned friends begin to tell him how he had offended God, a "fact" they believed to be self-evident in the face of his suffering. It is at this point that he begins to question their understanding of God and God's justice. The theology that Job begins to question is not just that of his friends but his own. He, too, shared the same theology, the same image of God and understanding of God's justice until his life situation made clear that there is something wrong

6. Farley, *Gathering Those Driven Away*, 71–81.

7. Farley, *Gathering those Driven Away*, 71–72; Gutierrez, *On Job*, xiv.

8. Gutierrez, *On Job*, esp. 79–81.

9. Farley, *Gathering Those Driven Away*, 5.

10. Gutierrez, *On Job*, 11–12.

with this theology. The doctrine of temporal retribution and the condemnation meted out because of it do not square with the God who comes as Divine Eros. The God whose justice such a simplified theology seeks to defend is exposed because of the reality of the suffering of the innocent and the protest of those who are unjustly condemned by such a theology.

Appropriating Farley: The Hope She Gives

Like others, I began my study of theology because I had God-questions. I longed to know and understand that for which, even in my youth, my heart longed. I thought that by studying theology and learning about God, I would grow in deeper intimacy with God. The great irony is that the deeper I went into the intellectual study of theology, the more difficult I found it to pray or participate in liturgy. The more my mind began to grasp what thinkers had to say about the history of Scripture, elements of the tradition, and of the Church, the less attentive I became to the movements within. Somewhere along the way, there grew a dissonance between my head and my heart. I experienced the exhilaration that came from my rational mind contorting, stretching, and expanding to try to grasp the paradoxes that constitute my faith tradition's understanding of God. But my heart, which leaps at the possibility of knowing God more, ached with a longing that only deepened with further education. And while all of this is part of my spiritual journey, somewhere along the way, theology became primarily a technical exercise with a set of rules and prevailing authorities to be followed, that of the Church and that of the academy.

As I read Farley's *Gathering Those Driven Away*, I was captivated by its inclusivity, by the profound wisdom that undergirds it. There is wisdom that enables the writer to dig deep into the truth that hides behind the many layers of expressions to describe Divine Eros at the very heart of the matter. This gives hope to a reader, like me, who recognizes but does not know how to articulate a shared experience of a connection with the Divine. As I read, I found myself thinking: Yes, that's it, precisely. It describes what I have learned. I agree, but I have been too afraid to allow myself to express the experience of such an expansive God in my theology.[11] After all, aren't doctrines there to precisely mark the parameters outside of which I, as a Catholic theologian, am not allowed to overstep?

11. In the area of spiritual writings, it was the work by Paul Coutinho and Richard Rohr that I found to capture the same liberating movement of experiencing Divine Eros.

My intuition has always been that theology begins with a profound encounter with the Divine, with the experience of an ecstatic union with the Beloved that gives birth to a loving knowledge of a relationship that always persists even if sometimes forgotten. But somehow, I struggle to find the freedom to do theology in this way. Without being aware of the debate, I fell into the trap of divorcing my theology from my spirituality even though the latter led to me pursue the former.[12] I, instead, find myself struggling to learn the language game of the dominant theology of my church and to learn to speak the academic and scholarly lingo of the academy, while always feeling inadequate to the task of expressing the depth of an encounter with Divine Love. Alternatively, Farley presents a work that demonstrates that not only is it possible to do theology by beginning with the grittiness of life where we encounter God, but in so doing, theology becomes, as both she and Gustavo Gutiérrez have declared, a love letter to God.[13]

By beginning with the encounter with Divine Eros in the lives of those who have been pushed aside and driven away, who suffer innocently and are condemned, we can learn to speak lovingly and truthfully about the meaning of the incarnation in all its richness and its liberating power. By attending to the beauty and the hope that remains even in the midst of the greatest of horrors and the most heartbreaking of circumstances, it is possible to discover the presence of God in our midst.

At the same time, commitment to and solidarity with those pushed out is coupled with contemplation, of silence and pauses that allow one to listen and attend to Divine Love.[14] Farley describes her work as "contemplation on the incarnation." She describes the importance of contemplation in the encounter with Divine Eros. When she does this,

---

12. Sheldrake notes how "spirituality provides solid foundations for judging the adequacy of our theological explanations," and, in the case of classical "spiritual texts" "frequently contain wisdom that theology has not taken seriously." See *Spirituality and Theology*, 395, esp. 93. It is noteworthy that, in a conversation with Farley, she described the work as a retrieval of neglected elements of the tradition. See also: Ashley, "The Turn to Spirituality?"159–70, and Schneiders, "The Discipline of Christian Spirituality and Catholic Theology," 196–212.

13. Farley, *Gathering Those Driven Away*, 5. Gutiérrez, *A Theology of Liberation*, xlvi.

14. Commitment to the struggles of the oppressed along with contemplation are the two elements of what Gutierrez calls "silence before God", which serves as the starting point of a liberation theology. See for example: Gutierrez, *Essential Writings*, 49–52.

the words are as if from a guru who lives in the everyday world. She does not diminish the struggling student who does not yet know how to focus but encourages her down the path of openness and encounter. In fact, the discipline or "hygiene" of the contemplative pause makes it possible to learn to be more and more attuned to God's presence, to begin to see God in all things. This echoes what St. Ignatius of Loyola invites retreatants to experience through the rigor of his Spiritual Exercises and through deepened awareness as a way of life.[15] This is what Job came to understand once he stopped his speaking and began his listening to God. This is what Gustavo Gutiérrez points to in his definition of theology as beginning with silence before God. And this is why Farley refers to her Christology as a "meditation." It is through spiritual exercises, through meditation and contemplation, that Ignatius invites practitioners of the Spiritual Exercises to come to know God and to know God through Jesus Christ. This is noteworthy for me because what I learned from St. Ignatius in the context of the Spiritual Exercise, Farley demonstrates in her Christology.[16]

A Liberating Theology, a Liberated Christology

Gathering Those Driven Away shows how Scripture and the writings of the Early Church Fathers and of great Christian mystics and theologians can help us come to know the God about whom they write and recognize this God as the one for whom our own hearts long and yearn. These works can teach us not only a theological language in order to deploy this in theological discourse, but also to discover the liberating God that they describe. I would like to highlight three elements of Farley's Christology that highlight the theme of liberation. First, I draw attention to her critique of the use of power in the construction of traditional dogma. Second, I note the importance of non-duality and apophasis in transcending the limiting nature of much God-talk. Finally, I look at

15. It is interesting to note the role of his personal encounter with God in the construction of the Spiritual Exercises. At the same time, the preaching and teaching that flowed from this encounter with Divine Love also led him into conflict with the authorities of the Catholic Church in his time. See for example, Modras, *Ignatian Humanism*, 18–22, and Ignatius of Loyola, "Autobiography," 91–99.

16. I was struck by the similarity of the use of "hygiene" in Farley and of "exercises" for Ignatius. In both cases, there is something to be gained by repetition, by the practices of contemplation, of putting oneself intentionally in the presence of Mystery.

the affective impact of considering the incarnation not in terms of the *Logos* but of *Sophia,* of particular significance for me as a woman who has unconsciously experienced marginalization by the concealment of the feminine in traditional teaching around the incarnation of the *Logos* into a male body.

To bring to light the role of power in the construction of orthodoxy and still be able to close with an embrace of the fullness of the divinity and humanity of Christ is a mark of integrity and confidence in the truth of the incarnation of Divine Wisdom. And what more powerful way to pull the rug out from arrogant dogmatism than to bring to light the ignoble political underpinnings of even the most sacredly held doctrine of the church? To be reminded of the history of a church composed of those who are excluded emerging as ones that exclude, not by the light of Wisdom but by the exercise of political cunning, casts doubt on the theological confidence with which many of its members continue to condemn and exclude today. The focus on the theological justification for declaring the likes of Arius heretics fails to accurately tell the story of the role of power in the church. Political expediency is given priority over trust in God and is done in a covert manner. This very temptation marked the history of Israel and the history of the church. Recall Isaiah inviting King Ahaz of Israel to trust God rather than political expediency to protect the sovereignty of Israel in the face of a Judah and Assyria alliance (Isaiah 7-8). The story has been and seems to continue to be one of an inability to trust God to preserve that which God has desired to bring into being. This lack of trust gives way to human cunning. History suggests that religious leaders repeatedly find it easier to rely on human ingenuity even when what is produced runs contrary to what they have come to know about God in their history as a people. Pope Francis describes how "the Church can become a museum piece or the possession of a select few . . . when some groups of Christians give excessive importance to certain rules, customs or ways of acting. The Gospel then tends to be reduced and constricted, deprived of its simplicity, allure and savor."[17] Often these "certain rules, customs or ways of acting" become efforts to defend constructions in the name of preserving the Gospel but in a manner that makes the reality of Divine Eros hard to believe. Who is this God that so desperately needs to be defended through the distortion of God's message?

17. Pope Francis, *Gaudete et Exsultate,* par. 58.

To expose the misuse of power in the construction not only of theology but even of firmly held doctrines requires confidence in the truth and fidelity of God. It requires confident faith that this God survives human insecurity and uncertainty. But such a profound trust in God is possible only with personal knowledge of God. Farley shows her readers the dangers of dualistic, ego-conscious thinking and language that not only leaves out the mystery of God but claims to capture God in nice, neat human categories. I cannot help but imagine her as a person who knows this God intimately. Through the journey of reading her work, I recognize the truth of what she describes and the incapacity to wrap my mind around it. But how can I expect to be able to capture in a neat conceptual package the product of the contemplation of the Divine Abyss that is both plentitude and emptiness all at once. After all, the dynamic of an encounter with Divine Wisdom, while the most real and deepest of encounters, is that which can least be captured in propositions without distortion. Only poetic rendering of the experience, which is how the prose of the book reads, can begin to communicate the incommunicable. And yet, because it is ultimately such an encounter with God that makes it possible for these words to ring true in the ears of hearers, it is through contemplation, through instructing her readers about the path that opens to an expansive God, that she prepares them for understanding her theology of the incarnation. She asserts the importance of the cultivation of a life of prayer, of contemplation, no matter how imperfect and seemingly inadequate. To grow in awareness of being in the presence of Divine Love is important for doing theology. Only a non-dual, what I would term mystical, knowledge or experience of God and the necessity of apophasis in the midst of this can lead to speaking about God with the humility and reverence that must flow from recognizing oneself as being enfolded in Divine Love.

By emphasizing non-duality and apophasis, Farley invites readers to recognize that the one about whom the rest of the book will speak is more than what the words will communicate. At the same time, this one permeates human experience. The inadequacy of words and of theology becomes clear in this profound theological treatise and yet it successfully uses words to make the incarnation meaningful and enmeshed in daily life. The reminder and invitation to move away from dualistic thinking, she suggests, is at the beginning of being able to understand the incarnation. I first began to understand in the context of prayer that such thinking is often born of judgment and division both within oneself and in our relationships.

She frees herself from the bonds of a narrow understanding of the tradition precisely by retrieving the forgotten elements of the tradition. The first three of the ten commands are not read as descriptions of a narrow allowable way of relating to God but as cautions against efforts to restrict God. The construction of images and graven idols are attempts to limit how God relates to humanity, something that those who are most eager to defend God often do. The invitation is to transcend the dualistic discursive thinking that characterizes much God-talk. Instead, she points to the way of non-duality and apophasis in any attempt to speak about the "Great Abyss." But can one come to recognize the revelatory potential of non-duality and the necessity of apophasis apart from an encounter with God that obviates the limits of all efforts to talk about God and to encounter God? She finds echoes of Hinduism and Buddhism in the wisdom of the Christian mystical tradition from which she draws. In her case, she travels through the path of non-duality and apophasis in order to construct a theology of the incarnation. The theologian can be trapped in the field of the conceptual if she hears the tradition without coming to know Divine Eros. To study the Christian tradition without being rooted in the "hygiene" of placing oneself before Wisdom and attending to her can serve to bind rather than to free. And ironically, the freedom that leads to what I would describe as a reverent Christology also enables her to recognize the Christ that is present beyond Jesus of Nazareth. The expansive God made known through Jesus Christ described in this book I came to know and continue to know not primarily through academic training but through spiritual practice.

The critique of dualistic thinking about God found in this work is not harsh and angry but corrective. The aims seems to be so that the reader becomes open to the possibility of recognizing the entrance of Divinity in the midst of humanity through all that has come into being through Divine Wisdom and in Jesus of Nazareth in a unique way. Farley is able to simultaneously hold the uniqueness of the person and natures of Jesus Christ that is found in the tradition and hold as firmly onto an expansive God whose love and truth exists beyond the limits of Jesus of Nazareth and the Christian Church. When she declares that Divine Wisdom is active and present in places outside the church just as truly as she became incarnate in the man of Galilee, she does not need to affirm— as my tradition does—that Wisdom is somehow *more* present and *more* fully understood in the Church. Only a person confident in the love of her God could so firmly embrace the idea that God loves all just as fully and passionately. And so, I am convinced that her theology of the incarnation is more than the product of good scholarship; it is the product of a life of faith, shaped by contemplation of Divine Love. It is the product of one who has encountered God and allowed herself to be taught by God.

Finally, the affective impact of a meditation on the incarnation as the incarnation of Divine Wisdom is powerful. She brings the feminine into the conception of the incarnation of God in a male form by focusing not on Logos but Sophia. And in this one move, Farley brings to light how a purely male conception of the incarnation can stand in the way of fully receiving the good news of the divine in me as a woman. That *she* became a man can enable women to see themselves as fuller participants in the possibilities opened up by the incarnation. That the incarnation does not just happen in a man or in men, that it happens in us, in others around us, and in all of creation when grasped with more than my conceptual mind, can liberate. Wisdom, God as *logos*, while entering the world in a unique way in the person of Jesus, is present in all that is created through *Sophia*, and She continues to be in the world, in all of creation, which is once again recognized to be sacred. How does Farley capture so well the mystical experience of Teilhard that enabled him to see the world permeated with spirit from its beginning and in all its parts? Can it be because she has seen the same God? And while Teilhard was silenced by his Church for his profound insight, Farley echoes over and over the words of the creed, with its meaning and consequence coming to full light in her high Christology.

Who is this personified Wisdom and what do we learn from looking at the life of Jesus of Nazareth? Wisdom is personified not only in this one man, although there is uniqueness in this personification. She is present to and in all of broken humanity and wounded creation. And the idea of savior once again becomes meaningful as Farley reminds us of how Wisdom enters into the suffering of our world and how suffering occurs not only because of the cruelty of a world that often fails to see the humanity of human beings and the sacredness of all creation, but also because of the failure to recognize our divinity. And as she constructs her theology of the incarnation, she continues to reveal the expansiveness and the depth of the love of Divine Eros, of Wisdom about whom she speaks. She calls on and calls out the tradition and does it with such dexterity and confidence because she knows of what she speaks.

Conclusion

I had always hoped that theology could be done in a way that comes out of life experiences as an expression of the encounter with the divine and echoes the wisdom of those in the tradition whose theology is an attempt to do the same. And maybe at some point I knew that it could. But somewhere along the way, I was so consumed by the need to get it right, I could not trust that what I came to know in my life of prayer could become the foundation for a solidly grounded, truth-bearing and not just ideas-bearing theology. I continue to hear inner voices reminding of the limits that are set on me by my tradition and my role as a Catholic theologian in a Catholic institution.[18] But this work invites me to trust the voice of Divine Wisdom encouraging the attempt to bring to expression the encounter with Divine Love, an encounter that takes place within the complexities of the world and the ambiguity of the church and academy.

In reading the book, I did not anticipate to be moved both intellectually and spiritually, that my deepest knowing about the expansiveness and depth of God's love could be held together with faith in Jesus of Nazareth as the unique incarnation of Love. What we need more than orthodoxy, "correct method," or the "right language" in doing theology is an encounter with the Divine. We need to trust that encounter and the powerful knowledge that flows from it, that the world is permeated with the presence of the God of love. At the same time, it is precisely the rootedness in an encounter with Divine Eros that gives birth to the right language. After all, did not Jesus say, "I will give you the words to speak." This work is not primarily about what others have said about Jesus, even as it draws from the words and wisdom of tradition. I am persuaded that this work is about the God whom the author has come to know through the encounter of Divine Wisdom incarnate in Jesus Christ. It is about Divine Wisdom in the flesh of the man with the long chain and the woman living an empty life of affluence. It is about the God of love present in the world's beauty and its brokenness. Farley's rootedness in and knowledge

18. Schneiders notes that theology until the Higher Middle ages was understood as "faith seeking understanding" and "understanding seeking transformation, transformation of self and world in God," where "the theologian was defined as the one who prayed truly." "[T]heology *was* spirituality understood not as an academic discipline but as living faith seeking understanding for the purpose of transformation in Christ." She argues that this definition of theology is something that may no longer be possible in a post-Enlightenment world of excessive fragmentation. "The Discipline of Spirituality and Catholic Theology," 199–200.

of the tradition is inspiring because it allows her the freedom to both critique and draw deeply from it to express the wisdom that she herself has found. This work is a faithful love letter to God written in the midst of pain. This is theology.

Bibliography

Ashley, J. Matthew. "The Turn to Spirituality? The Relationship between Theology and Spirituality." In *Minding the Spirit: The Study of Christian Spirituality*, edited by Elizabeth A. Dreyer and Mark S. Burrow, 159–170. Baltimore: John Hopkins University Press, 2005.

Coutinho, Paul. *How Big Is Your God?: The Freedom to Experience the Divine*. Chicago: Loyola Press, 2007.

Farley, Wendy. *Gathering Those Driven Away*. Louisville: Westminster John Knox, 2011.

Francis. *Gaudete et Exsultate*. Vatican City: Vatican Press, 2018.

Gutiérrez, Gustavo. *A Theology of Liberation: History, Politics and Salvation*. Maryknoll, NY: Orbis, 1988.

———. *Essential Writings*, edited by James B. Nickoloff. Maryknoll, NY: Orbis, 1996.

———. *On Job: God-Talk and the Suffering of the Innocent*. Maryknoll, NY: Orbis, 1987.

Ignatius of Loyola, "Autobiography." In *Ignatius of Loyola*, edited by George E. Ganss, translated by Parmananda R. Divarkar, 65–112. Mahwah, NJ: Paulist, 1991.

Modras, Ronald. *Ignatian Humanism: A Dynamic Spirituality for the 21st Century*. Chicago: Loyola Press, 2004.

Schneiders, Sandra M. "The Discipline of Christian Spirituality and Catholic Theology." In *Exploring Christian Spirituality: Essay in Honor of Sandra M. Schneiders, IHM*, edited by Bruce H. Lescher and Elizabeth Liebert, 196–212. Mahwah, NJ: Paulist, 2006.

Sheldrake, Philip. *Spirituality and Theology: Christian Living and the Doctrine of God*. Maryknoll, NY: Orbis, 1998.

Teilhard de Chardin. *Hymn of the Universe*. New York: Harper & Row, 1965.

ELEVEN

Recovering Care: A Conversation with Wendy Farley's Incarnational Approach to Being Together in Community

Thomas E. Reynolds

"We have gifts that differ according to the grace given to us."
(Romans 12:6)

IN JOURNEYING WITH MY son, who is diagnosed on the autism spectrum, "inclusion" has been a buzzword. It is commonly held up as an ideal by and for people with disabilities in efforts to create accessible communities. However, there are ways it can be problematic. While used to indicate practices aimed at welcoming people with disabilities into communal life as full participants, inclusion can instead entail representing difference as deviant and other, and in fact names kinds of difference as "outside" and thus anomalous, an "other" to be brought into a privileged "inside" that functions normatively as "us." As Miroslav Volf bluntly puts it, inclusion "implicitly portrays 'them' as the kind of people 'we' are not."[1] Sara Ahmed goes further, claiming that inclusion often functions as a "technology of governance" that makes "strangers into subjects, those who in being included are also willing to consent to the terms of inclusion." She notes how to be included is really "a way of sustaining and reproducing a politics of exclusion," differences made to deny themselves in order to be

1. Volf, *Exclusion and Embrace*, 58.

an acceptable part of the inside, managed by a sovereign center.[2] People with disabilities are often subject to such mechanisms. I have witnessed this in advocating with my son, and also fallen into such "inclusive" practices in parenting, despite my better desires.

In religious communities and society, inclusion can be reflected in different registers, such as tolerance, normalizing gestures of assimilation, and diluted forms of hospitality. First, with tolerance, different bodies are given minimal access and "put up with" in terms that condescend and guarantee the safety of the status quo by keeping the dominant system intact. Tolerance permits deviation, but seeks to control deviation by distancing it from an established center of power as something that remains "outside" and unable to fully participate (e.g., tolerating noises by disabled people in church, but considering them disruptive instead of communicative). Second, with normalizing gestures of assimilation, different bodies are accommodated but only insofar as they are remade and fixed/cured to reflect the normative "inside" as they gain access to participation (e.g., "taken care of" paternalistically to restrain otherwise unruly bodies or "restore" faulted bodies via curative and healing measures). Here also, romanticized notions of disability as "special" or "gifted" can become ways that non-disabled people project their own need to remake disability into a palatable and meaningful event, an ironic display of assimilative powers. Lastly, hospitality itself can be a false pretense reifying a binary between guest and host, the "host" retaining mastery of the home and the "guest" rendered dependent by receiving gifts of welcome: the home fully under the control of the host, the guest becoming a passive recipient of piecemeal acts of charity. All three of these modalities of inclusion manifest what political philosopher Iris Marion Young calls the "logic of identity," which, in an effort to provide unity and coherence to a community, either reduces differences to the same via management and control, or rejects differences as deviant and utterly other.[3] The effect is that, in the name of care and doing good, inclusion can marginalize, alienate, and harm.

Correctives to these problematic forms of inclusion depend upon several features: upon being noticed, valued, respected, and invited, upon accessibility as a co-creative community affair, and upon hospitable companionship. However, I want to push further and note how half-hearted

2. Ahmed, *On Being Included*, 163.

3. Young, *Justice and the Politics of Difference*, 98–99.

even these features can be if not grounded intentionally in genuinely *caring practices and values*. Practices of inclusion and access and hospitality are not one-time achievements, neither the first step nor the last step toward right relations with people with disabilities. Rather, they are parts of an ongoing—and never completed—process aimed at the full participation of all in sharing life together. They presume attentiveness and openness to people, a responsiveness that does not merely "allow for" participation but actively invites and empowers it in relationships of mutual giving and receiving. Robust inclusivity is only possible via ongoing invitation, access, and hospitality, and these are features of *caring* communities. Caring communities exhibit a form of togetherness within which people share in life together, bearing witness to one another with an attentive regard that is both compassionate and respectful in character. This threads the fabric of a shared experience of belonging, by which all become parts of one another in and through their differences, indeed, to the degree that there is longing for each other when some are absent.

In moving further to develop an understanding of care, there are rich resonances in Wendy Farley's work that can open up theological possibilities for reimagining and recovering care as an eros-filled feature of human togetherness. Care is a fundamental gesture that cannot help but "bear witness to a power that is stronger than what binds us" and what separates us.[4] The gospel testifies to such a power. Yet, in Farley's words, this "gospel does not remove us from the violence of the world or neutralize the lies it tells about us." Instead, holding us close with caring attentiveness, such power "listens to our pain and believes our stories. It tells us we are beloved and that we are essential to the story of Divine Eros."[5] In this way, bearing witness to the despised, rejected, and brokenhearted is fundamental to the gospel as good news, that story of being "knit and oned to God" and being "kept luminous and noble as when created."[6] And it is fundamental to becoming communities of care, communities in which relationships of mutual respect and reciprocity flourish in dynamic gestures of gift giving and receiving among all as partners and contributors. Care emerges within the envelope of desire for healing relation and connection with others, a desire that itself testifies to a goodness untrammeled by what harms and undoes life, that is deeper than our

4. Farley, *The Wounding and Healing of Desire*, xiii.

5. Farley, *Gathering Those Driven Away*, 5.

6. Julian of Norwich, *Showings*, quoted in Farley, *The Wounding and Healing of Desire*, 19.

scars and stronger than what binds us to a broken past, and that is wider in its stretch than the insidious exclusions and tepid inclusions that fetter human communities. It opens to the holiness of life together, to God.

In what follows, I want to explore themes of care as both a way to highlight creative insights from Farley and a means of developing a theological vision of care as a modality of witness that cultivates attentiveness, opens accessibility, and offers hospitable companionship as an embodied desire to be-with others within the arc of divine love. The goal of this essay is modest: it does not seek to produce any complete horizon of thinking, but rather outlines possibilities for recovering care, filling in details along the way with brief brush strokes. The hope is to evoke a sense that care is a response—an address—to and with one another that reaches passionately toward relational wholeness, and in so doing embodies divine Eros.

Toward Caring Together

I wish to begin somewhat counterintuitively by suggesting that the famous aphorism of pre-Socratic philosopher Empedocles is accurate—namely, that "like attracts like." It seems counterintuitive because a preoccupation with its own "likeness" is precisely what leads a community to exclude others who are "different" in so many cases. Farley speaks of the "rhetoric of binary opposition" that works its wiles here in Christian traditions, which creates "unity" via strategies asserting doctrinal "orthodoxy" against differences deemed heretical, and by moralistic appeals to "virtue" against differences deemed "sinful."[7] Others are driven away and excluded on behalf of a tribal god whose name has been identified with the likeness of a normate "us." Idolatry and its violence prevail. The insidious "we" of group identity looms large over many aspects of human life, including matters of disability and mental health. "We" tend to accept and care for those somehow like "us," relating most comfortably with those with whom something is shared according to standards of normalcy, drawing together around that common flame as distinct and separate from "them."

But what if "like" can be reconsidered beyond horizons of sameness, beyond assimilating to become "like us" or mainstreamed to function "normally," or even "included" through benevolent but paternalistic

7. Farley, *Gathering Those Driven Away*, 26–31.

gestures of "granting" space for allegedly "weaker" members, the "others"? What if "like" comes not from what we possess—as something given in advance and managed as property—but from divine Eros, which rises and refreshes itself in relationships as a grace both received and pursued, a communion that is not an identity of sameness but a web of together- ness and connection created in the sharing of differences as gifts?

Through the experience of parenting with my son, I have come to believe it is not possible even to begin imagining what such a web of connection means without reconsidering the moral postures and prac- tices that make fruitful life together possible. The term *care* thus seems appropriate, on many levels and in many registers, to speak of gift giv- ing and receiving. Here, it is important to build on the work done by Nel Noddings, Joan Tronto, and Virginia Held,[8] among others, who seek in feminist terms to imagine an "ethic of care." This has helped me to imagine wider ways of thinking about my relationship with my son, as an advocate and supposed care "giver." And in fact, it has made me painfully aware of how often care is distorted and malformed, both in my own actions and within the caring communities around me, particularly faith communities. Hence, I am interested in reimagining and "recovering" care as an essential way of being human together, and more, as part of what it means to be a vulnerable communion called church, the Body of Christ.

To be a caring community is to be an emblem of God's loving pres- ence in the world, giving and receiving as a people invested in each other as gifts of God. This is incarnational: it embodies divine care, renouncing the sovereign logic of unity and taking on fleshly multiplicity in beloved differences.[9] Drawing on Nicholas of Cusa, Farley stretches the implica- tions of incarnation here beautifully as both a metaphysic and a practice, suggesting that divine presence in Christ liberates us to bear witness to the face of Christ in the world. The face of Christ appears in another human face, and as I bear witness to this, I am brought into the arc of divine love shining through all and at the same time shining in each as if only through that particular form.[10] Divine care infinitely values the particular and radiates through its difference. And it rises and makes us "one flesh" with each other through the prism of incarnational love. Such

8. Noddings, *Caring*; Tronto, *Moral Boundaries*; and Held, *The Ethics of Care*.

9. See Schneider, *Beyond Monotheism*, 197.

10. Farley, *Gathering of Those Driven Away*, 180-183.

love is refracted transformatively through Christ, as the power of divine Eros, to loosen what holds us in bondage and open up what closes us off from embracing the image of God in each other and ourselves.[11] Farley elegantly sums it up:

> It is not the way of Divine Eros to despise what She has made. Becoming enfleshed, Christ reveals the sanctity of our own flesh. This sanctity is not something that is accomplished by way of perfection but is present precisely in the form of our existence: luminous, wounded, and infinitely diverse.[12]

In divine grace, differences reveal sacredness at the heart of all, the destitute and outcast gathered in as beloved. The community that lives in the space created by this momentum is one characterized by care. This is a community that risks struggle and care-fully holds pain as part of its sacred togetherness.

Creating Space for Care

Recovering care as a concrete value and practice, however, requires clearing a lot of ground. For the word has been used in unhelpful ways that flatten, distort, and even pervert a more textured meaning. Farley helps us proceed in her first book, *Tragic Vision and Divine Compassion*, by noting that caring for another's well-being is an intrinsic feature of love: "Love is the capacity to care for and enjoy the other; it is desire that has been freed from egocentricity."[13] This helps set up certain criteria for discernment in weeding out problematic conceptions.

First, care has often been imposed as a duty requiring self-immolating service to others. It is a distortion to suppose that when caring for another, one looks after, protects, and provides for another without regard to one's own welfare. This has been especially problematic for women, historically pressed into domestic labor as mothers caring for children and homemakers charged with providing hospitality.[14] But masochistic self-denial is not the stuff of "enjoying the other," which Farley rightly takes as essential to love. Desire unfettered by egocentricity is not self-effacing to the point of indifference or suffering. Rather, it is care, a

---

11. Farley, *The Wounding and Healing of Desire*, 100–106.

12. Farley, *The Wounding and Healing of Desire*, 104.

13. Farley, *Tragic Vision and Divine Compassion*, 77.

14. See Farley, *The Wounding and Healing of Desire*, 81-85.

desire for another's happiness that delights in and is emboldened by the good of another and their flourishing. Care in this way can be courageous and risk harm, not out of duty, but out of deep concern that passionately identifies with the preciousness of persons. And this opens the capacity for self-transcending postures of loving-kindness and compassion.[15] Put in negative terms, the absence of care—carelessness—can then be understood in terms of being insensitive or indifferent, as if one is not invested in something or someone enough to pay attention and find value. Much of what passes for love is careless.

Indeed, contrary to many traditional renderings, the commandment of Jesus to "love your neighbor as yourself" entails neither duty-bound nor self-sacrificial giving to another for their good with no thought of return. Rather, it seems to grant that a certain measure of love for oneself is an acceptable activity; the phrase does not say to love your neighbor instead of or against yourself. Of course, unfortunately, there are myriad theological resources for a self-sacrificial approach, such as notions of redemptive suffering that use "the way of the cross" as a prototype for love, valorizing deprivation and baptizing oppression.[16] Farley adds her voice to the growing chorus of theologians who see the damage this can cause, noting also how conceptions of original sin and substitutionary atonement truncate theological vision and foster harmful practices.[17] If the "love commandment" of Jesus means neither self-indulgent love (which would erase the other as instrument of self) nor complete self-denying or self-less love (which would erase the self as an instrument of another), the word "care" may be an instructive way of naming what is going on here.[18] It clears space for a middle ground, for conceptions of mutuality in relationships of giving and receiving and, in fact, can be an important qualifier to love, steering away from approaches that too quickly expend the self and obscure the crucial role of the passions in empowering care. Care delights and finds joy in the other, which expands the self, not constricts it. And, as Farley notes, it is easy to miss this and mistake obligation and guilt feelings for real love when desires are squelched, joy

---

15. Farley, *The Wounding and Healing of Desire*, 77–78.

16. For only several examples, Soelle, *Suffering*; Brock, *Journeys by Heart*; Ray, *Deceiving the Devil*; and Brock and Parker, *Proverbs of Ashes*.

17. See Farley, *Gathering Those Driven Away*, 31–35, 157–59.

18. For a good argument for this point, see Wolterstorff, *Justice in Love*, chapter 9.

depleted, and delight denied, held captive by oppressive powers or by excessive demands.[19]

If we take this seriously, moving the discussion forward, it becomes clearer that care cannot be reduced simply to the activity of serving others. First, it is not what "experts" or professionals do, providing a service for consumption. Neither, second, is it solely what is imagined to happen in the many kinds of care-giving roles we find ourselves in throughout our lives, where "taking care of" another becomes central—like infants or elderly parents, or as with my son—by providing for them in ways they are unable to do for themselves. In both cases, care involves administering or managing some form of beneficial assistance to another. But reduced to these modalities, care becomes a commodity, something packaged and reproducible, performed or delivered on call, as a service. It is no accident, then, that care is commonly referenced on the personal level as a "duty" (e.g., often a gendered, organized, managed, and administered social imaginary for women). And it is no accident that in bureaucratic contexts care is referenced in terms of an "industry," an organized complex of service delivery governed according to criteria of efficiency and productivity (e.g., the health care industry, managed care, or customer care). With these approaches, care is readily thinned out to an interest-driven economy of exchange, as if care is a "doing for," a technique or set of technologies oriented toward performance, which presumes knowledge, power, and privilege over another from a position of control and mastery. Care here can lose relational openness or vulnerability to another, as the one cared for remains a passive recipient (a patient) undergoing a process "done to" them. In fact, there is a potentially delusional "rightness" on the part of the caregiver, whose agenda "knows better," based in either expertise or experience.

A similar dynamic occurs in other, perhaps less calculative and exchange-driven instances when care becomes a matter of serving with "good intentions." Especially in faith communities, care is often seen as an activity that distributes goods aimed at benefiting others. While this may not be intrinsically harmful, the arc of the dynamic can easily slip into a condescending, benevolent paternalism. Care here becomes a "charity" handed out from a distance, from a nonreflexive and detached privilege that can mask self-preoccupation and unjust power relations. Such care displays its shallow affective demeanor when it appears as pity,

19. Farley, *The Wounding and Healing of Desire*, 86.

which perhaps desires passionate connection with another but operates instead from a condescending posture of self-protection. And as noted above with care in the theological shape of "disinterested benevolence" or *agape*, care not only can become masochistic self-denial but also ironically heartless, dispassionate, and uninterested in the genuine good of another, pretending to "know better" for another (e.g., not only burning heretics for their own good, but also institutionalizing people with disabilities for their own good) or strategically seeking to implement agendas occupied more with serving self or the status quo than the good of another (e.g., placing Indigenous children in residential schools to facilitate assimilation into North American society).

The above examples illustrate how easily care can be distorted and malformed, and in the name of doing good. Something is missing when care becomes (1) service deliverance tantamount to "doing for" and/or (2) a "know-how" with strategic aims, a technique or technology. As Farley suggests above, care is a feature of love as self-transcending delight: it (1) desires and attends to the preciousness and giftedness of others, (2) in a way that moves beyond the orbit of self-preoccupation and the logic of interest-driven economies of exchange. Instead, there is an opening toward relational mutuality and reciprocity. Care is truncated and malformed when mutuality is denied.[20] In the fullest sense, care flowers in interdependent relationships of vulnerable giving and receiving.

Becoming Care-Full

The perils and promises described above are especially real to me as a parent. Being in relationship with my son has taught me that caring is not merely a matter of "helping," of giving from a position of strength, but of recognizing vulnerability and becoming open to the ways I receive from others. Others—in ways that include "disabilities"—become essential not only to my own flourishing but also to the common good of the communities in which I flourish together with my son. This cultivates the power of giving through first receiving, receiving from him. Attending to his voice and life rhythm has summoned a much richer way of caring than would be possible on terms dictated by preplanned strategies for assistance developed out of my own agendas based on expectations of what

20. See Steinhoff Smith, *The Mutuality of Care*, especially chapters 2, 3, 7; and Nothwehr, *Mutuality*.

"parenting" means, especially gendered notions of "fatherhood." While matters of disability and mental illness loom large in my own experience, prompting me to reassess what care really means, the dynamic here opens up wider vistas for reconsidering care in relation to many shapes of human vulnerability and suffering.

The term *care* seems appropriate, on many levels and in many registers, to speak of this kind of gift giving and receiving. It is inherent in the way we find ourselves among others. There is care in all kinds of relationships (among family, friends, colleagues, lovers, etc.); it is defined by a range of social domains (in institutions, communities, small group, face-to-face, and for oneself); and it is active in various modes (as supervisor, employee, friend, child, student, spouse, counselor, pastor, etc.), the natures of which shift and change from context to context, conditioned by social and cultural frames of reference.

Throughout each level and register, however, there exists a basic pattern of care as both a *practice* and *value*.[21] As a practice, care is an action or gesture oriented toward the well-being of persons. This is usually what is meant by "caring for" others or oneself. There is an availing of oneself, an expenditure of energy, for the benefit of someone or some group, providing something that is considered good by the ones cared for or by a relevant advocate. The good of another for their own sake is the object of care. This is important, for it implies a relational correlation that depends upon a connection of trust between parties. Issues of justice and equity, then, are intrinsic to practices of care. For care mediates to another their worth and integrity, presuming a covenantal relation. The act of caring is never merely one-way. There is an exchange, which can be exploitative and unjust if the creaturely personhood and worth of another is overlooked or mistreated. This is why care also involves value.

Care is not merely a practice; it is also a moral posture and value, a disposition indexed by attentiveness and responsiveness to others that issues in a concern for their good. If the object of care is the good of the other, then its subject is passionate concern for the other, wherein one's own happiness connects with the happiness of another. This gets to the meaning of "caring about" someone. To care is to desire and be personally invested in another within what Martin Buber calls a "dialogical situation"—not that literal "dialogue" is necessary, but rather that a *communication of presence* is at play. This involves sharing space in some

21. See Held, *The Ethics of Care*, chapter 2; and Tronto, *Moral Boundaries*. This dual aspect of care is frequently highlighted in feminist ethics of care literature.

way—through body gestures, touch, listening, speaking, etc.—so that a connective reciprocity emerges. The face-to-face context is fundamental, in which a reciprocal validation emerges that expresses that each matters to the other, even if one party does not reciprocate in kind. And, agreeing with Farley, using the language "eros" conveys such connectivity with poetic power.[22] Eros is the creative power of self-transcending delight in being with another, which means interdependency and mutual vulnerability in an exchange of presence.[23] Eros is "rooted in joy" and "aroused by that which is intrinsically valuable and which always eludes totalization."[24] Another's preciousness evokes desire, but their worth and dignity call for a respect that resists both dismissal and assimilation. As a value, care involves a sympathetic apprehension of another's presence, such that one's own being is affectively aligned with the other's in compassion.[25]

As both practice and value, then, care is much more than a "doing for." It is, most profoundly, a being-with that rises through mutual vulnerability in connections of giving and receiving. Indeed, we only respond with care by first having received the presence of another, having been summoned into attentiveness and concern through a kind of call that enlivens response-ability. Arthur Frank suggests that care "is an occasion when people discover what each can be in relationship with the other."[26] And this happens in diverse ways. But in each, caring is something learned from each other, from listening to what is being communicated in a given instance, from receiving a specific summons for a particular kind of responsiveness, which requires sympathetic attentiveness. Openness to the other is elemental. Until one can accurately imagine what another is imagining of one's care, genuine mutuality has yet to emerge. Care does not simply remove burdens, but empowers by cultivating a wholeness that is relational. And empowerment in this sense comes from more than individual actions distributed to others deemed in need, but rather from trust and the growth of shared interest in mutual well-being between carer and cared-for.[27] We come to "take care." Susan

22. For a moving account of eros see Carson, *Eros the Bittersweet.*

23. See Farley, *Tragic Vision and Divine Compassion,* 76–78; *Eros for the Other,* chapter 3; and *The Wounding and Healing of Desire,* 13–16, 101–6.

24. Farley, *Eros for the Other,* 69.

25. On sympathetic relation and compassion, see Farley, *Tragic Vision and Divine Compassion,* 70–81.

26. Frank, *The Renewal of Generosity,* 4.

27. Held, *The Ethics of Care,* 35.

Parsons describes "taking care" as a way of understanding self and others not as accidentally related, self-sufficient individuals, but as woven into a web of relationships that requires keeping them steady and flexible enough to sustain well-being.[28] Care's most focused instance occurs in a face-to-face communication of presence that attends to the well-being of persons. But it extends from here to include all we do "to maintain, continue, and repair our 'world' so that we can live in it as well as possible."[29] It involves creating just conditions for mutuality. And as Virgina Held reminds us, there "can be no justice without care."[30]

Resonant with Farley's way of joining compassion and respect, Catholic ethicist Margaret Farley's (no relation) term "compassionate respect" can help us unpack the moral features of care's communication of presence.[31] Compassionate respect is a way of focusing attention on human vulnerability as a precious gift of God. Ethical implications arise in that care presumes the creaturely worth of persons, such that another's imperilment summons responsiveness that identifies with another sympathetically while also respecting their unique value. Care desires another's worth to be safeguarded. And when such worth is imperiled by suffering or injustice, care responds, seeking to provide for and protect. Wendy Farley puts it eloquently:

> To receive compassion is to receive respect. Compassion as a form of love includes a recognition of the value and beauty of others. Far from insulting the sufferer with gratuitous pity, it mediates to the other a sense of her own integrity . . . Compassion identifies suffering as an affront to this integrity, as an anomaly that threatens and defaces the sufferer.[32]

Pushing further, we might say that care, as compassionate respect, honors persons by paying attention to both equality and difference. That is, it treats someone as equal without therefore being made over and assimilated into the image of a normate center of power (which effectively erases difference) and as different without therefore being dismissed or marginalized as "deviant" and "abnormal" (effectively denying equality).

---

28. Parsons, "Redeeming Ethics," 212.

29. Fisher and Tronto, "Toward a Feminist Theory of Caring," 36–54.

30. Held, *The Ethics of Care*, 17.

31. M. Farley, *Compassionate Respect*.

32. Farley, *Tragic Vision and Divine Compassion*, 79.

Care, then, becomes fundamental to conditions of justice and right relationships.

With this mind, it is possible to move beyond Young's "logic of identity," discussed in the opening pages of this essay, to see that receiving others in compassionate respect is a genuine practice of hospitality. Such care-full hospitality entails no inside/outside binary, but rather a kind of circular gathering into which each guest is invited as hosts to one another, joined in relationships of mutual partnership and giving and receiving rather than dependent relationships of unilateral caring giving.[33] An attentive practice of caring listens and receives, letting-be the speaking voice of another and hearing how they perceive. In this way, the margins and the center, the guest and host, each circulates and shifts among the other, distinctions blurred. The listener comes to confront the biases, false assumptions, and unequal power quotients that obscure encountering the vulnerable difference of another. Furthermore, the listener responds, adjusting to the way of another by entering into their story. And the speaking voice of another grows into itself and gains dignity by being heard, respected, and accommodated. The dynamic shifts, then, as each trades roles and becomes an "other" for and with the other in an ongoing exchange of mutual welcome. Communities of genuine companionship and partnership are built upon this transformational process. And such companionship also entails a commitment to justice work confronting enduring systems of inequitable power relations, as vulnerability is not parceled out equally. But while care is basic to justice, norms of fairness and equity cannot do the work of empowering care, of appreciating and delighting in differences. Something more is needed.

Taking Care: Disability, Difference, and Provocation

I want now to build upon this discussion and speak of recovering care as a way of being open to difference in the form of disability—that is, more readily disposed to engage in relations of mutual welcoming and ongoing accommodation. But it is crucial to be "care-full" when speaking about care and engaging in caring relations with persons with disabilities. First, non-reciprocal modes of care as charity and/or service should be challenged. This, second, entails moving beyond ideals of inclusion and instead toward co-creative processes of collaboration and interdependence.

33. See Russell, *Just Hospitality*.

Part of this means moving beyond a discourse of what we "owe" each other by right, as a minimalist way of relating to ensure justice as sameness—i.e., equality before the law. Equality can lump all bodies together in a way that denies the diversity of disability experience. Thus, finally, it means paying attention to that which is different, bearing witness, and receiving its provocation as an invocation to care. It is within connections of care—shaped by the dynamic interdependencies of offering and receiving gifts of presence—that trust and covenantal commitments to an ongoing togetherness are fostered. But such togetherness is not possible without difference.

So rather than focus on what about people with disabilities "deserves" inclusion as a quality of likeness or sameness shared by non-disabled and disabled persons alike—i.e., a fundamental humanity, imago Dei, personhood, etc.—I want to focus on difference as something that interrupts sameness, that provokes and disturbs. This may seem an odd choice, for certainly I do not mean to deny the importance of imago Dei and personhood. Rather, my hope is that taking this different approach will bear fruit and something of the Spirit (Gal. 5:22) as a way of engaging with Farley's vision of incarnation as erotic connectivity.

Indeed, the togetherness of church, as the body of Christ, is a gift of the Spirit that trades upon bearing witness to differences and in fact holds differences as gifts of grace. Yet, as the earliest Christian communities knew, such grace is not an achievement but a discovery, and it comes through the practice of opening thresholds provoked into conversion, into transformation, through an invocation or calling. Invocation into what? One reading of the New Testament is that Christians are called into a "vulnerable communion," summoned to be a church not ordered by human achievements measured according to standards meted out by normalcy, but as a gift received, an aftereffect of welcoming differences in caring relations as God loves the world. Farley suggests that it "is precisely as beautifully diverse bodies that we share divinity." She continues: "We don't need to be saved from the form of human we embody. This is how Divinity plays itself: in the infinite plurality of particular forms."[34] What is shared together is not the product of some center of power deciding in advance for "us," imposing what we have in common, but rather emerges with and in our differences, which provokes recognizing each other's unique gifts and needs, thereby invoking response and swelling into an

34. Farley, *The Gathering of Those Driven Away*, 153.

incarnational crescendo of divine Eros. Provocation is an invocation, a summons into a relational liturgy of mutuality in care, a *koinonia* fellowship outlining the shape of God's presence. Accounts of Jesus' ministry in the Gospels and Paul's theology of reconciliation offer ample support for this point.

The grace I am talking about here is an opening to God, discovered as preoccupation with control loosens its hold, when efforts to manage or manufacture it become stilled. This is where I especially appreciate Farley's retrieval of contemplation as a path toward divination. It offers a kind of *spirituality of attentiveness* that disposes us to the divine Face radiating in all other faces, and does so through a way of negation (*via negativa*) that consents to live in the space of non-possession and vulnerability. In fact, God is not a being capable of being possessed; God is "no-thing" at all. Thus it is by negation that all names and images for the divine, which entrap us in cycles of idolatrous and violent closures, begin to fall away and we become available to receiving gifts of creaturely differences as divine blessings, indeed, as the grammar of divine expression. Contemplation rests in the divine as nondual *Ungrund*—a resplendent empty-surplus undoing all discursive framing in subject-object terms— and this has the effect of releasing the anxious and fear-ridden ego from the illusion of control, creating "room for sympathy and compassion" and deepening capacities for joy and delight.[35] Rather than possess God as a manageable term (an idol), salvation lies in the opening of desire, which beholds without grasping divine Eros in the embodied plurality of fleshly life. In fact, it soars with desire like a grace received, and lets-go of clinging in order to let-be all else. Instead of absolutes, we get vulnerable interdependency. "Instead of inerrancy we get desire," which "is the bridge between ourselves and the Beloved."[36] Contemplative practice, for Farley, enacts the truth that "desire is the royal road to the Divine." We come to know ourselves and others as luminous God-bearers, images of the divine not in sameness but in diversity.[37] The provocative summons of difference is the summoning of divine Eros. The apophatic moment of negation opens onto a cataphatic incarnational landscape of multiplying love, not a retreat and abandonment of the world.

35. Farley, *The Gathering of Those Driven Away*, 103.

36. Farley, *The Gathering of Those Driven Away*, 59.

37. Farley, *The Gathering of Those Driven Away*, 91.

Thus, in welcoming one another, we welcome the divine. In fact, as many biblical stories of hospitality attest, divine presence and blessing comes as a surprise in receiving others, loving one's neighbor, indeed, receiving the stranger, outcast, and despised *as* one's neighbor. Living in openness to God is connected to treating "the least of these" as Christ himself (Matt. 25:40), those from whom society expects nothing and for which society desires nothing being emblems of divine nearness. The "preferential option for the poor" in Jesus' ministry exemplifies God's solidarity with those driven away and with those who suffer. And further, the Beloved dwells with us in the deepest affliction and despair, even unto desolation on the cross. Whereas suffering can defraud persons of preciousness and worth, telling us we are God-forsaken, the passion of Jesus tells us we are not forsaken.[38] This gets to the core of care, divine and human, interwoven incarnationally. It is more than a social program or policy. It is a kind of theological thread woven deeply into human ways of being present to one another, which opens us toward encountering suffering in the face of others and responding with compassion.[39] And it energizes movement for the creation of just social and economic conditions for mutuality, in which hospitality and neighborly love are held up as ideals, widening the circle of care beyond kin and country to everyone in principle. All people deserve care, as God's love extends to all. And more, the excluded and marginalized receive a preferential care because of their situation on the "outside."

Caring Communities and Incarnate Eros

Rooted in God's incarnational attentiveness to humanity in Christ— "God's Erotic power in the flesh"—churches can become transformed into caring communities that receive people with disabilities with love and respect, opened to unanticipated gifts. This is not to say that disability itself is a gift, rather that it is *neither* a deficit or lack *nor* does it exhaust all that a person is (as defined by normalcy); disability is a bodily difference that provokes and unsettles the low expectations of communities. All people are gifts and have gifts. And communities often overlook this crucial point in engaging people with disabilities because of a negative expectation drawn from focusing on what is perceived as a bodily flaw

38. Farley, *The Gathering of Those Driven Away*, 164.

39. Farley, *The Gathering of Those Driven Away*, 195–96.

or deficit in need of remediation or "special" treatment. When ignoring the giftedness and gifts of persons, the community itself suffers from disabling mechanisms: carelessness. Care's attentiveness is wider than that of normalcy. Its aperture is opened, leaving room for the Spirit. In real ways, I have learned this from my life with my son, whose life calls out to me, "pay attention not to your way, but mine, and be with me." The life in him confronts me outsides the boundaries of agendas and expectations I may have planned in advance, and ushers me into a relationship that I can't control on my own terms, but which has opened up to new horizons of relational joy I could not have imagined otherwise.

Genuine care emerges in another's presence who makes it possible to risk enough to receive the gift of their presence. It comes in an attunement to another's rhythm and cadences—as if to say, "it is not about my way, but yours." This means a hermeneutic readjustment, an attentiveness that bears witness to another in the shape of a vulnerable responsiveness. It is from such responsiveness that accommodation to difference moves beyond assimilation and becomes expansive and transformative. A community is changed by adjusting its way of being to another's way of being. The story of "us" shifts by attending to and entering the stories of persons with disabilities. The process empowers humility, and perhaps patience, and the willingness to fail and begin again, sometimes amidst deep disorientation and struggle, even anguish. But it also cultivates, perhaps because of these, companionships that are life-changing and grace-filled. Such relational connections function like liturgies of care, ritual acts of welcoming of God amidst us in the lives of one another. And this points to how theology is transformed by care.

Bearing witness to one another as a way of living within divine Eros encourages theology to be more than simply a rational discourse. Prioritizing caring relations means, in Rebecca Chopp's way of framing it, recovering the language of testimony. In holding up a "poetics of testimony," and drawing from Paul Ricoeur, Chopp seeks to dislodge the view that witness and testimony should be judged by theoretical discourses—whether theological, historical, or philosophical. Testimony is a form of discourse through which suffering and hope are brought to language, often in truth-telling narratives that are fragmented, giving voice to people and experiences often ruled out of court by the power mechanisms implied in rational discourse. For Chopp, "poetics" grants space for such language, seeking "not so much to argue as to refigure, to reimagine and refashion the world."[40] Testimony is discourse that calls into question the ordering of discourse by dominant social imaginaries. Its language resounds with an "indisputable claim of existence," a claim of survival and hope that provokes listening and invokes new kinds of relationships.[41] Farley corroborates the point: "Someplace between the testimony to suffering and the longing to be free from suffering is a firm desire to *live*."[42] In this way, testimonies call for bearing witness, summoning a response (response-ability) that pays attention and aligns itself with the pain of others so as to foster a relational solidarity that serves with accountability and justice. Bearing witness is a being-with that seeks to honor the life-impulse in others so that their preciousness and goodness might be realized in *living well*. In essence, testimonies are provocative invocations to care. And in honoring them, theology itself is invited to become care-full, a witness to the claims of existence in others as the call of divine Eros into relations of compassionate respect.

This is important because, if faith communities are about forming Christian care givers/receivers who reflect God's erotic attentiveness, we need a radically different set of criteria to think about care than presently exists. Needed are communities cultivated by more than generous intentions and right beliefs, but instead by habits of care formed *with* people at the margins, habits that cultivate mutual partnerships of vulnerability open to the transformative power of God's grace together. And such grace often surprises and disrupts on the way toward transformation, coming unexpected and in ways that unsettle dominant normalizing mechanisms and relations. Care risks exposure to testimonies from others who call a normative "us" into question, undoing what has been taken for granted about "us" and opening up something more than "we" were before. As responsive, care then opens co-creative processes in which the unique contributions of others might be received (not based on predetermined ways) as gestures of giving (not based on what is pre-calculated as worthy of value). This means risk, being vulnerable to the claims of others. As parenting has helped me realize, risking relationships of care requires opening to another's way of being, which challenges and introduces change even as it allows the possibility of receiving the giftedness and gifts of another person.

---

40. Chopp, "Theology and the Poetics of Testimony," 61.

41. Chopp, "Theology and the Poetics of Testimony," 62.

42. Farley, *The Wounding and Healing of Desire*, 9. Italics in original.

In the end, "we" are members of an Eros-cultivated Body of Christ, each with gifts to offer in fragile earthen vessels making present God's loving solidarity with the world. Attentiveness to others in relationships of mutual care is a way being attentive to God, a spiritual act. It is a divine liturgy. It is incarnational.

Conclusion

Several features outline how our fragile earthen vessels "make present" God's loving solidarity. First, as Farley would concede, it is the creaturely gift of life that takes priority. Life seeks life, and in different ways. The preciousness of a person's humanity is not reducible to ability or disability, or to any particular set of features measured by normalcy. It radiates its own beauty and intrinsic worth—in smiles, laughter, gestures, and sometimes, even words—as loved by God and as a gift of God. The presence of a human being is a reservoir of abundance exceeding ways value might be attributed to it according to the economies of exchange that dominate social life. So, second, our response (our response-ability) to this preciousness is to pay attention to it with compassionate respect—creating space for its own ways of flourishing (not based on predetermined ways) and giving (not based on what is pre-calculated as worthy of value). This, third, traffics in a spirituality that welcomes others as loved by God, and indeed, as a way of loving God. Love of God and love of neighbor, the stranger, are twin elements wrapped in one dynamic. As Farley puts it, "Spirituality, compassion, and justice cannot be isolated from one another."[43] Indeed, they are joined in care as a way to cultivate a world in which the well-being of all is made possible.

Care is a life impulse, rising in an affirmation of the goodness of things as embraced by divine love. It is life seeking to flourish, caring for itself, reflecting divine Eros. But it does so incarnationally in disseminated forms, through caring for self and others. Communities of care participate in this Christic dynamic insofar as they embody reciprocities of giving and receiving among all participants, so that belonging—as invitation to, access for, and welcome by all—is enacted by each in matrixes of caring relationships. Such a vision, deeply informed by the work of Wendy Farley, may open up refreshing ways for faith communities to

---

43. Farley, *Gathering Those Driven Away*, 141.

actively anticipate the kin-dom of God, a future in which divine Eros will join all together most fulsomely in an extravagantly care-full embrace.

Bibliography

Ahmed, Sara. *On Being Included: Racism and Diversity in Institutional Life.* Durham: Duke University Press, 2012.

Brock, Rita Nakashima. *Journeys by Heart: A Christology of Erotic Power.* New York: Crossroad, 1988.

Brock, Rita Nakashima, and Rebecca Ann Parker. *Proverbs of Ashes: Violence, Redemptive Suffering, and the Search for What Saves Us.* Boston: Beacon, 2002.

Carson, Anne. *Eros the Bittersweet: An Essay.* Princeton: Princeton University Press, 1986.

Chopp, Rebecca. "Theology and the Poetics of Testimony." In *Converging on Culture: Theologians in Dialogue with Cultural Analysis and Criticism.* Edited by Delwin Brown, Sheila Greeve Davaney, and Kathryn Tanner. Oxford: Oxford University Press, 2001.

Farley, Margaret. *Compassionate Respect: A Feminist Approach to Medical Ethics and Other Questions.* New York: Paulist, 2002.

Farley, Wendy. *Eros for the Other: Retaining Truth in a Pluralistic World.* University Park, PA: Pennsylvania State University Press, 1996.

———. *Gathering Those Driven Away: A Theology of Incarnation.* Louisville: Wesminster John Knox, 2011.

———. *Tragic Vision and Divine Compassion: A Contemporary Theodicy.* Louisville: Wesminster/John Knox, 1990.

———. *The Wounding and Healing of Desire: Weaving Heaven and Earth.* Louisville: Wesminster John Knox, 2005.

Fisher, B., and Joan Tronto. "Toward a Feminist Theory of Caring." In *Circles of Care.* Edited by E. Abel and M. Nelson. Albany, NY: SUNY Press, 1990.

Frank, Arthur W. *The Renewal of Generosity: Illness, Medicine, and How to Live.* Chicago: University of Chicago Press, 2004.

Held, Virginia. *The Ethics of Care: Personal, Political, and Global.* New York: Oxford University Press, 2006.

Julian of Norwich. *Showings.* Translated by Edmund Colledge and James Walsch. New York: Paulist, 1978.

Noddings, Nel. *Caring: A Feminine Approach to Ethics and Moral Education.* Berkeley: University of California Press, 1986.

Nothwehr, Dawn M. *Mutuality: A Formal Norm for Christian Ethics.* Eugene, OR: Wipf & Stock, 1998.

Parsons, Susan Frank. "Redeeming Ethics." In *The Cambridge Companion to Feminist Theology.* Edited by Susan Frank Parsons. Cambridge: Cambridge University Press, 2002.

Ray, Darby Kathleen. *Deceiving the Devil: Atonement, Abuse, and Ransom.* Cleveland: Pilgrim, 1998.

Russell, Letty M. *Just Hospitality: God's Welcome in a World of Difference.* Edited by J. Shannon and Kate M. Ott. Louisville: Wesminster John Knox, 2009.

Schneider, Laurel. *Beyond Monotheism: A Theology of Multiplicity*. New York: Routledge, 2008.

SteinhoffSmith, Roy Herndon. *The Mutuality of Care*. St. Louis: Chalice, 1999.

Soelle, Dorothee. *Suffering*. Translated by Everett R. Kalin. Philadelphia: Fortress, 1975.

Tronto, Joan. *Moral Boundaries: A Political Argument for an Ethic of Care*. New York: Routledge, 1993.

Volf, Miroslav. *Exclusion and Embrace: A Theological Exploration of Identity, Otherness, and Reconciliation*. Nashville: Abingdon Press, 1996.

Wolterstorff, Nicholas. *Justice in Love*. Grand Rapids: William B. Eerdmans, 2011.

Young, Iris Marion. *Justice and the Politics of Difference*. Princeton: Princeton University Press, 1990.

TWELVE

Virtually Baroque:
A Postcolonial Interlude on the
Salvific Opacity of the Divine Eros

Kristine Suna-Koro

POSTCOLONIALLY SPEAKING, THE AFFIRMATION of opacity (*opacité*) distracts from absolute, possessive, and conquering truths—or so claimed the late Martiniquan postcolonial critic Édouard Glissant. Postcolonial opacity for Glissant engenders a celebration of the "irreducible singularity" of human persons, cultures, creative expressions, and languages without imposed simplification and domestication to reductive transparency.[1] Postcolonial opacity, according to Glissant, is a baroque attitude. It is a life-form that "protects the Diverse"[2] in the administered world of conquering dogmatic certitude and transparency.

What does Glissant's postcolonially baroque opacity—a right for which we all are invited to "clamor"—have to do with Wendy Farley's theological *Eros* of the incarnational Divine Abyss which unfolds as lucidly and poignantly as a neoclassical orchestral suite in her *Gathering Those Driven Away: A Theology of Incarnation?*[3] At the first glance, not much, at least stylistically. A closer reading, however, reveals that the

---

1. Glissant, *Poetics of Relation*, 190.

2. Glissant, *Poetics of Relation*, 62.

3. "We clamor for the right to opacity for everyone," Glissant, *Poetics of Relation*, 194.

resonances between Farley's incarnational theology and Glissant's post-colonial imaginary run deep.

The goal of this brief essay is to peregrinate through the network of fruitful convergences between Farley's tenaciously apophatic recuperation of the Incarnation of Divine *Eros* as both radically inclusive sapiential hermeneutics and as an ascetic spiritual practice from the "underside of Christian history," on one hand, and a Glissantian postcolonial baroque perspective as a practice of opacity and therefore, of counterconquest, on the other.[4] Amidst the conversation between these two very complex "undersides" of the Occidental socio-cultural and spiritual edifice emerges, I submit, an effective and restorative ecclesiological imaginary.

Namely, it is an imaginary of the church as the Body of Christ—envisioned, orchestrated, and performed—as a postcolonially baroque archipelago of divine love. Perceived simultaneously as "erotic" in the Farleyan sense and as postcolonially baroque, this Body can insert itself as a space of opaque, vivacious, and salvific dissent and healing in the world of endlessly proliferating cultural, political, and spiritual empires of coercive dominance. Its immediate vocation is to facilitate the sapiential liturgy of longing for Wisdom through Farley's eloquent adage of "pain seeking understanding."[5] The paramount mission of this Body is to embody Wisdom through pain which ultimately seeks not just understanding but also, I must add, redemptive transformation, as it reconvenes the shards of histories, bodies, spiritualities, knowledges, identities, and integrities within the graced archipelago of divine love and wholeness.

As if to parody the very idea of opacity, I must start with a very clear disclaimer. My peregrinations through Farley's *salut d'amour* to the Far-Near divinity do not presume to present a comprehensive inquiry of her intricate imaginary of the self-diffusive Divine *Eros* through multiple and complementary conduits of revelation that she delves into: trinitarian, incarnational, ascetic-apophatic, contemplative, artistic, ethical, and philosophical. It is impossible to do even meager justice to the whole breadth and depth of *Gathering Those Driven Away* in the present brief format. The intrigue of my present modest endeavor consists of highlighting two trajectories in *Gathering Those Driven Away*, namely, to suggest an ethically fruitful resonance for transdisciplinary wisdom if approached through a prism of postcolonial baroque. I will do it by teasing out motifs

4. Farley, *Gathering Those Driven Away*, 8.
5. Farley, *Gathering Those Driven Away*, 1.

of benevolent postcolonial ecclesiology as 1) baroque and therefore erotic (in a Farleyan sense) and 2) as opaque (in a Glissantian sense).

The Divine Eros, the Erotic Abyss: A Revelation of Veiled Love

To begin with, let's consider the trajectory of impenetrability amidst all the revelatory planetarity of what Farley calls "the visceral reality of apophatic divinity" of the Eternal *Eros*.[6] Affirmed and rendered virtually palpable with flying apophatic colors through a buoyant *via negativa*, the unfathomable God-head is the "Abyss of Divinity beyond all names and all negations."[7] It is, nevertheless, disclosed to us as love. It interabides with us as the incarnated eros against the long odds of perversely victorious logic and grammar of domination and hegemony—in the Trinity, in Christ as Wisdom and as the Word, and most paradoxically of all, even in us, humans. The Divine *Eros* is the foundation of all reality in which we can rest at least during our least idolatrous moments of truth, no matter how fleetingly, and do it even on this side of the beatific vision of *theosis* as we inscrutably and unbelievably keep "bathing in the Good Beyond Being who is holy in and beyond every name."[8]

Never mind how grumpy the intellectual indigestion of human minds steeped in the (peculiarly, though not exclusively Occidental) rationale of binarity may be, Farley never tires of emphasizing that the unnamable Abyss of Divine *Eros* becomes "refracted in Christ," in Jesus of Nazareth.[9] The refracted divinity migrates into historically embodied flesh and culturally embedded flesh and bones to "light the path by which humanity returns to the Divine Eros" through the supreme practice of love—divinization, *theosis*.[10] Farley lusciously reaffirms the classic spiritual wisdom that the path of divinization starts in, with, and through Christ as an attraction to fall in love with and to imitate in life. But the life of Jesus Christ is precisely the performative space "where the utter concreteness, uniqueness, and vulnerability of a particular human body

---

6. Farley, *Gathering Those Driven Away*, 91.

7. Farley, *Gathering Those Driven Away*, 205.

8. Farley, *Gathering Those Driven Away*, 61.

9. Farley, *Gathering Those Driven Away*, 11,

10. Farley, *Gathering Those Driven Away*, 170.

intersects with Erotic Wisdom."[11] This path leads "over the wall of reason to the garden where opposites coincide," where "unitive contemplation perfumes justice," and where salvation is most palpably both healing and transparency to Goodness as the human soul painstakingly recovers its own erotic profundity as the divine image.[12]

And yet: *sed contra*. Right in the middle of spiritual aspirations toward deifying transparency of mystical union, amidst the unique and maximal transparency of humanity to divinity in Christ, and amidst the radically corporeal economy of salvation that is permeated and "perfumed" by the interplay of Divine *Eros* and human desire for Her, the divine revelation must remain ever veiled on this side of the wall of unredeemed human consciousness. Even when its gaze is directed toward itself as a fruit of the Divine *Eros*. Farley tenaciously insists that "the deeper truths of creation are veiled."[13] There is no voyeuristic, perhaps even pornographic, transparency in this *Eros*. Concurrently, proceeding with a loyal "Pseudo-Dionysian" composure of apophatic reserve, Farley reiterates that the divine face itself ultimately remains veiled even amidst the most sensuous and enfleshed revelation.[14] The mystery of the Trinity remains unmastered and impenetrable, as does the mystery of the Incarnation. Evermore, the impenetrable mystery of Incarnation is "announced in an impenetrable interplay of success and failure, victory and defeat."[15]

All these mysteries and epiphanies (or sacraments, for a more Occidental theological taste) of the Divine *Eros* in the present dispensation come across as what Glissant would call baroque and opaque. They arrive as unmasterable except by reductive violence; as excessive because inscrutable except by idolatrous simplification. Thus the holy eroticism of Farley's divinity is akin to the sheer baroque imagery of God as in one of the most beloved Latvian Lutheran hymns by the Latvian poet and pastor Ludis Bērziņš (1870-1965), "Nearness and Farness" ("*Tuvums un tālums*").[16] In the hymn, the Divine remains sparsely named,

---

11. Farley, *Gathering Those Driven Away*, 132.

12. Farley, *Gathering Those Driven Away*, 185.

13. Farley, *Gathering Those Driven Away*, 14.

14. Farley, *Gathering Those Driven Away*, chapter. 7. Also see chapter 3. See also Pseudo-Dionysius, "Letter Three to Gaius," "But he [God] is hidden even after this revelation, or (. . .) even amid the revelation,"1069B, 264.

15. Farley, *Gathering Those Driven Away*, 7.

16. *The Hymnal of the Evangelical Lutheran Church of Latvia and in Exile*, 173.

except through explicit capitalization, as the "One" and as "Redeemer." Yet this "One" reigns over nearness and farness, dew-filled valleys, misty mountains, fertile fields, austere rocks, distant lands, and foreign islands through a monumental, indeed baroque, exuberance of grace. "The One" reigns by scattering, doling out, unleashing, and even drenching the creation in the divine blessing as the Latvian phrase "*svētību šķiezdams*" describes it. Grace is doled out, as it were, sloppily, hyper-generously, perhaps even wastefully: all of these meanings co-inhere in the Latvian verb "*šķiest.*" And this is how the unfathomable and yet intimately bountiful Eros enters into our bodies and minds—in a strangely, I want to suggest, baroque way.

However, it is worth underscoring that among the mysteries of the Divine Abyss is the mystery of human personality, an *imago* of the unfathomable divinity with its own profound opacity of love, affliction, identity, hopes, as well as unique historical and cultural idiosyncrasies. Yet the opacity does not stop here. The flipside of this kind of creaturely opacity reaches deeper, since it is irresponsible to overlook a habitually idolatrous human desire that often (and tragically) recognizes divine indwelling neither in revelation, nor in its own humanity, nor in fellow human persons. Thus the erotic interface of the God-world relationality, as Farley's account instigates, bodies forth not merely as the dark splendor of the ever sumptuous, ecstatic, and exuberant divine opacity through its non-utilitarian and steadfast loving-kindness but also as marked by the existential opacity of routine living with all its joyous intricacies and barely nameable cruelties. Nevertheless it is the intertwinement of the uncreated and the created opacities—keeping in mind that dissimilarity is always greater than similarity across the trans-ontological continuum —that leads me to the other trajectory in Farley's neoclassical *Gathering* that I cannot resist pondering over through a postcolonially baroque key.

Opacity as Postcolonially Baroque:
Envisaging a Counterconquest

Why even bother to wrestle with the almost incomprehensible French-Creole linguistic jungle of the Martiniquan postcolonial poet and theorist Édouard Glissant for theological purposes? How could his postcolonial musings on baroque and his doggedly pursued "right to opacity for everyone/*nous réclamons le droit à l'opacité*" from one of the many undersides of the Occident and its globally projected modernity be of use in conversation with Farley's crisp and supple neoclassical theo-poetics thematically and methodologically? What, after all, is *this* baroque?

Today we are aware of many faces and etymologies of baroque, indeed of multiple baroques. There is, of course, the historical European, or colonial(ist) baroque. But there is also neobaroque, understood as "the New World discourse of countermodernity."[17] Some scholars favor more precision and specificity when it comes to understanding baroque in the context of colonialism. They name it coloneobaroque.[18] Sometimes the entanglement of the historical European baroque and colonial escapades is theorized through the imaginary of Baroque New Worlds.[19]

Baroque is understood as a historical style in visual art, architecture, music, philosophy, spirituality, theology, and politics roughly in between 1600 and 1750, in Europe as well as its internal and transmarine colonies. The historical baroque as an era and as a style is an internally diverse socio-cultural phenomenon. Curious discrepancies, even apparent contradictions abound. For instance, the obsession with systematic knowledge vis-à-vis the unreliability of sensual knowledge is what Lois Parkinson Zamora calls the cerebral and logical branch of baroque, while an ever thickening expressive opulence and excess was also being enthusiastically sought after through the sensual and theatrical branch of baroque as if to savor the *barrôco* (an irregular, lumpy pearl in Portuguese) aspect to exhaustion in opulent ornamentation, frenzied elaboration, and sensual exuberance in art and music.[20]

Yet baroque is also reclaimed and revamped as a transhistorical rationality, a spiritual comportment, a subjectivity, and "an orientation of taste."[21] The revamped baroque prefers performative excess, eccentric syncretism of genres, proliferation of variation, ornamentation and

17. Kaup, "Neobaroque," 128.

18. Eggington, "The Corporeal Image," 108.

19. See the sumptuous collection of essays *Baroque New Worlds*.

20. See Zamora, *The Inordinate Eye*. Also, Perreira and Fastiggi's *The Mystical Theology of the Catholic Reformation* sketches, through a rather un-baroque flatness of presentation, the feverish intensity of both baroque impulses, the cerebral-systematic and the florescence of mystical theology (think of Teresa of Avila and Bernini in one breath) during the multifaceted baroque modernity.

21. Calabrese, *Neo-Baroque*, xii.

non-linear imagination. This notion of baroque continues to enjoy a "surprising afterlife . . . beyond its natural boundaries."[22]

Yet the baroque that I invoke here from the luscious menu of baroques is the specific neobaroque of polydimensionality.[23] It manifests in the decolonizing un-official baroque "from below" as a vehicle and style of postcolonial expression.[24] Above all, it is the "underside" baroque of postcolonial hybridity, the baroque of ironic reversals of and hybrid dissents against the imperial projects articulated by authors such as Alejo Carpentier.[25] But above all, it is the creolizing baroque of Édouard Glissant. It is the baroque as counterconquest.[26] This baroque is "based on breaking limits, or excessiveness"[27] and the "bleeding of borders"[28] with the intention to modulate—through opacity and hybridity—the illusions and, indeed, the idolatries that have been fabricated in the colonialist ideology of dualistic transparence of reality, ethics, and divinity.

Undoubtedly, baroque's deep confluence with the Occidental coloniality of power must be recognized. Yet, as Zamora notes, "it is one of the few satisfying ironies of European imperial domination worldwide that the baroque worked poorly as colonizing instrument."[29] In this context, Glissant's baroque advocates for and performs, in his writings, opacity as the ever mobile instrument of counterpoetics that resists the "bureaucratic reason"[30] of the imposed imperial ideologies of transparence.

Glissant has tirelessly promoted opacity as principle of creative defiance against the modern Occidental instrumental reason which craves to master and possess everything through clarification and, therefore, reduction.[31] He is not enchanted by the culture of audit, transparency, the

22. Harbison, *Reflections on Baroque*, x.

23. For Calabrese, neo-baroque is not a simple "return" but a "search for and valorization of, forms that display the loss of entirety, totality, and system in favor of instability, polydimensionality, and change," *Neo-Baroque*, xii.

24. Kaup, "'The Future is Entirely Fabulous,'" 233. Kaup, among others, argues, that baroque as a tool of absolutist, colonialist, and religious Counter-Reformation ideology was in profound tension with the subversive baroque aesthetics thus engendering the hybrid Latin American/Caribbean alternative modernity/countermodernity.

25. Salgado, "Hybridity in New World Baroque Theory," 317.

26. The term was introduced by Lima, *Baroque New Worlds*, 1–27.

27. Lima, *Baroque New Worlds*, 195.

28. Eggington, *The Theater of Truth*, 18.

29. Zamora, "New World Baroque," 127.

30. I borrow here the term from McLure, "The bone in the throat," 729–45.

31. Glissant, *Poetics of Relation*, 189.

instant gratification of accessible writing, and hardnosed utility: "Western thought has led us to believe that a work must always put itself constantly *at our disposal*."[32] To dismantle the infinite forms of oppression, Glissant declares faith in "the production of 'opaque' works,"[33] without the need to justify them against the Occidental requirements of transparency.[34]

Reading Glissant theologically, I contend that opacity is like a protocol against the idolatries of colonizing transcendence, both the uncreated and the humanly intersubjective, as far as the latter belongs to the order of *imago Dei* as a created mystery. Originating from his reflections on the colonial linguistic dispossession and denigration of oral cultures and folklores through the exaggerated prestige of (Occidental) writing, Glissant's creolizing plea is for a metaphysical recognition of the uniqueness, the irreducibility, and the dense aura of historico-cultural specificity of the complex human identities of various undersides on a planetary level. To make the globalized postcolonial modernity more underside-friendly, Glissant seeks "that which is not obvious, to assert for each community the right to a shared obscurity (*le droit à l'opacité mutuellement consentie*)."[35]

Opacity is not a reversal to "barbarism."[36] Nor is it the simply "obscure."[37] Rather, for Glissant, it is "a positive value to be opposed to any pseudo-humanist attempt to reduce the scale of some universal model. The welcome opaqueness (*la bienheureuse opacité*), through which the other escapes me, obliging me to be vigilant whenever I approach."[38] At the end of the day, opacity is "that which cannot be reduced, which is the most perennial guarantee of participation and confluence."[39] Most importantly, opacity is an ethical exigency. Through opacity, "every Other is a citizen and no longer a barbarian (. . .) The right to opacity would not establish autism; it would be the real foundation of Relation, in freedoms."[40]

32. Glissant, *Caribbean Discourse*, 107.
33. Glissant, *Caribbean Discourse*, 154–55.
34. Glissant, *Poetics of Relation*, 190.
35. Glissant, *Caribbean Discourse*, 161.
36. Glissant, *Poetics of Relation*, 189.
37. Glissant, *Poetics of Relation*, 191.
38. Glissant, *Caribbean Discourse*, 162.
39. Glissant, *Poetics of Relation*, 191.
40. Glissant, *Poetics of Relation*, 190.

Glissant's clamor for opacity is not meant to merely resist the on-going linguistic imperialism of the Occidental colonial languages such as the homogenized Anglo-American and French. It is also to advance an ethically invested comportment toward minoritarian—expected and unexpected—voices within the open totality of the worldliness (*mondi-alité*), the whole-world (*Tout-Monde*). Thus Glissant's counterpoetics of opacity constitutes the existential and ethical pivot of his poetics/aesthet-ics of Relation. It is also the aesthetics of counterconquest that deeply, often without any recognition, structures the whole-world, ever radically interrelated, ever interdependent, ever in the movement of "unpredict-able and unforeseeable" creolization.[41] Glissant's planetary metaphysics of Relation is grounded in opacity; it is "built on the voices of all peoples, what I have called their inscrutability (*opacité*), which is nothing, after all, but an expression of their freedom. The transparency encouraged by misleading imitativeness must be shed at once."[42]

Now, that spacious, luscious, and jumbled imaginary of the whole-worldly Relation, grounded in opacity, is baroque. For Glissant it is baroque precisely as the counterpoetics of transparency.[43] Certainly it is also a metaphysics, a world-view, or a hybrid "being in the world."[44] Glissant's baroque goes beyond the historical Euro-baroque, which was a "compensatory strategy of excess . . . wrapped around a vacuum"—a language of abundance and insufficiency of those who can really no lon-ger possess any certainty after the Copernican revolution.[45] And the very texture of Glissant's postcolonial baroque is opaque and hybrid. Precisely as such, it liberates as it continues the movement of "rerouting . . . the rationalist pretense of penetrating the mysteries of the known with one uniform and conclusive move"[46] by disturbing or shuddering dogmatic certitudes through bypasses, proliferation, redundancy.[47] Finally, the

41. Glissant, *L'Imaginaire des langues*, 90. My translation.

42. Glissant, *Caribbean Discourse*, 255–256. Celia Britton argues that opacity con-nects Glissant's endeavors to Gayatri Chakravorty Spivak's prioritization of muted subaltern voices that always struggle to speak: "'The right to opacity', which Glissant claims is more fundamental than the right to difference is a right *not to be understood*," in Britton, *Edouard Glissant and Postcolonial Theory*, 19.

43. Glissant, *Poetics of Relation*, 79.

44. Glissant, *Poetics of Relation*, 78.

45. Glissant, *Caribbean Discourse*, 250.

46. Glissant, *Poetics of Relation*, 77.

47. Glissant, *Poetics of Relation*, 78–79.

postcolonial baroque is a "generalization of *métissage*."[48] It is a baroque
come to age, opaque enough to accommodate the "way of living the
unity-diversity of the world," all the way into the thicket of the "unstable
mode of Relation"—the fluid, open, unpredictable, uncertain totality of
the whole-world.[49]

To sum up: the postcolonial baroque—such as Glissant's—labors to
unshackle the axiological hierarchy of the dominant Occident modernity with its obsessions with purity, transparency, and certainty, through
prioritizing a whole carnival of unapologetic opacities. At our time of
convoluted postcolonial globalization and seismic shifts within world
Christianity, the dialectic of opacity/transparency can be rendered baroque, that is, rendered hospitable to the fecund irregularities of life and
mind, imagination, and liberative action. And the ability to live with
opacity, despite being so keenly eradicated in today's hurried world of
simplification, efficiency, and ruthless utility, can be the route to a more
convivial, indeed, a baroque humility: "The thought of opacity distracts
me from absolute truths whose guardian I might believe myself to be. Far
from cornering me within futility and inactivity, by making me sensitive to the limits of every method, it relativizes every possibility of every
action within me."[50] Be it politics, history, or ecclesiology—opacity resonates with the textures of erotic tenderness since

> transparency no longer seems like the bottom of the mirror in
> which Western humanity reflected the world in its own image.
> There is opacity now at the bottom of the mirror, a whole al-
> luvium deposited by populations, silt that is fertile but, in actual
> fact, indistinct and unexplored even today, denied or insulted
> more often than not . . . [51]

To conclude this section, one thing must be mentioned here, if
somewhat proleptically: there is a strand of thought within the postcolonial baroque that expresses something of an allergic reaction to
emptiness. It harbors a sort of *horror vacui* toward clearly demarcated
and transparent spaces deemed empty of life, grace, value, art, goodness,
meaning, and health. In other words, this strand harbors compassion

---

48. Glissant, *Poetics of Relation*, 78.

49. Glissant, *Poetics of Relation*, 79, 171.

50. Glissant, *Poetics of Relation*, 192. Glissant also asserts that "widespread consent
to specific opacities is the most straightforward equivalent of nonbarbarism," 194.

51. Glissant, *Poetics of Relation*, 111.

toward those to be silenced, or "civilized," or streamlined into those alleg-edly "empty" spaces only to be governed and told what to do and how to be. That, however, is a longer conversation. For now, I will probe deeper into the resonances between the Farleyan "carnivalesque" ecclesiological imagination and opacities of postcolonial baroque.

The Indispensable Dispensables: The Baroque Catholicity of the Body of Christ

Ecclesiology, according to Georges Florovsky, "is but an 'extended Chris-tology', the doctrine of the 'total Christ', *totus Christus, caput et corpus*."[52] No doubt, this is a very "high" ecclesiological model. Yet it is superbly resonant with certain, still embryonic postcolonial conjectures about the superlative hybridity of Christ, the second person of the Trinity, as "true God from true God" (the Nicene Creed) and yet fully and genuinely hu-man. While it is impossible to delve into several fascinating recent theo-logical endeavors in constructive Christology, suffice it to say here that a profoundly hybrid, creolized, or mulatto Christ as *caput* translates rather organically into a notion of hybrid church as Christ's *corpus*.[53]

Hybridity entails genuine and irreducible difference and thus it is the perennial "third space" wherein even the greatest imaginable dif-ferences coexist, concur, interpenetrate, sometimes harmoniously and sometimes dissonantly, even agonistically. Certainly, in the Chalcedo-nian two-natures/one-person imaginary of Christ, the trans-ontological difference between divinity and humanity concur ideally and harmoni-ously without separation and without annihilating fusion. It is particu-larly pertinent to the state of glorified or deified humanity of Christ after Ascension. But of this glorified hybridity in relation to Christ's *corpus* as the church it is currently possible to speak only under judicious escha-tological and apophatic provisos. While the glorified hybridity of Christ remains opaque precisely because of its uncreated, darkly luminous per-fection beyond human imagination and language, the hybridity of the *corpus* is shot through by the opacity I spoke of earlier as pertinent to the complex mystery of humanity as erotically created and yet sinful *imago*. While the glorified hybridity of the second person of Trinity, the *caput*,

---

52. Florovsky, "The Ever-Virgin Mother," 52.

53. See, for example, Kwok, *Postcolonial Imagination*, especially chapter 7; Burrus, "Radical Orthodoxy and the Heresiological Habit"; Bantum, *Redeeming Mulatto*.

is always already consummated as a post-resurrection reality, it is equally true that the church, even as *communio salutis,* remains opaque precisely because it is a *communio viatorum.* As such, the church is a decidedly unfinished symphony. Rather, it often speaks and acts as a blundering assemblage ever vulnerable to idolatrous and hurtful ways and means, as Farley's *Gathering* itself so poignantly attests.

As a *communio viatorum,* the Body of Christ is opaque in its imperfection and yet also opaque in its abundant diversity[54] of wayfarers without bureaucratizing them into reductive pigeonholes of identity and bland orthodoxy. The church materializes as a genuinely hybrid and inclusively baroque *corpus* precisely if it is envisaged and practiced, in Farley's words, as "the carnival of humanity," for, "without the carnival of humanity, Christ's body is incomplete."[55] The baroque opacity of this ecclesiological carnival of *corpus Christi* accommodates under its wing the whole palooza of life-worlds and life-forms, assumed in their fullness of overflowing human density by the Divine Word/Wisdom to be redeemed. Remember the classic theological maxim: what is not assumed cannot be healed . . . Hence, as Farley argues, without those driven away by virtue of their gender, sexuality, race, ethnicity, ability, immigration status, and you name what else on the black list of toxic (or "con")–orthodoxies, "the full range of the Divine Eros would be unfulfilled."[56]

Moreover, the church "requires the voices of those driven away . . . burned or consigned to silence," for without their, as it were, opacity *in via* toward salvation, the eschatologically exuberant, hybrid, baroque, and maybe even hyper-generous and slightly wasteful wholeness, "the body of Christ is hopelessly maimed and dismembered."[57] In other words, humanly created silences, omissions, exclusions, reductive transparencies, white-washed spots of history and human experience do not merely show a lack of taste for a certain baroque theological sensibility of plenitude rather than scarcity of (divine) love and (human) life. More

---

54. I am alluding to Glissant's aesthetics of planetary, non-universalizing and yet transversal diversity: "Diversity (*Le Divers*), which is neither chaos nor sterility, means the human spirit's striving for a cross-cultural relationship (*une relation transversale*), without universalist transcendence. Diversity needs the presence of peoples, no longer as objects to be swallowed up, but with the intention of creating a new relationship," Glissant, *Caribbean Discourse,* 98, 255.

55. Farley, *Gathering Those Driven Away,* 225.

56. Farley, *Gathering Those Driven Away,* 5.

57. Farley, *Gathering Those Driven Away,* 5.

grievously, they show the inability to discern the Body of Christ, to use a more biblical expression.

Furthermore, the Body of Christ is situated within the precious historico-theological ambiguity of theological imagination about what/ Who is the true (*corpus verum*) and/or mystical (*corpus mysticum*) Body of Christ: the church or the Eucharist?[58] The ambiguity here need not present a problem—at least from a baroque perspective of anamorphosis, or a baroque parallax, wherein an image can appear or disappear depending on one's viewing angle. Such ambiguity, perhaps indeed opacity, is nothing else but a radically hospitable polyvalence and polyphony of redemptive meaning and experience. After all, it is the Eucharist, the Ur-Mystery of the *opus Dei*—cosmic, hypostatic, as well as deeply personal and irreducibly social and political—that engenders the church as the Body of Christ. This Body—opaquely uniting many in one—is tasked as divinely convoked instrument of salvation. Within this redemptive convocation, salvation as Shawn Copeland insightfully observes, is precisely "salvation in human liberation as an *opaque* work, that is, a work that resists both the reduction of human praxis to social transformation and the identification of the gospel with even the most just ordering of society."[59]

And now it is time to return—theologically—to that irreducible Glissantian opacity at the bottom of the mirror of human lives, identities, and desires. But I return to this creaturely opacity precisely as being *in via salutis*—in the process of being saved. On and through this path, the whole carnival of human opacities becomes divinely graced to painstakingly voyage into the erotic profundity of, as Farley calls it, the "spotless mirror" of divine image.[60] In other words, I return not to announce a triumphant arrival as realized eschatology—but rather to make a few suggestions about the convocation of voyagers toward *theosis* through the opaque lens of postcolonial baroque.

The Body of Christ:
An Opaque Archipelago of Divine Eros

Ecclesiology as well as Christology can soar high. And yet, no matter how high an ecclesiology soars, church as the sacramental Body of Christ

58. On the historical developments of this dialectic, see de Lubac, *Corpus Mysticum*.

59. Copeland, *Enfleshing Freedom*, 102. Italics added.

60. Farley, *Gathering Those Driven Away*, 178.

was historically perceived as *corpus permixtum* on this side of the beatific vision—a mixed flock, an imperfect convocation of Christ's disciples.[61] As such it is circumscribed by thickly ambiguous imperfection while still embroiled in the toil of being "in" the world and yet no longer merely "of" the unjust world. But the church can be understood as *corpus permixtum* in more senses than one. It can be perceived and embodied as a rightfully baroque *corpus permixtum* precisely if and when it lives spaciously as both the mystical and the true Body of Christ without contradiction or competition between these two dimensions of Christ's presence in the world after Ascension.

Moreover, as Bernd Wannenwetsch has recently reflected on the early Christian eucharistic practices, it is precisely the mixed nature of offering diverse gifts to be consecrated and partaken as the Body of Christ that gathers those who embody the differences and inequities of the creation as we know it today. Speaking of individual worshippers contributing various quantities and qualities of wine and bread for the eucharistic celebration, Wannenwetsch observes:

> Although each believer was *individually* represented in the elements (having brought these herself), these elements were now presented for consecration in a *mixed form*, thus representing no longer just the believers individually but the community as a whole. The elements, which were brought to the altar, were in a heightened sense *corpora permixta*: containing an irreducible mixture of expensive and cheap wine, offered by rich and poor members of the community respectively. Purity of taste, it might be said, had to be sacrificed for the sake of symbolic representation of the Church as a whole in these elements: the Church with all its members, with all the aspects of its corporate existence, success and failure, conflict and reconciliation.[62]

The opaque benevolence and porous hospitality of the Body of Christ borders on sloppy excess (remember Bērziņš' hymn?) and all that allegedly wasteful fervor of endless baroque variations. As such it also exudes the apophatic enfleshment of salvation and its eschatological entanglements so captivatingly expressed by Jesus himself in the parable of the weeds growing among wheat (Mt 13:24-30). And finally, as such, as ever-bent on crossing borders, the Body of Christ is like an opaque "archipelago" of Divine *Eros*—to use one of the most evocative Glissantian

---

61. De Lubac, *Catholicism*, 69.

62. Wannenwetsch, "Eucharist," 138.

terms for inclusivity, healthy equality, patient ambiguity, and hospitality toward fragile histories and connections. The church as the archipelago of Divine *Eros* is inaugurated through the sacrificial love of Christ, sustained through the exuberant grace of the Creator, and transfigured through the countless life-saving detours of the Holy Spirit for the salvation of the whole creation.

The church as a postcolonially baroque archipelago of Divine *Eros* is hybrid[63]—poly-vocal, poly-racial, poly-gendered, poly-cultural, and poly-centric. Thus, as any typically baroque entity, it is very hard to police. In other words, this ecclesial archipelago is not only sacramental but downright liquid[64]—ever open to variation and transformation. It is embedded in the great living Christian tradition. Yet is not deep-frozen in its own institutionalized and bureaucratized deviations and oppressions. But most importantly, this archipelago is opaque: fecund with patience toward the Triune economy of salvation in which the revelation is simultaneously disclosed and hidden; in which all divine names —and all human lives and identities—retain their irreducible depth and breadth, harmonies, contradictions, surprises, unpredictable interactions and outcomes. Finally, this archipelago ensures the right not to be easily understood on demand and not to be preemptively judged before the harvest (Mt 13:30). Within such sacramental archipelago, the "carnival of whole humanity" can indwell, suspended in the erotic opacity of divine patience (2 Pet 3:8–10) toward all those whom sinful habits of minds and bodies, as well as cultural and historical inertia, are ever ready to drive away or weed out before the eschatological harvest. This archipelago subsists in the opacity of patient and spacious divine power which, despite another token conundrum of intellectual indigestion, can often appear as foolishness or mere weakness (1 Cor. 1:25).

But above all, the hospitable opacity of this archipelago is a most reliable sacramental mirror of the Divine *Eros*. The Divine *Eros* is reflected in the world through the convocation of Christ's disciples if and when it bodies forth as a postcolonially baroque *corpus permixtum*—opaquely inviting and gathering even those typically considered "dispensable," and enjoying and suffering divine patience and its unpredictable surprises on the long and arduous road of engodding (*theosis*). Certainly, the actual historical lives of the members of Christ's Body are often as unreliable

---

63. See Baker on the ecclesiology of hybridity in his *The Hybrid Church in the City*.
64. See Ward, *Liquid Church*.

sacramental signs of the Divine *Eros* as it gets. But that, too, is part of the opaque economy of salvation which, after all, is a decidedly unfinished symphony individually, interpersonally, ecclesially, and on the ever evolving planetary level. Nevertheless, what takes redemptive precedence, within the opaque archipelago of Christ's Body, is the spacious perseverance amidst perennially unanswered questions, still unfinished identities and yet unhealed wounds of body, soul, and spirit. This perseverance leans into the fecundity and opacity of divine grace and the truly unfathomable "love divine, all loves excelling," as Charles Wesley would sing when spoken and written words alone are no longer apophatically good-mannered to say even what God is not.

And so, to conclude: I clamor for the ecclesial comportment of postcolonially baroque opacity for the sake of us all within the erotic archipelago of divinity—the Body of Christ in this scandalously unjust and unredeemed world and also in a church that is often devilishly difficult to distinguish from this world. Of course, short of idolatry, of transparently revealed divine love there can only be an eschatology. In the meantime, here and now, I look for solace and empowerment in the opaque and unpredictable *sapientia* of counterconquest. That is to say, the postcolonially baroque Body of Christ lives and moves as a redemptively opaque archipelago of Divine *Eros* in which indeed no race, gender, culture, ethnicity, sexuality, or class "possesses the monopoly on beauty, on intelligence, on vigor, and there is enough room for all in the *rendezvous* of victorious conquest,"[65] to borrow the words of another Martiniquan postcolonial thinker, Aimé Césaire. In other words, no one who desires to enter is ever *driven* away from the postcolonially baroque archipelago of Christ's true and mystical Body. There is enough roomy opacity for all to be welcomed into a *rendezvous* with the Divine *Eros* which exuberantly excels over everything and anything we dare to experience and imagine as love.

Bibliography

Baker, Christopher. *The Hybrid Church in the City: Third Space Thinking.* Aldershot: Ashgate, 2007.

Bantum, Brian. *Redeeming Mulatto: A Theology of Race and Christian Hybridity.* Waco: Baylor University Press, 2010.

Britton, Celia. *Édouard Glissant and Postcolonial Theory: Strategies of Language and Resistance.* Charlottesville: University of Virginia Press, 1999.

---

65. Césaire, *Cahier d'un retour au pays natal,* 57–58. My translation.

Burrus, Virginia. "Radical Orthodoxy and the Heresiological Habit: Engaging Graham Ward's Christology." In *Interpreting the Postmodern: Responses to Radical Orthodoxy*, edited by R. Radford Ruether and Marion Grau, 36–53. New York: T&T Clark, 2006.

Calabrese, Omar. *Neo-Baroque: A Sign of Times*. Foreword by Umberto Eco. Translated by Charles Lambert. Princeton: Princeton University Press, 1992.

Césaire, Aimé. *Cahier d'un retour au pays natal*. Présence Africaine, 1983.

Copeland, M. Shawn. *Enfleshing Freedom: Body, Race, and Being*. Minneapolis: Fortress Press, 2010.

Eggington, William. "The Corporeal Image and the New World Baroque." *South Atlantic Quarterly* 106:1 (2007): 107–27.

———. *The Theater of Truth: The Ideology of (Neo)Baroque Aesthetics*. Stanford: Stanford University Press, 2010.

Farley, Wendy. *Gathering Those Driven Away: A Theology of Incarnation*. Louisville: John Knox, 2011.

Florovsky, Georges. "The Ever-Virgin Mother." In *The Mother of God: A Symposium*, edited by E. L. Mascall, 40–56. Westminster: Dacre Press, 1959.

Glissant, Édouard. *Caribbean Discourse: Selected Essays*. Translated by J. Michael Dash. Charlottesville: University Press of Virginia, 1989.

———. *L'Imaginaire des langues: Entretiens avec Lise Gauvin*. Paris: Gallimard, 2010.

———. *Poetics of Relation*. Translated by Betsy Wing. Ann Arbor: University of Michigan Press, 1997.

Harbison, Robert. *Reflections on Baroque*. Chicago: The University of Chicago Press, 2000.

The Hymnal of the Evangelical Lutheran Church of Latvia and in Exile. Pieksamaki, Finland: Raamattutalo: Latvian Evangelical Lutheran Church in Exile, 1992.

Kaup, Monika. "'The Future is Entirely Fabulous': The Baroque Genealogy of Latin America's Modernity." *Modern Language Quarterly* 68:2 (2007): 221–41.

———. "Neobaroque: Latin America's Alternative Modernity," *Comparative Literature* 58:2 (2006): 128–52.

Kwok, Pui-lan. *Postcolonial Imagination and Feminist Theology*. Louisville: Westminster John Knox Press, 2005.

Lima, José Lezama. "Chapter 2 from *La expression americana*, 'Baroque Curiosity' (1957)." In *Baroque New Worlds: Representation, Transculturation, Counterconquest*, edited by Lois Parkinson Zamora and Monika Kaup, 112–240. Durham and London: Duke University Press, 2010.

Lubac, Henri de. *Catholicism: Christ and the Common Destiny of Man*. Translated by Lancelot C. Sheppard and Elizabeth Englund, OCD. San Francisco: Ignatius Press, 1988.

———. *Corpus Mysticum: The Eucharist and the Church in the Middle Ages*. Translated by Gemma Simmonds. University of Notre Dame Press, 2007.

McLure, Maggie. "The bone in the throat: some uncertain thoughts on baroque method." *International Journal of Qualitative Studies in Education* 19:6 (2006): 729–45.

Perreira, Jose, and Robert Fastiggi. *The Mystical Theology of the Catholic Reformation: An Overview of Baroque Spirituality*. Lanham: University Press of America, 2006.

Pseudo-Dionysius: *Pseudo-Dionysius: The Complete Works*. The Classics of Western Spirituality. Translated by Colm Luibheid. Edited by Paul Rorem. New York, Mahwah, NJ: Paulist Press, 1987.

Salgado, César A. "Hybridity in New World Baroque Theory." *Journal of American Folklore* 112 (1999): 316–31.

Wannenwetsch, Bernd. "Eucharist and the Ethics of Sacrifice and Self-Giving: Offertory Exemplified." In *Liturgy and Ethics: New Contributions from Reformed Perspectives*, edited by Pieter Vos, 131–48. Leiden and Boston: Brill, 2018.

Ward, Pete. *Liquid Church*. Peabody: Hendrickson, 2002.

Zamora, Lois Parkinson, and Monika Kaup, eds. *Baroque New Worlds: Representation, Transculturation, Counterconquest*. Durham: Duke University Press, 2010.

Zamora, Lois Parkinson. *The Inordinate Eye: New World Baroque and Latin American Fiction*. Chicago: University of Chicago Press, 2006.

———. "New World Baroque, Neobaroque, Brut Barroco: Latin American Postcolonialisms." *PMLA* 124:1 (2009): 127–42.

THIRTEEN

To Be and to Become Divine:
Nondualism in the Theology of Wendy Farley

John J. Thatamanil

"You are of divine being," namely in the ground of the mind, is a statement of observation; whereas "Become the Son of God," namely by new birth, is a statement of exhortation. This step from a descriptive to a hortative discourse will have consequences for Eckhart's ontology. What we are, void and divine in our inmost being, we have yet to become. In detachment, what is given becomes ordered; identity by nature becomes the process of identification; nothingness becomes annihilation.

—Reiner Schürmann[1]

To Be and to Become Divine

TWO POWERFUL MOTIFS OF divine immanence resonate together in Wendy Farley's work: *becoming* divine and *being* divine. What history and lineage divide—becoming divine motifs are found predominantly within Christian traditions and being divine motifs primarily in Hindu traditions—Farley unites under the sign of nonduality.[2] Nonduality is a

1. Eckhart, *Wandering Joy*, 164–65.

2. Of course, to speak of these motifs as divided by traditions is far too neat. Religious traditions are wide rivers into which many streams flow and so the becoming

198

driving intuition that structures her work, *Gathering Those Driven Away*, and in the light of nonduality, the differences between these two ways of imagining and conceptualizing the divine-human relationship seem less urgent than what they both share. Farley's apophatic sensibilities also serve to relativize differences between these two theological imaginaries; no linguistic frame can capture precisely the relationship between world and divinity because divinity defies conceptualization. Hence, both frames make possible for Farley a thinking of divine presence in the very materiality of the world and, in so doing, offer a radical extension of the notion of incarnation within Christian theology. Incarnation, in Farley's work, does not refer solely to the historical Jesus but becomes, and necessarily so within a nondualist framework, a way of speaking about the whole of creation. The world itself is an incarnation of divinity, and we ourselves can become sites of incarnation.

The theological itinerary that leads to Farley's vision is not straightforward as it requires more than the "mystical" movement into the divine life as classically conceived. The threefold of purgation, contemplation, and illumination/union is vital to Farley, so much so that it serves to structure Farley's book, but Farley calls for and performs another kind of labor, namely a sociopolitical purgation that goes beyond confession of personal sin. Farley asserts that the church has marginalized and driven away its most vulnerable, creative, and dissenting minorities and, in doing so, has broken the church, body of Christ. Moreover, she contends that those driven away often articulated more capacious conceptions of incarnation than currently available in the ruptured church's regnant orthodoxies. The theologian must therefore work to heal this broken body, as no fractured church can speak with conviction about the integrative power of divine love when its own broken life tells a different tale. The theologian is compelled to do this work of healing and to (re)discover the treasured wisdom that the exiled hold in memory. For Farley, at the heart of this treasury is an understanding of incarnation as the means by which God calls Her beloved creatures *to be and to become* divine.

For some readers of *Gathering Those Driven Away*, this fluid and explicit integration of becoming divine and being divine motifs will be a source of concern. Writers within becoming divine traditions often seem

---

divine motif can be found in Hindu traditions and the being divine motif in Christian traditions, as this chapter will shortly demonstrate. It is, nevertheless, meaningful to speak of prevailing tendencies within traditions so long as these tendencies are not reified.

uneasy about the proximity of their traditions to nondualism and so have protested that *theosis* is not nonduality. The protest is issued because nonduality is too easily and often identified with pantheism; *theosis*, by contrast, offers deep intimacy with divinity without denying the distinction between world and God. After all, there is no possibility of becoming divine for what is already and from the very first divine. Deification demands distinction, if not duality, which is only subsequently transcended as God *becomes* all in all, and creation is taken into the divine life while yet remaining creation and not the creator *simpliciter*. Time matters. Matter matters. What once was not divine subsequently becomes so, and God's entry into creation in Jesus the Christ makes such becoming possible. The entry of the divine into creation by way of incarnation renders time and materiality into sites for deification.

Within the province of nonduality, as classically conceived in Hindu and Buddhist traditions, temporality matters, albeit in a different key. Vast timescapes may be required—indeed countless lifetimes—for persons to come into the knowledge of nonduality, understood either as the discovery that one is Brahman or that one's true nature just is Buddha nature, but time matters only to disclose what is already the case or to remove obscurations that cover over inherent divinity. There is no question of divine infusion—of uncreated energies infusing materiality—because ultimate reality is never separated from conventional reality.[3]

Even these hasty generalizations intimate that weighty matters hinge on the difference between becoming divine and being divine traditions. Do these differences matter to Farley? Should they matter to Farley's readers? For Farley, such distinctions, however significant, do not pose an insuperable bar that would prevent a studied integration of motifs drawn from both conceptual frames. What permits Farley to synthesize theological resources from both being and becoming divine traditions? What theological ontology makes this integrative worldview possible? Are there prior thinkers who do not police the distinction between these two motifs? Is there a lineage in which Farley stands that offers precedent for troubling the distinction between becoming and being divine? Most importantly, what can we learn from Farley's approach to integrating elements from both these ways of imagining immanence?

---

3. For a Hindu account of divine inflowing that escapes the simplistic assertion that being divine is the sole imaginary in the East, see the work of Michelle Voss Roberts, *Dualities*.

In what follows, I shall argue that the interpretive freedom that permits Farley to draw resources from both frames is rooted in a distinctive tradition of theological ontology. For Farley, these two imaginaries cannot be dichotomized. Both linguistic registers deliver common animating and salvific truth that is of greater consequence than their differences. Both being and becoming divine traditions fund and authorize a commitment to contemplative practice. Both drive adherents to move beyond juridical accounts of atonement. Most importantly, both traditions invite devotees into participation in the divine life even if the nature of that participation is differently imagined and conceived.

On the ontological front, Farley stands within an important if somewhat neglected Christian tradition of theological ontology, one in which the vocation of human life is, to quote Reiner Schürmann speaking of Meister Eckhart, "to become what we already are." The peculiar logic of this position is difficult to grasp and articulate; human beings are, in some sense, already divine and have always already been so. And yet, this truth must be brought to fruition. It must be accomplished; what *is* must nonetheless *be actualized.* Although there are many ways in which to articulate the significance of Farley's work for constructive theology, her work is important precisely because she offers a contemporary revivification of this neglected theological imaginary, one that necessarily requires the integration of being and becoming divine motifs.

And yet, the logic of this particular theological framework is difficult to puzzle out: What need is there to become what one already is? Surely, the most apropos metaphoric register for a being divine tradition is one that appeals to tropes of unveiling or removing obscurations. In the world's religious traditions, some customary tropes that are deployed for being divine ontologies are those of polishing a mirror to remove dust or dispelling clouds that hide the bright, ever-shining sun. These imaginaries make clear that work needs to be done; spiritual disciplines are necessary, but they do not bring about ontological transformation because none is needed. Human beings already are what they need to be.

Becoming divine traditions within the Christian family generally assert that the precondition for becoming divine is present incipiently in human beings. That human beings can become divine means that there is within us an intrinsic nobility that grounds and makes possible becoming divine; that precondition is that we are made in the *imago dei*, the image of God. But the lineage in which Farley stands is more radical than conventional formulations of the *imago dei* tradition. Within an important minority strand of the Christian tradition, the notion of the *imago dei* is radicalized to mean not merely that we are capable of receiving *ad extra* the infusion of divine energies; rather, *imago dei* is understood to refer to a point of ontological indistinction between soul and divinity. I refer in particular to the lineage of the Beguine mystics Mechthild of Magdeburg and Marguerite Porete, to whom Farley frequently appeals throughout *Gathering Those Driven Away*. In both thinkers—as well as in the writing of Meister Eckhart—there are intimations (Mechthild) and even explicit assertions of an uncreated dimension of the soul (Porete and Eckhart) that is eternally one with Godhead. The vocation of the human being within this tradition is not merely to discover this indistinction but to abide within it or, in still other language, to let one's inhabitation in indistinction so thoroughly permeate one's manner of existence in the world that one's life in time and the body becomes itself incarnation. Wendy Farley's theology stands in this tradition of incarnation both as what the human being always already is and *yet also a human vocation*, a becoming that must be brought about.

Farley's theology is promising precisely because it is a contemporary constructive articulation of this sometimes violently suppressed strand in Christian traditions.[4] But Farley does not merely reproduce classical Beguine theology. Rather, she generates a twenty-first-century constructive Beguine theology, one that is richly attentive to the Christian liberation and feminist theologies and indebted to an extra-Christian inspiration in Tibetan Buddhist notions of nonduality. Farley is what Marguerite Porete would sound like if the latter had access to Gutiérrez, queer theory, and the Dalai Lama. The result is a radical theology of incarnation, one that grounds a life marked by the union of contemplation and justice, a theology that genuinely gathers together those who have been driven way— mystics condemned and burned alive, the poor, the queer, the broken and violated bodies of women, and even the religious other.

In what follows, I will offer a reading of Farley's creative integration of being and becoming divine motifs to understand better the distinctive logic of this synthesis and its promise for constructive theology. As I have already indicated, several questions arise that admit of no easy resolution. They are threefold: First, how do the tropes of the being and becoming traditions hang together? Can they really be integrated or are they incommensurable? This question is, of course, not just tropological but

---

4. Those familiar with medieval mystical traditions will know that Marguerite Porete was burned at the stake in Paris on June 1, 1310.

ontological. Behind the question of tropes is puzzlement about how one can insist that human beings must become divine if they already are. The second question is one about the appropriate mode of access to divinity or ultimate reality. In nondual traditions, the ultimate mode of access to divinity is typically by way of knowledge, namely knowledge that one's true nature just is not other than ultimate reality whether understood as Brahman or Buddha-nature. Longing for ultimate reality especially in the key of love or devotion is usually understood as propaedeutic to knowledge. One yearns for ultimate reality *only for so long as* one takes ultimate reality to be other than oneself. Hence, devotion is given a role in early stages of spiritual life, but such yearning is understood as a penultimate mode of engaging ultimate reality. In the end, knowledge surpasses desire because divinity is no longer understood as something that stands over against me. Love or compassion for human beings and other sentient beings may follow from knowledge of nonduality; one may become the site of perfect love and compassion, but one no longer yearns for ultimate reality as though it were something that stands over against the one who yearns for it.

By contrast, in those traditions in which God or ultimate reality is, at least in some sense, distinct from if not wholly other to the human seeker, yearning and love for God is vital to the spiritual life and never surpassed by a mode of engagement with ultimacy that is more final. It is far more likely that knowledge will play a penultimate and preparatory role for devotion. Knowing that one is distinct from ultimate reality can prepare the soul for an understanding of its true nature and relationship to ultimate reality on which the soul depends. Love and longing for intimacy with ultimate reality or even union-in-distinction/communion is the goal but not knowledge of nonduality. These differences, for example, mark out the terrain for the sharp debates within the Hindu tradition between the absolute nondualism (*kevaladvaita*) of Sankara, which privileges knowledge (*jnana*), as opposed to the qualified nondualism (*visistadvaita*) of Ramanuja, which stresses devotion (*bhakti*). What then are we to make of an imaginary in which one becomes what one already is? What is the relationship between love and knowledge within such a framework? These are intriguing questions to bring to Farley's *Gathering Those Driven Away*.

A third and final issue also needs clarification, although it can only be taken up rather briefly within the confines of this chapter: the nature of the human predicament. Here, too, matters of affect and ontology intertwine. Is it the case that we human beings forget our innate divinity but are always and nonetheless divine? If so, what brings about that forgetting, and how is remembering made possible? Or is it the case that we are most assuredly not divine but rather estranged from the divine? If there is a real divide from the divine that is due to creation itself, a distance that is not itself a consequence of a fall into predicament, then presumably that distance is the precondition for human longing and eros for the divine; as such, this longing can, need, and must never find fruition in an erasure of difference, but finds its fulfillment instead in the growing intimacy of love. The human predicament then would be understood as longing misplaced, of longing for what is other and less than divinity. But given the clear differences between how the human predicament is understood within being and becoming divine traditions, and given the sharp history of contention between traditions committed to different ontologies and theological anthropologies, how is the human predicament to be understood in the work of a thinker who seeks to wed these traditions together? Is such a marriage possible, or is it doomed from the start?

Language and Ontology

Before proceeding to the work of answering these fundamental questions about whether being and becoming divine traditions can be integrated in any consistent fashion, it must be demonstrated that Farley does seek to accomplish such integration. It is a straightforward matter to show that Farley routinely interweaves tropes of being and becoming divine throughout *Gathering Those Driven Away*. The following passage is typical:

> Divinization remains unsatisfied with the milk of right belief and decent behavior. It craves the meat that liberates us from whatever is unworthy of our divine selves. It ignites a different desire: why not be flame? Christians as diverse as Athanasius, Angela of Foligno, and Friedrich Schleiermacher believe the incarnation is a cosmic event through which Divinity became human *so that* humanity could become divine. Christ may not provide exclusive access to our divine nature, but the incarnation is an invitation to awaken to our deepest desires and truest identity.[5]

5. Farley, *Gathering Those Driven Away*, 170.

While the whole of this passage can be read as consonant with the *theosis* tradition, another note is plainly sounded: Farley's affirmation that human beings possess a divine nature and must awaken to our "truest identity." Here the idioms of being divine traditions are interwoven with a more traditional Christian language of becoming divine. Farley goes so far as to (re)define "divinization" as "the desire to experience more fully *what is already the case*. It is the process of sanctification for those already justified."[6] Again, Farley weds *theosis* as typically understood—the second sentence which interprets sanctification as divinization is wholly in keeping with the orthodox becoming divine tradition—with the first sentence which stands in the being divine tradition. To speak of "what is already the case" is to assert that in some sense, human beings are already divine.

The same integration of motifs is found in Farley's claim that "Divinization emancipates us from obscurations that deny us our true identity. Through increasing intimacy with the Divine we come to the state where we are incapable of hurting or wounding anyone; and discover psychologically nonviolent ways of relating to those who harm us. Divinization fosters the human capacity to participate in the divine *eros* and *caritas* for the world."[7] The language of removing obscurations to disclose one's true identity is plainly derived from a being divine framework, whereas the language of "increasing intimacy" with the divine and "participation" is drawn from the becoming divine tradition. Again, although these idioms are smoothly juxtaposed, questions linger about how they fit together. What ontology or imaginative frame makes it possible to hold these modes of discourse together? The mind that desires consistency is not easily silenced.

Thankfully, there is nothing merely ad hoc about Farley's project. What is articulated in *Gathering Those Driven Away* is a theological vision in which God is a nondual and nameless reality that underlies and undergirds all creation. This reality is utterly different from anything whatsoever as it is no-thing, but precisely because it is no-thing whatsoever, it is nearer to everything than it is to itself. Readers familiar with the apophatic theology of Nicholas of Cusa will recognize these theological moves, and not surprisingly, Nicholas is a regular interlocutor in *Gathering Those Driven Away*. For example, Farley appeals to Nicholas's "On

---

6. Farley, *Gathering Those Driven Away*, 171 (emphasis added).

7. Farley, *Gathering Those Driven Away*, 173.

the Vision of God" in order to render more capacious the very idea of incarnation. Christ is to be seen in every human face:

> This ascent into imageless darkness wherein we see the unveiled beauty of Christ's face is what makes it possible for us to recognize Christ in human faces. Ascent to uncreated darkness helps to break the hold of the ego-mind so that we can encounter the unveiled beauty glimmering in the mobile beauty and suffering of every face. The Divine Emptiness is the simultaneity of otherness and sameness. It is always the same as itself, divine, in such a way that it can be manifest only through infinite variety. Or rather, itself empty of otherness and sameness it is displayed in the infinite diversity of actual faces.[8]

God, or here Christ, is beyond the dichotomy of same and other and so may be called "not-other" to use Nicholas's own term (*non-aliud*). God is emptiness, a no-thing that is refracted in every thing and to be seen therein.

And precisely because God is not-other, nonduality obtains between the human being and divinity. Now, this is a noteworthy claim on Farley's part even though she stands in a venerable, albeit neglected, tradition in making it. I know of no contemporary constructive theologian who weds together apophasis and nonduality so intimately.[9] To begin with, nonduality (*advaita*) is a term derived from Hindu and Buddhist traditions and so rarely deployed in Christian theological circles. Moreover, apophatic theology is often employed to opposite effect, namely to assert *infinite distance* between God and beings. Kevin Hector has recently made this observation about Jean-Luc Marion's theology. Marion's theology, as presented by Hector, is resonant with Farley's version of apophasis. For Marion too, any God who can be fit to the size of a concept would not be God. God necessarily exceeds all conceptualization. Therefore, as Hector shows, Marion suggests that discourse about God ought to be understood as "de-nominative" or "non-predicative" and as performing the work of praise and not as offering a conceptual description of the divine nature.[10] Although Farley does not offer a full and formal account of the nature of language about the divine, she would not differ in the main with Marion's

8. Farley, *Gathering Those Driven Away*, 181.

9. For my own efforts in this direction, see Thatamanil, *Immanent Divine*.

10. Hector, *Theology without Metaphysics*, 16–17.

commitment to apophasis, save in one crucial respect: Marion's discourse of distance. Hector calls attention to this feature of Marion's work:

> Because God is the One who gives-to-be all that is (*es gibt*), it follows that an act of giving, charity, or donation is prior to being/s; this means, on the one hand, that the radical distance of God from being/s *must* be acknowledged, and, on the other, that this distance *can* be acknowledged. All that is—and the fact *that* anything is—depends upon a prior act of charity, an act that is necessarily misunderstood if conceived of as if it stood within the realm of that which it gives to be; hence the distance of the Gift must be acknowledged. . . . Marion concludes, then, that Charity is the only name suitable for God, since this name alone signifies that which is infinitely qualitatively different from all being/s.[11]

Farley would contend that Marion's apophasis does not go far enough, as the conceptual asceticism that apophasis calls for is aborted by a thinking in which concepts of self and other, far and near, remain in operation. The God who is at a remove, at a distance, remains a God to whom the category of distance remains applicable. Pseudo-Dionysius, the father of Christian apophasis, is unlikely to be content with this partial dethroning of the conceptual register. It is, at any rate, out of keeping with Farley's reading. For her,

> The *via negativa* is a Christian practice intended to dissolve the mind's attachment to concepts and integrate nonduality into awareness. Pseudo Dionysius deploys names and concepts to gradually extinguish both: the divine nature "is not soul nor mind nor does it possess imagination, conviction, speech, or understanding . . . it is not wisdom, neither one nor oneness, divinity nor goodness, nor is it spirit. There is neither speaking of it nor name nor knowledge of it. Darkness and light, error and truth—it is none of these. It is beyond every assertion and every denial."[12]

For Farley, the conceptuality of near and far and hence any discourse of distance must be dissolved by an apophasis truly worthy of the name. Here, she stands squarely in the tradition of Marguerite Porete, who undoes talk of God's distance:

---

11. Hector, *Theology without Metaphysics*, 18–19.

12. Farley, "Duality and Non-Duality," 139–40.

> His farness is greater nearness, because from nearby, in itself,
> it better knows what is far, which [knowing] always makes her
> [the Soul] to be in union by his will, without the interference
> of any other thing which may happen to her. All things are one
> for her, without a why, and she is nothing in a One of this sort.[13]

Porete's *coincidentia oppositorum* of transcendence and immanence is the fruit of a deeper apophasis than Marion's, and it is precisely that thoroughgoing depth that concludes in nonduality.

Farley deploys the term nonduality carefully so that it is not misconstrued by ordinary habits of mind that make ready recourse to same versus other dualistic thinking. These constricted patterns of reflection inevitably reduce nonduality to pantheism by making divinity *the same as* humanity and world. As Farley puts it, the "accusation" of pantheism, "is itself embedded in a simple reversal of the logic of duality. Instead of thinking of God as 'totally other' than creation, God is conceived of as 'the same' as creation."[14] But neither assertion is on target: "For apophatic theologians the distinction of same and other, so crucial for beings, is irrelevant to Divinity. Applying either side of it, sameness or otherness, to God can have a kind of truth to it, but both are equally problematic."[15]

Apophatic theology and its negations do not serve in Farley's account to place divinity at an infinite distance from beings. Spatial language of distance is shown to be inappropriate inasmuch as it renders Divinity into an-other who is else-where. A thoroughgoing apophasis requires a more rigorous *ascesis*. She writes,

> The *via negativa* attempts to interrupt this way of thinking about
> Divinity. Rather than conceiving of Divinity as a being with cer-
> tain characteristics, this approach unpins our minds from the
> habit of conceiving of everything in terms of beings. Beings are
> the same as themselves and different from others. They have
> their own separate and distinct existence. They come into being
> and pass out of it. God is not a being, even a super-being; God
> is not a being at all[16]

The subtlety of this language does much to explain why Farley feels free to deploy both being and becoming divine idioms. Because God is the

---

13. Marguerite Porete, *The Mirror of Simple Souls*, 46.

14. Farley, *Gathering Those Driven Away*, 83.

15. Farley, *Gathering Those Driven Away*, 83.

16. Farley, *Gathering Those Driven Away*, 65.

source and ground of creaturely being, God is not other than the creature. The creature cannot exist apart from divinity. Still more can be said: the creature's being simply is divinity, as it has no being apart from divinity. For these reasons, the discourse of being divine is neither mistaken nor inappropriate. In the most radical language employed by Farley's primary theological inspiration, Marguerite Porete, the soul can be said to preexist in the divine ground prior to time and creation.

And yet, the creature *qua* creature is not divine. She remains a particular and delimited this, a something and not a no-thing—a being among beings, which the divine most certainly is not. God is not a being, not even the most elevated of beings. In this respect, Farley shares a deep affinity with Tillich's ground of being theology, although her discourse is shaped primarily by Neoplatonic motifs of God as the Good *beyond being*.[17] Indeed, God is so far beyond being that it would be truer to speak of God as a no-thing or nothingness itself. The question then is what is the relationship between the "somethingness" of the creature and the nothingness of God?

Two theological tropes present themselves at this juncture, each tied to a respective set of contemplative practices: tropes of *becoming* and tropes of *unbecoming*. Within a more conventional and orthodox (also Orthodox) frame, finite creatures become divine as they are infused by uncreated divine energies. The Orthodox tradition, especially as inspired by Gregory Palamas, is prepared to speak of the creature as becoming divine and even becoming uncreated as the eternal energies of divinity enter and transform the creature.

In the second imaginary, the creature is not infused by divine energies but leaves behind its somethingness by *unbecoming* or becoming nothing. By a rigorous *ascesis* that is volitional as well as cognitive, the creature unbecomes by willing nothing, surrendering even the will to will what God wills. If one can will what God wills, the creature remains to will and to love. Only when even this creaturely remainder is surrendered does it return to that primal and aboriginal ground of nondual indistinction.

To which of these tropes does Farley appeal? The answer, as the reader may by now suspect, is both! Discourses of becoming and unbecoming are interfused in Farley's writing; she stands under the inspiration

17. See for example her claim, "The incarnation is the embodiment of the Divine in a human form. The Goodness Beyond Being becomes meat (*carne*)." Farley, *Gathering Those Driven Away*, 63.

of both Palamas and Porete, even though the latter enjoys priority, as the Beguine's theology is more rigorously nondual. When commending hesychastic commitment to embodied discipline, Farley appeals to Palamas's discourse of deification: "when the saints contemplate this divine light within themselves, seeing it by the divinizing communion of the Spirit . . . then they behold the garment of their deification, their mind being glorified and filled by the grace of the Word, beautiful beyond measure in His splendor."[18] For Palamas, human beings don the garment of deification when infused by the deifying energies of divinity by the power of the Holy Spirit. That operation occurs *ad extra*. But given Farley's apophatic dismissal of the language of spatiality, this dimension of Palamas's theology is not pertinent in Farley's reading.

What matters most to Farley is a Neoplatonic conviction that the movement out from the abyss of divinity to the world and the movement from the world into divinity is but one work of divinity in which God as Wisdom/Logos is the fulcrum. It is proper to speak of the world as distinct from divinity, but it is also right to speak of the world as the self-giving and diffusion of divinity. The world's being is not-other than divinity, and the world's return to divinity is also accomplished by divinity. The fluidity of Farley's understanding of the God–world relation is fully manifest in her appeal to the work of John Scotus Eriugena. Farley cites this father of Celtic Christianity who writes in his commentary to the prologue of John:

> And now you [the Evangelist] call him "light" and "life, because this same Son, who is the Word, is the life and light of all things that are made through him. . . . Observe the forms and beauties of sensible things and comprehend the Word of God in them. If you do so, the truth will reveal to you in all such things only he who made them, outside of whom you have nothing to contemplate, for he himself is all things. For whatever truly is, in all things that are, is he.[19]

To Eriugena's striking language, Farley adds, "Pantheism, panentheism, absolute qualitative distinction: all true—and all inadequate to the infiltration of the cosmos by Divinity."[20] All these formulations fall short—although given her nondualism, "absolute qualitative distinction"

18. Farley, *Gathering Those Driven Away*, 172.

19. Farley, *Gathering Those Driven Away*, 125.

20. Farley, *Gathering Those Driven Away*, 125.

is likely to be most problematic—but the intention of Farley's appeal to Eriugena is unmistakable: the world is shot through with divinity. The relationship between God and world is nondual. Given divine presence and given the inadequacy of all linguistic frames, the usual distinctions between being and becoming divine traditions cannot be sustained. Moreover, the concrete disciplines found in becoming divine traditions and those traditions that speak of unbecoming into divine nothingness serve to undo "the distance" between divinity and humanity, even if the idiom of unbecoming seems to best capture Farley's core commitment to the inherent divinity of the self.

Modes of Access to Divinity: On Knowing and Loving God

If both sets of discourses and their attendant therapeutic regimes serve to erase notions of rigid and radical separation between divinity and humanity, between God and world, then questions about the relative adequacy of these frameworks may hinge on the questions identified earlier in this essay, namely those concerning modes of access to divinity and affectivity—the priority of love over knowledge or vice versa—and questions about the human predicament. On the question of the most efficacious mode of access to divinity, Farley's work surprises. Customarily it is safe to suppose that the more rigorously nondualistic a theologian is, the more likely it is that she will emphasize the priority of knowledge over love: knowledge that *one is divine* surpasses *love of the divine*. This logic does not neatly apply within Farley's theology.

On the soul's journey to divinity, Farley is clear that love must be the driving force. Reason must be left behind as love drives the soul to where reason cannot go. And yet the itinerary of love culminates in a knowing beyond reason, a nondual knowledge in which the soul discovers that the object of the soul's love already lies within the soul's home ground. The result: love and knowledge enjoy an unusual intimacy. Farley's commitment to nonduality does not diminish the worth of love nor does love unilaterally triumph over knowledge. Ultimately, Farley insists that only divinity reconnects us to the Divine. Here, she cites Porete:

> I have said that I will love Him.
> I lie, for I am not.
> It is He alone who loves me;
> He is, and I am not. . . .

And by this am I impregnated.
This is the divine seed and Loyal Love.[21]

God loves the soul and loves Godself in the soul. God must love Godself in me. Appealing to Porete, Farley writes, "only . . . divinity loves the Divine, not as something alien and other, seated far away, 'way beyond the blue,' but near at hand, closer even than one's own heart or breath. We crave Divinity not only to console us in our misery but because we are light and we long for radiance. Only Christ ascends to heaven because there is nothing but Christ. Light from light, a light that burns within us too."[22]

Here then all talk of the ways by which one can come to God and the relative superiority of those ways seem irrelevant. Ultimately, only God can bring human beings to God, and God can do this work in us because we are never separated from God. The longing for God is already God at work in us. Hence, for Farley, there is no reason to suppose that knowledge must supersede love or that love must supersede knowledge. Conceptual knowledge of the divine mystery is, of course, impossible, but intuitive nondual knowing is possible. However, if Love is itself divine and our love for divinity is itself the divine in us, then Farley's version of nondualism need not posit a moment in which love falls away as the distinction between creature and creator is annulled. Knowledge of divine nearness never dispatches with love; nondual knowledge and love commingle. Love and knowledge collaborate so that we can become what we already are: light from light.

Nondualism and the Question of the Human Predicament

Thus far we have seen that virtually all the dichotomies that mark the distinction between being and becoming traditions seem to dissolve in Farley's version of apophatic theology. What about the matter of the human predicament? Those traditions which posit that human beings are ontologically alienated from divinity make it plain that there can be no talk about the inherent divinity of self. If human estrangement from divinity is real rather than apparent, one might become divine after human sinfulness is addressed, but if alienation is real, no recourse to a nondual theological framework is possible.

21. Farley, *Gathering Those Driven Away*, 178.
22. Farley, *Gathering Those Driven Away*, 178–9.

By contrast, nondual traditions speak in the key of forgetting when identifying the human predicament. Such forgetting is the cause of the human predicament and not an ontologically real alienation or separation from divinity. Where does Farley stand on this question? On this point, Farley comes down decisively on the side of forgetting and so stands squarely in the being divine tradition. The wounds inflicted by suffering cause us to forget our dignity and obscure from view the beauty of the world: "This is the fall: to be asleep and unaware of the beauty of the present moment."[23] Farley unambiguously rejects atonement theories which assert that, "God is angry, as angry as Nero or Caligula, and demands blood to satisfy his righteous rage."[24] Moreover, she is clear about the core ontological matter: "Divinity is the groundless ground of all that is and is also the deepest truth of the human soul. It is this erotic groundlessness that constitutes our own divine image."[25] Therefore, there can be no talk about a real separation from divinity.

> Our condition is one of suffering and affliction, of sin and the *perception* of God-forsakenness. Mother Christ meets us by coming to us in our extremity. The Beloved seeks us in our destitution where we have been divested of the beauty of spiritual beings. Or to put this in another way, it is as creatures destitute and suffering that we bear the divine nature."[26]

Even in the midst of acute and degrading suffering, Farley insists that human beings bear the divine nature. We suffer mistakenly from the "perception" of God-forsakenness but the truth is that we never are. Here, she operates from a nondualist frame through and through.

Moreover, Farley's commitment to the inherent dignity of the human being makes her acutely sensitive to the mysterious power of suffering. Suffering is so acute and eviscerating of any sense of innate worth that human beings, when caught in its painful grip, find it easy to believe in atonement theories that assert their worthlessness and justify the eternal torments of hellfire:

> Because our minds are contorted by suffering, the idea that we all fell in the Garden of Eden and were sinful from before our birth is easy to believe. Our worthlessness is so deep that the

23. Farley, *Gathering Those Driven Away*, 223.

24. Farley, *Gathering Those Driven Away*, 212.

25. Farley, *Gathering Those Driven Away*, 66–67.

26. Farley, *Gathering Those Driven Away*, 155 (emphasis added).

few years of our life are insufficient to contain it. Tracing it back through a primordial past expresses the metaphysical and essential nature of our worthlessness. That God is angry with us makes sense: of course God is enraged, he has every right to be.

As Farley proceeds, it becomes clear that among the things that human beings need to be saved from are atonement theories such as these because they serve only to exacerbate the power of suffering to wound and defraud us of our innate sense of worth.[27] From within the confines of such theories, taken literally, no royal road can be found to the territory of nonduality.

On the whole, Farley holds open a variety of soteriological options so long as they result eventually in real and genuine participation in the divine life; she acknowledges that it is possible to move into divinity even within a theological frame that begins with conventional atonement theories, so long as justification leads eventually to sanctification understood as *theosis*. Human beings are made for divinity and nothing less than becoming divine will satisfy. Nonetheless, Farley opposes any soteriology that would risk eviscerating human dignity and so will not grant to ransom and substitutionary theories of atonement anything more than provisional psychological validity. Human beings bear innate worth not just because they are capable of becoming divine but because the soul's ground is not-other than the divine ground. Here, one finds in Farley's work a clear preference for and commitment to being divine traditions over becoming divine traditions even if her work customarily posits a certain fluidity between the two frameworks.

Wendy Farley's work is significant for a host of reasons. First, she fruitfully troubles the putatively impermeable boundary between becoming and being divine traditions. This opening will require extensive deliberation. Second, Wendy Farley's work holds great promise for contemporary theology precisely because it is a creative appropriation of historically deep resources derived from medieval Christian mystics like Mechthild, Marguerite, and Nicholas of Cusa. These thinkers in turn stand in an antique lineage extending to Pseudo-Dionysius, among others. Therefore, hers is a theological program that cannot easily be dismissed as an exercise in ungrounded and superficial novelty. Finally, Farley offers to contemporary constructive theology a Christian nondualism that also holds tremendous interreligious promise. Especially intriguing are

27. Farley, *Gathering Those Driven Away*, 158.

potential lines of conversation with Buddhists that Farley broaches in the body of *Gathering Those Driven Away*. Farley's nondualism is perhaps the most important offering to comparative theology since Paul Tillich's nearly nondualistic ground of being theology. For these many reasons, we eagerly look forward to the further development of this singular theological vision.

Bibliography

Eckhart, Meister. *Wandering Joy: Meister Eckhart's Mystical Philosophy*. Translated by Reiner Schürmann. Great Barrington, MA: Lindisfarne, 2001.

Farley, Wendy. "Duality and Non-Duality in Christian Practice: Reflections on the Benefits of Buddhist-Christian Dialogue for Constructive Theology." *Buddhist-Christian Studies* 31 (2011): 135–46.

———. *Gathering Those Driven Away: A Theology of Incarnation*. Louisville, KY: Westminster John Knox, 2011.

Hector, Kevin. *Theology without Metaphysics: God, Language, and the Spirit of Recognition*. New York: Cambridge University Press, 2011.

Porete, Marguerite. *The Mirror of Simple Souls*. Mahwah, NJ: Paulist Press, 1993.

Thatamanil, John. *The Immanent Divine: God, Creation, and the Human Predicament*. Minneapolis: Fortress, 2006.

Voss Roberts, Michelle. *Dualities: A Theology of Difference*. 1st ed. Louisville, KY: Westminster John Knox, 2010.

FOURTEEN

Canon, Comparison, and Other Lovers

Michelle Voss Roberts

ALTHOUGH PEOPLE REFLECT UPON God in many genres, only a small range of these works appears in the discipline of systematic theology. The authors regularly referenced are the "usual suspects," the big names in the field: Gregory of Nyssa, Augustine, Thomas Aquinas, Karl Barth, Paul Tillich. Wendy Farley is no stranger to these men and their works, but she draws from a still-deeper pool of theological wisdom that includes a range of non-canonical sources—the "others" of the Christian tradition toward whom, and from whom, divine eros nevertheless flows.

For Farley, neglected and excluded voices sensitize us to aspects of the tradition we might not otherwise notice. They "open up possibilities for theological reflection that are absent when one remains within the lineage of traditional theology."[1] The very dominance of the dominant tradition is an obstacle. The Church is tempted to forget that its creeds and doctrines are not the faith itself but part of an ongoing process of discerning the divine mystery. In association with empire, the Church has taken Caesar's power as its own and crushed those who testify to other kinds of spiritual efficacy. For these reasons, little-read sources become major authorities in Farley's thought, including authors who do not write in recognizably theological genres, have been condemned as heretical, or belong by genealogy to another religious tradition. I use the

---

1. Farley, *The Wounding and Healing of Desire*, xi.

term "non-canonical" for these sources: they lie outside both the Christian scriptural canon and the mainstream theological tradition.

What do such sources accomplish in Farley's work? In *Gathering Those Driven Away*, extra-canonical sources from the first centuries voice the impact of the Roman Empire upon the Jewish and Christian communities, as well as Jesus' challenge to the kind of power that empire represents. The Didache offers simple practices for developing the loving-kindness characteristic of Jesus' alternative community. The Gospel of Mary Magdalene witnesses to Jesus' friendship with women and Mary's authority as an apostle. "Heretical" voices from the underside of the church's growing power—from Origen, Pelagius, Meister Eckhart, and Marguerite Porete, to the feminist, queer, and liberation theologians of today—bear further witness to the love of Christ. Lyrics from folk songs, the music of the outcast, punctuate Farley's writing. She invokes folk tales that weave a counter-narrative to the world's logic. She cites her own children as sources of the wisdom that is incarnate in everyday life.[2]

Farley also looks beyond sources internal to the Christian tradition, leaving traces of engagement with Buddhist wisdom and practice throughout her work. Farley writes out of the vision of reality she has encountered in a quietly interreligious path:

> I rediscovered Christ after I met His Holiness, the Dalai Lama. Like Thomas, I had to see to believe. A human body can contain and radiate the Divine. . . . I had never seen or really believed in incarnation: human being fully lit by an unwavering divine presence. After that, I found myself falling in love with Christ, entirely against my will and confounded by my intellectual and spiritual formation.[3]

Like the marginal voices in Christianity, the comparative encounter with other religious traditions helps Farley to retrieve Christianity's forgotten wisdom. Buddhist thinkers redirect her to proponents of non-duality within her home tradition such as Friedrich Schleiermacher, Marguerite Porete, and Meister Eckhart. Buddhist meditation reminds her of techniques for developing compassion in Pelagius and the Didache. The

---

2. Farley, *Gathering Those Driven Away*. Folk tales and songs are also major sources in Farley, *The Wounding and Healing of Desire*, chapters 5 and 6.

3. Farley, *Gathering Those Driven Away*, 134.

Buddhist tradition also fosters important spiritual habits such as attention to suffering and a method of negative "theology."[4]

In keeping with Farley's practice of reading neglected and excluded
voices that sensitize Christians to aspects of their tradition they might not
otherwise notice, I propose to read a major work in Christian monastic
theology, Bernard of Clairvaux's *Sermons on the Song of Songs*, together
with a Hindu work few Christians have encountered, Rupa Gosvamin's
Ujjvala-nilamani. Both texts offer guidance for a contemplative life based
in scriptures that depict the love relationship of divinity and the soul in
vividly erotic terms. In both texts, interpretation of the scriptural love relationship runs the risk of becoming a private, individual quest of union
with the divine. Farley's treatment of eros provides a crucial third leg of
this comparative (love) triangle. The following comparative excursus illustrates how the role of others in the individual's love relation with God
can emerge more clearly when one reads Bernard's sermons alongside
Rupa's work.

Krishna's Lovers

The *Ujjvala-nilamani* (*UN*) is Rupa's treatise for the most advanced practitioners of the sect of Krishna devotion known as Gaudiya Vaisnavism.
Its title denotes a bright, shining (*ujjvala*) sapphire, or alternately, a blue
jewel of erotic passion (*ujjvala*).[5] In Rupa's earlier work, the *Bhakti-
rasamrta-sindhu* (Ocean of the Nectar of Devotion), he outlines the
community's worship, culminating in five increasingly intimate modes of
devotional love: peaceful meditation, service, friendship, parental love,
and erotic love.[6] The *UN* is Rupa's exposition of the highest kind of love.
Rupa's work can be seen as an extended commentary on the primary
scriptural text of the tradition, Book X of the *Bhagavata Purana*, which
has been described as "the 'Song of Songs' of ancient India."[7]

Book X of the *Bhagavata Purana* narrates the story of Krishna as a
charming young man in Vraj, a rustic region of North India that is home

4. Cf. Farley, *Gathering Those Driven Away*, chapter 3.

5. Translations from the *UN* are my own. I follow the Sanskrit text of Rūpa
Gosvāmin, *Ujjvalanīlamaṇiḥ*, in consultation with the paraphrase in Rūpa Gosvāmin,
Śrī *Ujjvala-nīlamaṇi*. Because diacritic markings are unlikely to be helpful for many
readers, I have restricted their use in this essay to references in the footnotes.

6. See Rūpa Gosvāmin, *The Bhaktirasāmṛtasindhu of Rūpa Gosvāmin*.

7. Schweig, *Dance of Divine Love*, 8.

to cow-herding folk. This descent of divinity is not an avatar of power, although the boy Krishna performs many miraculous feats to protect his friends. Rather, it is the consummate avatar of divine love. Krishna defeats demons with an air of playfulness, and his mischievous pranks serve only to endear him to the hearts of everyone around him. His love defies conventional morality as the mere sound of his flute lures the cowherding women and girls (*gopis*) out of the beds of their sleeping husbands to tryst with him in the forest. Krishna sports for a while with the *gopis*, but then he suddenly disappears from their midst. The distraught women search the forest for their beloved. Mad with grief, they imitate his charming habits and pastimes. Soon, they discover evidence that Krishna has slipped away to enjoy particular intimacy with one, favored *gopi*, whom the Gaudiya Vaisnava tradition has identified as Radha.[8] In the climax of the tenth book, the *gopis* converge upon a forest clearing and perform the circle dance known as the *ras lila*. Krishna graciously multiplies himself so that each woman thinks she is dancing with him alone. The moral of the tale is that each devotee can experience divine love in full.[9]

One of the most striking things about the love story of Krishna and Radha as it unfolds in Gaudiya Vaisnava literature is the number of players in it. The couple is surrounded by friends, parents, and rivals. Rupa explores these characters in minute detail. He describes ninety-six qualities Krishna displays as a lover. Krishna sometimes acts as a husband (*pati*), other times as a paramour (*upapati*). He is undyingly faithful to Radha, but in his love play he also exhibits characteristics of insincerity (being with one woman but thinking about another), cheating (saying another woman's name), and arrogance (not trying to hide the evidence of his other affairs) (*UN*, ch. 1). Krishna plays multiple roles and, as we shall see, so do those who love him.

Krishna grows up to be a king with thousands of queens, his *svakiya* ("one's own," i.e., married) lovers. By contrast, his *gopi* lovers in Vraj are either young unmarried girls or married to another man (*parakiya*) (*UN*, ch. 3). For many participants in the tradition, the supreme risk of this adulterous love is the superior model for devotion. The age, mannerisms, and experience of these women span a spectrum of love scenarios. Some

8. Some of the most passionate poetry in the tradition depicts the vicissitudes of their relationship. See Kṛṣṇadāsa Kavirāja Gosvāmī, Śrī *Govinda Līlāmṛta*. The earlier influential poetry of Jayadeva is another fine example: Miller, *Love Song of the Dark Lord*.

9. See Bryant, *Krishna: The Beautiful Legend of God*.

*gopi*s are more mature and expert in the ways of love, while others are shy and naïve. Some are easily angered, others easily appeased. Some are proud and jealous (a trait known as *mana*); others are more likely to be heartbroken (*UN*, ch. 5). A hierarchy of leaders (*nayikas*) and followers emerges among them (*UN*, ch. 6). They organize themselves into rival camps, some loyal to Radha, others determined to impede her relationship with Krishna for the sake of her rival, Candravali (*UN*, ch. 8–9).

Like Radha, Krishna has a circle of friends who assist him in various ways. They dress him, arrange his trysts, and entertain him. All of his companions love him dearly, and his most intimate friends are privy to his secret love affairs with the *gopi*s (UN, ch. 2). The friends of the couple serve as messengers between them (*UN*, ch. 7). Some of their most intimate companions are permitted to assist in their love play. Later Gaudiya Vaisnavas imagine particular characters serving the couple betel leaf, applying fragrant sandalwood paste to cool their bodies, and fetching their discarded garments.[10]

The imaginative play of the love-mad *gopi*s becomes a paradigm for devotees in this tradition: devotees are to discover and then play out their true spiritual identity as one of Krishna's lovers. Each follows in the path of that particular *gopi* and cultivates her persona through meditation. Although Radha remains Krishna's favorite, and her unique identity is off limits to devotees, the multiplicity of *gopi*s in the narrative provides numerous subordinate models for imitation.[11] Every spiritual disposition has an exemplar. Each devotional persona is empowered to enjoy a particular flavor in the *rasa* (taste, savoring) of divine love, and only the totality of the devotees' experiences can encompass the full range of sentiment.

Maidens and Friends of the Bridegroom

This too-brief description of Rupa's work may illustrate several points of contact with the traditions stemming from the biblical Song of Songs.

10. For example, Rupa Gosvamin's devotional identity centers upon a thirteen-and-a-half-year-old girl with dark yellow complexion, dressed in a sari patterned with peacock's feathers. She is Radha's intimate friend, whose role in the *lila* is to serve betel nut to the lovers. Haberman, *Acting as a Way of Salvation*, 91.

11. Scholars hotly debate the degree to which devotees are to imitate the various scriptural exemplars. See Dimock, *The Place of the Hidden Moon*; Haberman, *Acting as a Way of Salvation*; and Wulff, *Drama as a Mode of Religious Realization*.

Bernard's sermons on this short book of Hebrew wisdom literature sketch contours of the soul's love relationship with God that run parallel to the Krishna story. Like the *UN*, this text is not for the undisciplined, but only for advanced practitioners (Serm. 1.12). Both texts comment on scripture with an essentially erotic theme. They evoke a dialectic of divine presence and absence, with all of the emotions that attend such a love affair (Serm. 51, 57). Both also contemplate the mysterious ability of God to love many souls as if they were one (Serm. 69.2) and of the soul to experience this love "as though she alone were looked on by him" (Serm. 69.8).[12]

Although Bernard frequently calls his monks to be mindful of the monastic community, the presence of other people is often ancillary to the individual's experience of God. Much of his text encourages private mystical experience in the mode of a *single* couple, the divine Bridegroom and his Bride.[13] Who is this Bride? Bernard's sermons illuminate two options: the Church (Serm. 68) and the individual human soul (Serm. 69). There is an implicit plurality in the first option, for the Church is made up of many Christians. This multiplicity does not receive much focus, however, as the Bride-Church functions as a single character: she "signifies not one soul but the unity or rather unanimity of many" (Serm. 61.2). When the Bride is the soul, the temptation to focus solely on the private contemplative life can become even greater.[14]

Reading Bernard's sermons side by side with Rupa's exegesis alerts the observer to characters that Bernard mentions almost in passing: the friends of the Bridegroom and the maidens accompanying the Bride. Bernard invokes these characters to explain why the main characters sometimes speak of one another in the third person. For example, Bernard

12. Citations follow Bernard of Clairvaux, *On the Song of Songs I–IV*, trans. Kilian Walsh and Irene M. Edmonds. Vols. 4, 7, 31, and 40, Cistercian Fathers Series (Kalamazoo, MI: Cistercian Publications, Inc., 1971, 1976, 1979, 1980). Sermons (Serm.) 1–20 can be found in vol. I, 21–46 in vol. II, 47–66 in vol. III, and 67–86 in vol. IV.

13. One of Bernard's foremost interpreters describes the work as "entirely centered . . . on the two persons spoken of, namely, Christ and his Bride." Leclercq, "Introduction," 309. Following Leclercq, I capitalize both "Bride" and "Bridegroom" as titles for the leading characters except when I cite directly from sources that do not capitalize these words.

14. Leclercq elaborates upon the unity of the Bride, including the relation of the pastoral/communal and contemplative/individual orientations, in "Introduction," 317–323. For a discussion of various medieval Christian treatments of the identity of the Bride (as individual, as Mary, and as Church), see Astell, *The Song of Songs in the Middle Ages*.

imagines the Bride speaking about the Bridegroom to his attendants (Sg. 1:11, Serm. 42.1) and altering her manner of speaking for the sake of the maidens (Sg. 2:3, Serm. 49.1; Serm. 24.2, 51.4, 67.1, 77, 78). If we follow such references beyond these formal concerns, we may begin to realize an expanded cast of characters for God's lovers.

Bernard cautions that "not all those whom you see today waiting on the Bride and hanging around her, as the expression is, are friends of the bridegroom." Rather, some of his purported friends are self-interested, adorning themselves as brides rather than as attendants (Serm. 77:1). Although the friends and attendants might fittingly aspire to be lovers, the Bride ultimately leaves all others behind to go to her Beloved (Sg. 3.4, Serm. 79.2). The couple's true friends possess the virtues of self-control, innocence, and patience (Serm. 70.8–9). They are the watchmen of Song. 3:3, who "watch over and take care of the bride" (Serm. 77.2). These guardians of the church include the apostles, martyrs, angels, saints, and spiritual directors (Serm. 77.3–6). They "give her tidings of her beloved" (Serm. 78.6) and sustain her with the creed (Serm. 79.2). Angels also fill this role, sending messages and gifts and occasionally "[bringing] them into each other's presence, either snatching her up to him, or leading him down to her" (Serm. 31.5).

The "maidens" who "love without measure" (Sg. 1:2) receive attention in several short passages. Bernard likens the maidens to the new members of the monastic community, who "are not well equipped to penetrate sublime truths. Still infants in Christ, they must be fed with milk and oil." Their "indiscreet zeal" causes them to invent extra vigils and fasts contrary to the moderation of the common life (Serm. 19.7). These monks/maidens make importunate demands of their superior: "their feminine appetites and conduct still untempered, they nevertheless cling to the bride in the hope of making progress" (Serm. 52.1). They are the "daughters of Jerusalem," instructed "not to stir my beloved or rouse her until she pleases" (Sg. 2:7)—a commandment that allows the community's leader to enjoy the "contemplative repose" of the Bride (Serm. 53.1).

The maidens, then, are friends of the Bride. They are less advanced in the love of God than either the Bride or the Bridegroom's close friends. Sermon 23 homologizes them to the virgins of Jesus' parable, who "follow at a distance" (Matt. 26:58) when the Bride enters the rooms of the King (Sg 1:3). "They are still undeveloped, they can neither run with an energy to match that of the bride, nor achieve the ardor of her desire" (Serm.

23.1). The Bride does not forget them. They may be impatient in her absence, but she exhorts them to wait and assures them of a share in her joy (Serm. 23.1). Some of them are likely to be jealous of her "unique glory" and to "murmur against her . . . for in almost any group of young maidens [one finds] some who curiously watch the bride's actions, not to imitate but to disparage them" (Serm. 24.2–3). The Bride must, therefore, speak with discretion when she returns, lest the maidens find her "overbearing and insufferable because of the impetuosity of spirit that she seems to have brought back from the wine-cellar" (Serm. 49.5).

The friends and maidens exemplify various stages on the way to becoming a lover of Christ. Some companions are more intimate than others, such that they enter the "rooms of the King" (Sg. 1:3; Serm. 23.5–8). As Bernard discovers, "the King has not one bedroom only, but several. . . . For he has more than one queen; his concubines are many, his maids beyond counting. And each has her own secret rendezvous with the Bridegroom" (Serm. 23:9). As examples, Bernard cites the women who anointed Jesus' feet and head, Thomas who touched his side, John who reclined on his breast, and Paul who ascended to the third heaven. Each person finds his or her own place, depending on their virtue:

> Who among us can see the difference between these various merits, or rather rewards? . . . There are many rooms therefore in the Bridegroom's house; and each, be she queen, or concubine or one of the bevy of maidens, finds there the place and destination suited to her merits until the grace of contemplation allows her to advance further and share in the happiness of her Lord, to explore her Bridegroom's secret charms. (Serm. 23.10)

In such key moments, the Song and its commentary encourage readers to acknowledge the multiplicity of experiences of union with the divine.

In mining the Sermons for evidence of others, I have noted the significance of the maidens and the friends of the Bridegroom. After exploring their multiplicity of experience, however, Bernard reasserts the singularity of the Bride: "no maiden, or concubine, or even queen, may gain access to the mystery of that bedroom which the Bridegroom reserves solely for her who is his dove, beautiful, perfect and unique" (Serm. 23.10).[15] The plurality of God's lovers sits uneasily in a text oriented toward the unique inner chamber of divine union.

---

15. Bernard is consistently circumspect regarding his own experience of God, though he describes "the bedroom to which I have sometimes gained happy entrance" as the place where God the Bridegroom rests: "Alas! how rare the time, and how short the stay!" (Serm. 23.15, cf. 23.16).

Comparison

Comparison of the erotic devotion in these two traditions illuminates the multiplicity of experiences of divine love in each paradigm. Just as the Krishna of the *Bhagavata Purana* presents himself for adoration as a king, child, and friend, the biblical Bridegroom appears in various roles. Bernard writes,

> You must already have noticed how often he changes his coun-
> tenance in the course of this love-song, how he delights in
> transforming himself from one charming guise to another in the
> beloved's presence: at one moment like a bashful bridegroom . . .
> at another coming along like a physician with oil and ointments.
> . . . Sometimes, too, he joins up as a traveler with the bride and
> the maidens who accompany her on the road . . . as a wealthy
> father [cf. Luke 15:17] . . . or again like a magnificent and power-
> ful king. (Serm. 31.7)

For Bernard, these varied tastes of devotion, called *bhakti rasas* in Rupa's tradition, "titillate in manifold ways the palate of the soul" (Serm. 31.7).

The lovers of God also play various roles. After observing the *go-pis*, we notice a host of friends and companions in the Song tradition, each of whom may become lovers of God in their own way. Some *go-pis* love Krishna directly, in competition with one another, while others (their subordinates) assist their leader and love Krishna only indirectly. The friends in the Song function resemble the latter model, even if they aspire to love God directly. The Bride is not a rival to the maidens but a mother who helps them: "But now see how the maidens anticipate their own reward in that of their mother, how they regard her recompense and enjoyment as their own, how her admission consoles them for the bitter-ness of their rebuff" (Serm. 23.2). The rivalry of the *gopis* heightens the emotional tension of Krishna's love story, but Christian monastic spiritu-ality aims to foster the love of other Christians. Emotions of devotional love in both communities run the spectrum from joy in the presence of the Beloved to pain in his absence (Serm. 32.2). Yet whereas the jealous indignation (*mana*) of the slighted *gopi* lends charm to the narrative in which Krishna's infidelity is only part of his divine play, Bernard must prohibit anger and jealousy among his monks (Serm. 24.2–3).

Although the differences between God's many lovers do not utterly disappear in the identity of the singular, allegorized soul in either tradi-tion, Bernard's rhetoric tends in that direction. When Bernard introduces the queens, concubines, and maidens (Serm. 23), he withholds from them the title of Bride. Though he claims to have experienced the peaceful contemplation of the "King's bedroom," he writes, "Whether this be the same room that makes the bride so jubilant I do not dare to affirm" (Serm. 23.16). No individual may presume to claim the highest union that is the privilege of Christ and his Church. With a surprising echo of the Gaudiya Vaisnava practice of identifying not with Radha but with one of the subordinate *gopis*, Bernard instructs, "So we shall be lovers of the bride and loved by the Bridegroom" (Serm. 24.8). The Bride that enters into union with God is an ideal figure: the true Church. Individual souls comprise this figure, but their particular experiences lack fruition until they are fully conformed to the eschatological Church.

If we introduce Farley's eros for the other as a third interlocutor in this comparison, we more clearly observe the limitations of Bernard's unifying tendency. Farley encourages us to ask: Who has been driven away? In the beautiful round dance with Krishna, each devotee would like to think that she alone is dancing with her Beloved; yet Radha must live painfully with the knowledge that her rival, Candravali, is also truly beloved of Krishna. Their rivalry plays out onstage in the Gaudiya Vaisnava dramatic tradition, as well as in the larger competition between the Gaudiya Vaisnavas and other sects. Bernard's exclusions appear even more prominently in the text of his sermons. The Bride is, first and foremost, the Church. Bernard fulminates against heretics at several points, especially those he suspects of having improper sexual relations (Serm. 64–66, 80).[16] Despite his use of the feminine as a positive symbol, he has difficulty extending his monastic theology to actual women.[17] His rhetorical equation of black skin with sinfulness (Serm. 25) bolsters his support of the Second Crusade against the Muslims.[18] His disparaging and supercessionist comments about Jews are almost too frequent to count (cf. Serm. 14, 29.1, 58.7, 60.1–5, 73:1–2, 75.12).[19] He cannot bear to think of these others as lovers of God.

Farley advocates the use of non-canonical theological sources because such exclusionary tendencies, while they shore up a sense of community, can also close the Church off from the life-giving flow of divine

---

16. Kienzle, "Tending the Lord's Vineyard."

17. See Lytje, "The Interior and the Abject"; and Damrosch, "*Non Alia Sed Aliter.*"

18. Holsinger, "The Color of Salvation."

19. Cf. Serm. 14, 29.1, 58.7, 60.1–5, 73:1–2, 75.12.

love. "The witness of the great diversity of Christ's lovers is of an entirely different order than some tepid obligation to be inclusive. The church requires the voices of those driven away because these are ones that Wisdom herself uses."[20] The warmth of the divine embrace must not make us cold to divinity's other lovers.

Reading Farley's incarnational notion of eros alongside two erotic forms of faith—Bernard of Clairvaux's sermons *On the Song of Songs* and Rupa Gosvamin's *Ujjvala-nilamani*—has encouraged attention to the nature and role of others in the individual's love quest for God. Mystical union in both traditions may be tempted toward cozy interiority, on the one hand, and furious jealousy of others, on the other. But the divine eros knows no bounds, and it shines all the more brightly when reflected at the boundaries of familiar theological authority.

This comparative perspective, aided by Farley, witnesses to the multiplicity of divine eros and invites an opening to the other. No longer "shackling our theology to the relentless assertion of authority," we attend to "books and bodies that moved boldly beyond what institutions could tolerate."[21] Could the *gopis* become models of devotion for readers of the Song? Could their rivalry be an occasion to explore the diversity of devotional love? What other sources might inform the Christian theological canon? Which other lovers have Christians still not yet recognized as paramours and Brides of the divine?

Abbreviations

Serm.	[Sermons] *On the Song of Songs* of Bernard of Clairvaux
Sg.	Song of Songs
UN	*Ujjvala-nilamani* of Rupa Gosvamin

---

20. Farley, *Gathering Those Driven Away*, 5.

21. Farley, *Gathering Those Driven Away*, 8.

Bibliography

Astell, Ann W. *The Song of Songs in the Middle Ages*. Ithaca and London: Cornell University Press, 1995.

Bernard of Clairvaux. *On the Song of Songs I-IV*. Translated by Kilian Walsh and Irene M. Edmonds. Vols. 4, 7, 31, and 40, Cistercian Fathers Series. Kalamazoo, MI: Cistercian Publications, Inc., 1971, 1976, 1979, 1980.

Bryant, Edwin F. *Krishna: The Beautiful Legend of God: Śrīmad Bhāgavata Purāṇa, Book X; With Chapters 1, 6 and 29-31 from Book XI*. New York: Penguin, 2003.

Damrosch, David. "*Non Alia Sed Aliter:* The Hermeneutics of Gender in Bernard of Clairvaux." In *Images of Sainthood in Medieval Europe*, edited by Renate Blumenfeld-Kosinski and Timea Szell, 181–195. Ithaca and London: Cornel University Press, 1991.

Dimock, Edward C. Jr. *The Place of the Hidden Moon: Erotic Mysticism in the Vaiṣṇava-Sahajiyā Cult of Bengal*. Chicago: University of Chicago Press, 1966.

Farley, Wendy. *Gathering Those Driven Away: A Theology of Incarnation*. Louisville: Westminster John Knox, 2011.

———. *The Wounding and Healing of Desire: Weaving Heaven and Earth*. Louisville: Westminster John Knox, 2005.

Gosvāmī, Kṛṣṇadāsa Kavirāja. *Śrī Govinda Līlāmṛta: The Eternal Nectarean Pastimes of Śrī Govinda*. Translated by Advaita Dāsa. Vrindavan: Rasbihari Lal & Sons, 2000.

Gosvāmin, Rūpa. *The Bhaktirasāmṛtasindhu of Rūpa Gosvāmin*. Translated by David L. Haberman. Delhi: IGNCA and Motilal Banarsidass, 2003.

———. *Śrī Ujjvala-nīlamaṇi*. Translated by Kuśakratha Dāsa. Edited by Pūrṇaprajña Dāsa. Vrindavan: Rasbihari Lal and Sons, 2006.

———. *Ujjvalanīlamaṇiḥ*. Vrindavan: Gauḍīya Vedānta, 2003.

Haberman, David L. *Acting as a Way of Salvation: A Study of Rāgānuga Bhakti Sādhana*. Delhi: Motilal Banarsidass, 2001.

———. Introduction to *The Bhaktirasāmṛtasindhu of Rūpa Gosvāmin*, translated by David L. Haberman, xxix–lxxiv. Delhi: IGNCA and Motilal Banarsidass, 2003.

Holsinger, Bruce. "The Color of Salvation: Desire, Death, and the Second Crusade in Bernard of Clairvaux's Sermons on the Song of Songs." In *The Tongue of the Fathers: Gender and Identity in Twelfth-Century Latin*, edited by David Townsend and Andrew Taylor, 156–186. Philadelphia: University of Pennsylvania Press, 1998.

Kienzle, Beverly M. "Tending the Lord's Vineyard: Cistercians, Rhetoric, and Heresy, 1143–1229. Part I: Bernard of Clairvaux, the 1143 Sermons and the 1145 Preaching Mission." *Heresis* 25 (1995) 29–61.

Leclercq, Jean. "Introduction to Saint Bernard's Doctrine in the Sermons on the Song of Songs." Translated by Elias Dietz, OCSO. *Cistercian Studies Quarterly* 43.3 (2008) 309–325.

Lytje, Maren. "The Interior and the Abject: Uses and Abuses of the Female in the Middle Ages." *Culture and Religion* 5.3 (2004) 287–319.

Miller, Barbara Stoler. *Love Song of the Dark Lord: Jayadeva's Gītagovinda*. Edited and translated by Barbara Stoler Miller. New York: Columbia University Press, 1977.

Schweig, Graham M. *Dance of Divine Love: The Rāsa Līlā of Krishna from the Bhāgavata Purāṇa, India's Classic Sacred Love Story*. Delhi: Motilal Banarsidass, 2007.

Wulff, Donna M. *Drama as a Mode of Religious Realization: The Vidagdhamādhava of Rūpa Gosvāmī*. Chico, CA: Scholars Press, 1984.

Consider Silence

Marcia W. Mount Shoop

Consider silence
an option
consider silence
oppression
long gusts of unspoken
collisions of truth and consequences
and erotic quiet
delight in havens
riddled with a lonely
song
empty-wise
gather into sacred void
divine darkness
alien embrace
your familiar
settle into waves of voices
surrender there, there
to burning Power within
without permission
find flesh rising
ashes of ravaged ones
who return silent cords
with the groans of giving birth
and fingertips dance out
round sounds of a new, old world

~ ~ ~

IF I DIDN'T GET out of bed by 3:30am and if I wasn't driving out of the driveway by 4:00am then I had no chance of making it. Every Monday morning of the second year of my PhD program this was the drill. I had to make it from Charlotte, NC, to Atlanta, GA, in time for my Schleiermacher seminar that met bright and early Monday mornings. It was almost a four-hour drive and, keeping in mind the snarl of arriving at rush hour in Atlanta, I had this ride down to a science.

It was a strange journey. My mind was tired and busy turning the wheels of the transition I needed to make from my life in Charlotte as the wife of an NFL football coach to the life of a graduate student in religious studies at Emory University. I inevitably got sleepy on the drive and would start to feel the heaviness of my eyes involuntarily closing. No amount of windows open, music blaring could wake me up. Even resorting to drinking a Mountain Dew for a jolt of caffeine didn't do the trick for this non-caffeine drinker. My mind would get foggy and my thoughts would meld together. Schleiermacher and Kant and Whitehead (my three courses that term) would ooze around in my sleepy head along with football plays and checklists about whether I had turned the burner off on the stove. Sometimes, I would even hallucinate. I remember one time in particular when my windshield wipers morphed into winged-like arches.

By the time I arrived at Emory I felt as if I had been through something akin to a combined near-death experience and bizarre drug trip. Moving from that to a doctoral-level discussion on a 19th-century German theologian could have been torturous enough to make even the most dedicated student question, "Is this worth it?"

Instead, how and what I learned those Monday mornings around the seminar table fed a deep aquifer of vitality in me. While I love Schleiermacher's theological anthropology and I am a sucker for parsing out dense texts with others (hence the trifecta of Schleiermacher, Kant, and Whitehead all in one semester), it was not simply the text itself that made the experience so revitalizing. It was the mode of encounter Wendy Farley made space for in that and other classes she taught and still teaches.

During the mid- to late nineties, when I was studying at Emory, Wendy was beginning her practice of meditation and sacred silence. She decided, as an experiment, to begin our Schleiermacher seminar each session with extended, meditative silence. For most (if not all) of us this way of starting a doctoral seminar was unfamiliar, perhaps strange, and maybe even dubious for some.

Knowing my own frenetic prelude to arriving in class and how fatigued I would be, I feared that this quiet stillness would be the perfect invitation to sleep, that my body would need to simply nod off. But far from inducing sleep, it was an awakening. Remarkably, only a few weeks into this practice I began to be almost thirsty for it before class—it set itself ahead of me on my morning journey as an oasis of calm and Holy attentiveness. The sensation of being open and the luxury of focusing on my breath was, indeed, something that tasted like the freshest, coolest water on a hot, dry day.

I also began to see the radical ways that we were being nurtured in and by this silence. It was a quiet revolution. We were seizing the way women had long been silenced in the academy, especially in the theological tradition, for our own life-giving use. And at the same time we were embracing a transcendent quality to what it means to be human beings together exploring the contours of redemption. As I look back now, I think how else could we have "gotten" what Schleiermacher's *Gefühl* is all about except by practicing a mode of non-cognitive awareness in community. It emptied us and filled us simultaneously; and it embodied our interdependence with each other and with a Divine impulse that we cultivate peace. And so we drank in the embodied interdependence of Schleiermacher's theological anthropology.

And the flowering that this wash of vitality and interdependence cultivated and hydrated continues to unfold and grow new shoots for many of us who studied with Wendy at Emory. She made space for us to be rigorous and collegial, attuned to fine intellectual points and viscerally aware of the limits of our cognition. She helped to form many of us as scholars not afraid to deal with the rawest kinds of pain (trauma, abuse of power, suffering) and the most tenacious spaces of societal ruptures (religious difference, homophobia, cultural myopia) with an eye toward redemptive threads.

As I live into my life these days as an independent scholar, I realize more and more the blessings of feeling "authorized" to claim my voice in contentious places. Wendy helped me and continues to encourage me not to mask the power of women's voices to be a transformative force. She was a midwife when my own theological voice began to emerge. And her mentoring and friendship now that I am no longer a student in her classroom continue to coax and clarify how I take up space in the many contexts I move in and out of in my work. This dynamic of finding, claiming, and writing theology in my voice is complicated and nurtured still as I carve out my work without an institutional home to grant me legitimacy. And my voice continues its entanglement with the fertile and formidable potency of silence/ing and audibility.

The questions I ask in and through my work about my own voice flow into a broader line of query about what exactly it means to do theology anymore. Perhaps because I move in and out of multiple contexts with my work (church, academy, etc.), these questions seem increasingly pressing, and silence spiders its way through it all with radical liberation and its own particular kind of paralysis. Women are coming into our own as theologians even as more and more outside of seminary and ecclesial settings see theologians as relics of a Christian-dominated past in the study of religion. The guild of religious studies seeks to unshackle itself from this christocentrism and locate itself in the world of human sciences. To that end religious studies increasingly privileges the knowledge gained from ethnography, anthropology, linguistics, and sociology. And substantive attention to theological poetics and construction gropes for its footing and its fold. For me, it is in these seismic shifts in the world of doing theology and being a theologian that I find the gifts of a "Farleyan" theological mode.

Wendy models in her teaching and writing that we engage the full robustness of Christianity when we attend to those cast out of the power structures.[1] Wendy's work and style embodies its own paradigmatic turn from the mentalities of orthodoxy toward an expanded canon.[2] This expanded canon is coupled with a willingness to let context and experience, from suffering to delight, define the contours of theological construction. Her ability to hear, feel, articulate, and integrate the spoken and unspeakable layers of suffering, resistance, and redemption set the tone of her theological sensitivity. And she has increasingly embodied the courage to speak clearly from pain in her own life in her work—a risky business in the world of academic conversation. This risk also carries a lifeline to the integrity of her work as it seeks strands of shared recognition for what is both true and possible in human life.

1. Her *Gathering Those Driven Away: A Theology of Incarnation* is a potent explication of the necessity of such an approach to understanding the transformational impulse of Christianity.

2. Emily Holmes describes this widening of the theological canon in her introductory essay in *Women, Writing, Theology*, 9.

The distinctive gift of studying with Wendy is perhaps how this mode of doing theology has found room to take on a constructive methodological identity. And in that identity I have come to recognize and claim a profound paradigmatic shift in how I both integrate and work out of the categories and understandings of the study of religion. I signal this methodological identity in the construction of theology as "bold vulnerability."[3]

This boldly vulnerable methodological identity that I claim in my own work reverberates with Wendy's voice and disposition toward the task of theology. And not just that, her constructive creativity and sensitivity echo in it all as well. Specifically her attention to tragedy, desire, and incarnation frame and form this constructive spirit. In and through these three categories, silence/ing and voice/ing wear the pathways of a generously open space. Tragedy expands our gaze on the human condition beyond the category of sin to include "radical suffering."[4] Desire courses through a robust understanding of sentience and humanity's created nature to help us catch more vivid glimpses of Divinity's fingerprints on and in us. Dualism becomes a strange artifact of an ill-fitting concept of what it means to be human. And incarnation breathes into theological constructions vitality that lets Christ's generosity and compassion seep in in a mode distinct from the calculus of familiar atonement theories.

This constructive mode coupled with attention to an expanded canon and experience make space for rich and thick theological anthropologies. And these complicated frameworks for understanding what it means to be human stitch themselves through multifarious theological explorations around questions that expand beyond the traditional loci of Christian systematic theology. The gaze and grist of constructive theology begins to shake loose of its sectarian identity. And the points of contact in larger conversations about human meaning ripple out into spaces not before conducive to theology's frameworks. And the dance of silence/ing and audibility stretches and constricts in ironic twists of novelty, misunderstanding, sparks of recognition, and poetic suggestion.

In my own work this dance invites my concentrated attention on bodies as the location of theological narrative, poesis, and metaphor.[5] The open spaces and constraints of constructive theology both authorize

3. "Embodying Theology: Motherhood as Metaphor/Method," in *Women, Writing, Theology*, 233–52.

4. Farley, *Tragic Vision*, 64–65.

5. Mount Shoop, *Let the Bones Dance*.

and resist this paradigmatic shift toward the body. The foci of how we are made and how we can flourish are not novel ones. Indeed, I share my subject matter with the seminal texts of orthodoxy and with the men who wrote with their own fears and anatomies camouflaged as ontologies and metaphysical claims. Writing from my own anatomy, however, seems to automatically signal a provisional argument that only applies to particular contexts and constituencies. Part of this need to sequester the work of women like me is, to be sure, a defense against further erosion of a worldview that is crumbling around us. Quieting the voices of women who write and embody theology in an age in which theology itself is suspect is a strange conspiracy. Theology is dying, and women are gestating and birthing new/old worlds of theological vitality.

This rhythm and flow of languishing/thriving/waiting/risking/tasting takes me back to that classroom at the bottom of the stairs in the Graduate Division of Religion at Emory that was my destination on those dark fall mornings. The vibrations of silent theological wanderings and surrender formed and shaped me then. And I breathe into that boldly vulnerable mode of writing my voice into a tradition as it decays and regenerates. And the erotic quiet feeds me, and us, still.

Bibliography

Farley, Wendy. *Gathering Those Driven Away: A Theology of Incarnation*. Louisville, KY: Westminster John Knox, 2011.

————. *Tragic Vision and Divine Compassion: A Contemporary Theodicy*. Louisville, KY: Westminster/John Knox. 1990.

Holmes, Emily. Introduction. In *Women, Writing, Theology: Transforming a Tradition of Exclusion*, edited by Emily Holmes, 9. Waco, TX: Baylor University Press, 2011.

Mount Shoop, Marcia W. *Let the Bones Dance: Embodiment and the Body of Christ*. Louisville, KY: Westminster John Knox, 2010.

————. "Embodying Theology: Motherhood as Metaphor/Method. In *Women, Writing, Theology: Transforming A Tradition Of Exclusion*, edited by Emily Holmes, 233–52. Waco, TX: Baylor University Press, 2011.